Susan Glaspell and Sophie Treadwell

Routledge Modern and Contemporary Dramatists

Barbara Ozieblo and Jerry Dickey

Routledge
Taylor & Francis Group

LONDON AND NEW YORK

First published 2008 by Routledge
2 Park Square, Milton Park, Abingdon, Oxon OX14 4RN

Simultaneously published in the USA and Canada
by Routledge
270 Madison Ave, New York, NY 10016

Routledge is an imprint of the Taylor & Francis Group, an informa business

© 2008 Barbara Ozieblo and Jerry Dickey

Typeset in Sabon and Georgia by
Keystroke, 28 High Street, Tettenhall, Wolverhampton
Printed and bound in Great Britain by
TJ International Ltd, Padstow, Cornwall

British Library Cataloguing in Publication Data
A catalogue record for this book is available from the British Library

Library of Congress Cataloging in Publication Data
Ozieblo, Barbara.
Susan Glaspell and Sophie Treadwell / Barbara Ozieblo and Jerry Dickey.
p. cm. – (Routledge modern and contemporary dramatists)
Includes bibliographical references and index.
1. Glaspell, Susan, 1876-1948—Criticism and interpretation.
2. Treadwell, Sophie, 1885-1970—Criticism and interpretation.
3. American drama—20th century—History and criticism.
I. Dickey, Jerry R. (Jerry Richard), 1956- II. Title.
PS3513.L35Z82 2008
812'.52—dc22   2007036118

ISBN10: 0–415–40485–1 (hbk)
ISBN10: 0–415–40484–3 (pbk)
ISBN10: 0–203–92993–4 (ebk)

ISBN13: 978–0–415–40485–3 (hbk)
ISBN13: 978–0–415–40484–6 (pbk)
ISBN13: 978–0–203–92993–3 (ebk)

Contents

Plates

Acknowledgements

We would like to thank Maggie Gale and Mary Luckhurst, editors of the Routledge Modern and Contemporary Dramatists series, for wishing to include Susan Glaspell and Sophie Treadwell, thus acknowledging their significance in the history of the theater of the twentieth century. Their support and comments have helped shape the final text. Our thanks also to Minh Ha Duong for guiding us through the process of publication. The rest of our acknowledgements are separate.

Barbara Ozieblo

Most of the material for the part on Susan Glaspell comes from my research over the last twenty years which culminated in *Susan Glaspell: A Critical Biography*, published by the University of North Carolina Press in 2000. There, I thanked in name all the librarians who aided me in my search for documents and information; now I simply wish to reiterate my thanks and appreciation. I also wish to thank the community of Susan Glaspell scholars, and the university and commercial theaters that are doing so much to make Glaspell better known to a wider public.

I would like to thank Steve Bottoms, director of the Glasgow Studio Theatre production of *The Verge*, for responding to emails enquiring about the production and the photographs. In spite of all my efforts, I have not been able to locate the photographer, Leslie Black. My thanks to Sam Waters and Nick Budden of the Orange Tree Theatre, Richmond, who helped me reach the photographer of their production of *The Verge*, Paul Thompson, who kindly gave his permission to reproduce a photograph of Act I. Also to the Billy Rose Theatre Division of the New York Public Library for the Performing Arts, Astor, Lenox and Tilden Foundations, for use of three photographs: of Susan Glaspell, of the production of *Trifles* and of *The Verge*. I would also like to thank MaryRose Devine, photographer, and Michael Bloom and Alex Roe of the Metropolitan Playhouse, New York, and Margaret Loesser Robinson, who played Madeline in *Inheritors* at the Metropolitan Playhouse, for being extremely helpful and cooperative. Unfortunately, we could not include a photograph of that production.

I am grateful to the faculty of the Department of English at the University of Málaga for allowing me to organize my teaching so as to give me almost eight months with no classes – time that I could dedicate entirely to this project. I am particularly grateful to Martha C. Carpentier, Vice-President of the Susan Glaspell Society, and to Noelia Hernando-Real, member of the SGS, for reading my manuscript and for making insightful – and incisive – comments.

Jerry Dickey

I would like to offer special thanks to Bonnie Travers of the University of Arizona Library Special Collections for her continued aid in my research and for organizing a special Treadwell exhibit in the fall of 2006. I am deeply indebted as well to Berlinda Parra of the Roman Catholic Diocese of Tucson for not only providing permission to quote from Treadwell's works but for many thoughtful conversations about Treadwell and her literary estate. My analyses of Treadwell's plays in performance were greatly enriched by discussions with several individuals associated with professional theaters – Deborah Martinson, Steven Scott Mazzola, Andrew White, and Jack Marshall of The American Century Theater – and especially Michael Kinghorn, now of the Guthrie Theater.

Several individuals and institutions helped provide photographs for this book: the University of Arizona Library Special

Collections; the Billy Rose Theatre Division of the New York Public Library for the Performing Arts, Astor, Lenox and Tilden Foundations; Janine Stanford of the Royal National Theatre, London; Alena Melichar; and Kirstin Lunke of the Arena Stage.

Finally, I would like to thank Miriam López-Rodríguez for many gratifying and challenging discussions about Treadwell's life and work. And for her constant support and encouragement, Deborah Dickey cannot receive enough of my gratitude.

The rights to Sophie Treadwell's works are owned by the Roman Catholic Diocese of Tucson: A Corporation Sole, from whom production rights must be obtained. Enquiries should be addressed to: Manager, Fiscal and Administrative Services, Diocese of Tucson, PO Box 31, Tucson, AZ 85702. These works are reprinted here by permission of the Diocese of Tucson. Proceeds from the printing or production of Sophie Treadwell's works are used for the aid and benefit of Native American children in Arizona.

Introduction

Barbara Ozieblo and Jerry Dickey

Overview

This volume offers an introduction to the lives and careers of
two of the most significant American women playwrights of
the modern era: Susan Glaspell and Sophie Treadwell. Glaspell
and Treadwell wrote during a time of rapid change in American
society, as ideas of progressive modernism challenged and
supplanted the Victorian, traditionalist world into which both
women were born. Biographically, both women moved from
small Midwestern or rural Western locales to become actively
engaged in the modernist bohemian culture of New York City,
the center of progressivism in politics and art during the first
few decades of the twentieth century. As writers, both employed
a variety of media – including journalism, fiction, and drama – to
examine and redefine women's roles in modern society, including
the exploration of such issues as suffrage, sexual freedom,
society's moral double standard for the sexes, and women's rights
for autonomous identities both within and outside of marriage.
Yet their traditional upbringings and subsequent marriages to
well-known and sometimes domineering husbands contributed
to personal conflicts in their desires for career and family that can
be seen in both their own lives and in some of the central female
characters of their dramas. At times, Glaspell's and Treadwell's
search for a sense of community took them to Europe as expatri-
ates and relative outsiders – Glaspell to Delphos, Greece, and
Treadwell to Vienna and later Torremolinos, Spain. Finally, both

women survived the deaths of their husbands by many years, later wrote more fiction than drama, and ultimately returned to the United States – Treadwell initially to Newtown, Connecticut, and ultimately to Tucson, Arizona, and Glaspell to Province-town, Cape Cod.

Both Glaspell and Treadwell are best known today for a single, oft-anthologized play – *Trifles* by Glaspell and *Machinal* by Treadwell – that used journalistic accounts of women murdering their husbands as springboards for original, dramatic statements about gendered behavior and sexual inequities. Although both dramatists wrote in dramatic styles ranging from the realistic, well-made play to the expressionistic and highly symbolic, it is in the latter area that they are receiving much recent critical attention. In plays such as Glaspell's *The Verge* and Treadwell's *Machinal* and *Intimations for Saxophone*, these dramatists achieved a melding of feminist ideals with experi-mental form that hitherto had been found only in American women's fiction.

Modernist American theater

The theater in America at the beginning of the twentieth century was dominated by Broadway, and the Theatrical Syndicate controlled by business entrepreneurs converted theater into a commercial rather than an artistic enterprise. Thus, plays that had succeeded in Europe, particularly in London, were preferred to plays by American playwrights because theater managers could look forward to good box-office results. The star system that had developed throughout the nineteenth century allowed specific actors and theater managers to flourish, encouraging them to ignore innovation and to continue performing acknowledged financial successes. Although there were isolated productions of the new modern dramas by European playwrights like Henrik Ibsen, as well as Ibsen-influenced American plays like James A. Herne's *Margaret Fleming* (1891), Broadway plays rarely ventured far beyond the boundaries of Victorian morality or explored the serious concerns of a rapidly changing American society. As Glaspell later described in *The Road to the Temple*:

We went to the theater, and for the most part we came away wishing we had gone somewhere else. Those were the days when Broadway flourished almost unchallenged. Plays, like magazine articles, were patterned. They might be pretty good within themselves, seldom did they open out to – where it surprised or thrilled your spirit to follow. They didn't ask much of *you*, those plays. Having paid for your seat, the thing was all done for you, and your mind came out where it went in, only tireder. . . . What was this "Broadway," which could make a thing as interesting as life into a thing as dull as a Broadway play?

(Glaspell 1927: 248)

It was this situation of stagnation and prevailing commercial incentive that gave birth to the little theaters, the germ of the off-Broadway movement in the United States.

The little theater movement

The little theaters in America grew at an astounding rate. In her recent study of the little theater movement, Dorothy Chansky notes that sixty-three of such theaters emerged between 1912 and 1916, with perhaps as many as 5,000 in existence by 1926 (Chansky 2004: 5). Some of the earliest and best-known little theaters included the Chicago Little Theater, the Washington Square Players and the Provincetown Players in New York. Many of these theaters were united by a common desire to revitalize American theater, largely by embracing and adapting European theatrical influences, encouraging the production of new plays, including those by American writers, and by using the theater to explore social issues with an eye toward inspiring a widespread cultural reawakening. Most little theaters performed in makeshift or converted spaces and employed excessively modest production means. While a number of the leaders and early participants in these theaters were technically amateurs in the world of theater, many of them had achieved at least some degree of recognition as journalists, painters, writers, or academics. Contrary to the practices of the Broadway commercial theater, these little

theaters initially eschewed specialization, often affording participants the opportunity to work in multiple areas of theatrical
production as writers, actors, designers, technicians, and publi-
cists, thus providing the all-round training that Edward Gordon
Craig considered necessary for the theater of the future (Craig
1905: 68). Their repertoires embraced plays with a wide variety
of subjects and styles.

The one-act play, which prior to this time had often been
relegated to popular stages in the form of vaudeville sketches,
curtain-raisers or after-pieces, found a welcome home on the
modest, little theater stages. As J. Ellen Gainor has noted,

> The one-act form presumably promised to the amateur
> theaters a convenient marriage of form and philosophy for
> artistic as well as social ends. Taking the form the critics had
> identified as originally for the "masses" would have been
> fitting for artists dedicated to socialism, at the same time as
> one-acts served their performance needs.
>
> (Gainor 2001: 13)

Both Glaspell and Treadwell utilized the one-act play form for
their early dramas.

The Provincetown Players

Many critics credit the Provincetown Players with helping
develop both a new American drama and an audience receptive
to theatrical experimentation. William Archer, the first British
translator of Ibsen, acknowledged the work of the Provincetown
Players with the following eulogy: "In the region of Washington
Square or Greenwich Village, or ... among the sand dunes
of Cape Cod – we must look for the real birthplace of the
New American Drama" (Archer 1921). George Cram Cook and
Susan Glaspell began offering plays in the summer of 1915 in
Provincetown, Massachusetts. The success of Glaspell's *Trifles*
and Eugene O'Neill's *Bound East for Cardiff*, Glaspell and
Cook's desire to renew America through the theater, O'Neill's
need for a theater that would perform his plays, and Jack Reed's

– future author of *Ten Days that Shook the World* – enthusiasm spurred the group of playwrights and amateur actors to create the Provincetown Players.[1] In the fall of 1916 they rented a brownstone on Macdougal Street, in New York's Greenwich Village just off Washington Square, and called their theater the Playwrights' Theater. Reed wrote up a series of resolutions that would govern their activities; the first of these aptly condensed their attitude to the job in hand:

Be it resolved:

That it is the primary object of the Provincetown Players to encourage the writing of American plays of real artistic, literary and dramatic – as opposed to Broadway – merit.

That such plays be considered without reference to their commercial value, since this theatre is not to be run for pecuniary profit.

(Quoted in Kenton 1997: 29)

The Provincetown Players, dubbed "experimenters without an exchequer" by their unofficial historian Edna Kenton (*ibid.*: 31), began their adventure with donations from members and financed their productions by selling subscriptions to seasons of plays – organized as a club or little theater they were not authorized to sell tickets. Initially, the "true amateur spirit" predicated by Cook (*ibid.*: 35) prevailed and, except for two salaried, full-time officers, none of the members were paid for their dedication to the project. It was not until the astounding success in 1920 of Eugene O'Neill's *The Emperor Jones* that the Provincetown Players turned their sights on Broadway and gave in to the allure of professional theater. As a result, the latent animosities and rivalries flared up and eventually led to the dissolution of the Players in 1922 (Ozieblo 2000: 169–90). But, before this happened, they had "produced ninety-seven plays by forty-six American playwrights" (Kenton 1997: 158), so fulfilling their goal of creating a stage on which American playwrights could experiment and develop their artistic talents. After a year's interim, however, O'Neill and others took over the theater, calling themselves the Experimental Theater Inc. – although they continued to be known by the old name of the Provincetown Players regardless of Glaspell's protests (see Ozieblo 2000: 227–34).

From the outset, women played a prominent role in all facets of the Provincetown Players. Judith Barlow notes that "More than a third of the plays performed by the Provincetown were written or coauthored by women, an astonishingly high percentage considering the scarcity of works by women on the commercial stage, then and now" (Barlow 1995: 260). Most of these plays placed female characters in positions of centrality in the action, and repeatedly explored themes of emotional and sexual fidelity, as well as the definition of women's roles by marriage, career, and social class. As opposed to Broadway's dominance by the star actor, the Provincetown Players placed a primary focus on the writer and director, and as Cheryl Black has pointed out, women occupied positions as the latter in over half of the group's productions (Black 2002: 167). In her study *The Women of Provincetown*, Black argues that "Provincetown provided its women a space from which to challenge sexually segregated theatrical practice by becoming directors, designers, playwrights, and managers. To the degree that they succeeded, they could claim with evidence that, in theater, 'women's place was everywhere'" (*ibid.*: 146). In both subject and practice, then, women theatrical artists with little theaters like the Provincetown Players reflected the evolving attitudes toward women's place in American society and contributed to a redefinition of their roles.

Unlike Glaspell, however, Treadwell's involvement with the little theater movement was minimal, since she participated with the Provincetown Players only for a short time early in their existence. Instead, she typically sought to bring reforms to the commercial Broadway theater while similarly seeking to expand women's traditional social roles.

Women playwrights

Although the Puritan influence in America had converted theater into a place of corruption, women playwrights, such as Judith

Sargent Murray in the eighteenth century and Anna Cora Mowatt in the nineteenth, had worked to assert the theater as a place of respectable entertainment that could, at the same time, be a way of educating the public, especially as to women's role in society. This work was continued by playwrights such as Rachel Crothers, who dedicated her life entirely to the theater on Broadway, as actress, director, and playwright. Her best-known early plays, such as *A Man's World* (1910) and *He and She* (1920), are heartfelt expressions of the injustices that artistic, talented, ambitious women face in patriarchal society. Other women playwrights of the early twentieth century include Zoë Akins, Zona Gale, Alice Gerstenberg, Georgia Douglas Johnson and, of course, the Provincetown playwrights who worked with Susan Glaspell – Edna St. Vincent Millay, Djuna Barnes, Neith Boyce, and Mary Carolyn Davies among them. Gertrude Stein's modernist, highly innovative plays were neither performed nor known in the first decades of the century, although her work gained recognition and became increasingly influential as the century progressed.

What do we mean by feminist theater?

The definitions of "feminist theater" have been varied and range from simple statements of intention to more theoretical concerns related to the use of stage strategies and devices. The notion of a feminist theater in the USA began with the women's movement of the 1960s, when theatrical performances were consciously used to raise women's awareness of their oppression in patriarchal society. The painter and performance artist Judy Chicago, founder of Womanhouse, where she collaborated on performances such *Ablutions*, gives a good working definition of what feminist theater should do when she states:

> When we performed, the audience was usually shocked, then fascinated by the fact that we were bringing the "private" sphere into the light, making the private public, and in so doing, taking a large step toward bridging the culture chasm between men and women.
>
> (Chicago 1975: 129)

Although both Glaspell and Treadwell brought women's issues "into the light" in their plays, the fact that their protagonists do not always fully succeed – in the terms of the twenty-first century – in their endeavor to seek freedom from social constraint has induced a questioning of their feminism. Glaspell scholar Sharon Friedman stated the problem in one of the earliest published articles on feminist drama:

> However, feminism as theme should not be understood as simply a call for women's rights on the part of the playwright or her characters. Rather, it may be a statement about a feminine consciousness, the feelings and perceptions associated with a female character's identity as a woman.
>
> (Friedman 1984: 70)

In 1914, the theater critic Florence Kiper protested at the idealized image of women in plays written by men: "It may be true enough that the idealization and worship of women is a purifying influence for men – but such worship is rather hard on the women" (Kiper 1914: 928). She called for more women to write for the stage and augured that "The literature that will be written by woman as a revealer of that so-called mystery, herself, will probably not sentimentalize femininity" (*ibid*.: 930).

Feminist critical theory and the theater

Initially, feminist theater in the 1960s was about applying women's perspectives to women's experiences and to presenting an image of women with which one could identify, rather than rejecting it as a figment of the male gaze or desire. Hélène Cixous, dramatist and one of the so-called French feminists who revolutionized American feminist theory in the 1970s and 1980s, has asked:

> How, as women, can we go to the theatre without lending our complicity to the sadism directed against women, or being asked to assume, in the patriarchal family structure

that the theatre reproduces ad infinitum, the position of victim? . . . For in every man there is a dethroned King Lear who requires his daughter to idealize him by her loving words and build him up, however flat he may have fallen, into the man he wishes to appear.

(Cixous 1977: 133)

The rediscovery of earlier American women dramatists, part of the challenge that feminist critics faced in all areas of research, widened the field and led to a need for theoretical approaches that would throw light on women's theatrical production. Studies such as those by Gayle Austin, Helen Keyssar, and Elaine Aston made critics question the concept and search for a definition of "feminist theater." One of the principal debates that has arisen is related to the use of realism by feminist playwrights. This debate explores the need to create new, alternative ways of presenting women's lives on stage.

Realism has frequently been considered a patriarchal device that strengthens the power of established authority. As such, it has been rejected. However, the arguments for realism in the theater are multiple (see Murphy 1987; Schroeder 1996). In the first place, if the objective of a feminist theater is to bring attention to the wrongs that women suffer, we should question whether an innovative work that explores and creates new theatrical conventions would be understood by the audience for whom it is intended. For example, Gertrude Stein's highly experimental *The Mother of Us All* (1945–46), although a stimulating theatrical experience, will not raise the average audience's awareness of the history of the women's movement.

One should also remember that the roots of realism in the American theater lie in the desire to escape the conventions of the melodrama and comedy that predominated on Broadway at the end of the nineteenth century. Realism was a strategy of revolt, as in James A. Herne's *Margaret Fleming*. Glaspell and Treadwell experimented with dramatic form, interweaving realism with other "-isms" that were replacing one another with great speed as the most avant-garde style in Europe. As J. Ellen Gainor has rightly pointed out:

Whereas expressionism and symbolism, to give just two examples, evolved rather distinctly in Europe, these and other forms of modernist creativity arrived in the United States virtually simultaneously. American artists felt free to explore in combination elements of modernism's signature techniques.

(Gainor 2001: 74–75)

The use of other models for feminist theatrical criticism has been examined, and even when these originate with male critics or theorists, they have been adapted for the analysis of drama by women whenever they appear to be useful. The German dramatist Bertolt Brecht's theories on epic theater and the V-effect have been effectively used by critics such as Janelle Reinelt, and Helene Keyssar has shown how the Russian literary theorist Mikhail Bakhtin's notions of the dialogic and the carnivalesque can be useful tools for the analysis of women's drama. Strains of discourse originating in psychoanalysis, as all the variants of postmodernist criticism, may be profitably applied to explorations of work by women playwrights.

The plays of both Glaspell and Treadwell are good examples of how European stage conventions were adopted in America and quickly converted into an original and innovative mode of expression. As already indicated, Glaspell's *The Verge* and Treadwell's *Machinal* and *Intimations for Saxophone* eschew realism for a highly feminist expressionistic form; their other plays, although perhaps less obviously experimental, show how they struggled with theatrical forms to achieve a voice of their own.

Part I

Susan Glaspell

Barbara Ozieblo

1 Life and ideas

The life, thought, and writing of Susan Glaspell (1876–1948) are characterized by vivid contrasts and sharp ambiguities, identified by Mary Papke as her "dualist and conflictual vision of human experience" (Papke 2006: 7), thus presenting a challenge for those readers who are anxious to pigeonhole early twentieth-century women into an essentialized compartment as feminists. Glaspell was undoubtedly a feminist of her times, but she was also a modernist reformer who firmly believed that she could improve society, not by marching with zealous acolytes but by bringing attention through her writing to the injustices and social ills that troubled her. As she explained in an interview given in 1921, "I am interested in all progressive movements, whether feminist, social or economic . . . but I can take no very active part other than through my writing" (Rohe 1921: 4). For a time, she saw the solution in socialism, and in her novel *The Visioning* (1911) she argued that this imported ideology "tempered by a purely American idealism, garnered from an amalgam of Emerson's transcendentalism, Nietzsche's overcoming, and Haeckel's oneness" (Ozieblo 2000: 47), could bring about a transformation of society. However, her feminism, socialism, and idealism were always controlled by the tension that arose from the inevitable clash of her convictions. Her firm belief in individual freedom of choice and freedom of speech was challenged by a belief just as firm in one's obligations and responsibilities to friends, family, and society, while her modernist desire to break out and seek new ways of life conflicted with her Victorian upbringing in a traditional, religious family.

The contrasts that today we see in her work were also apparent in her appearance: one friend described her as "a delicate woman with sad eyes and a sweet smile who seemed as fragile as old lace, until you talked with her and glimpsed the steel lining beneath the tender surface" (Langner 1952: 10). Early photographs depict her as a pensive, romantic young woman with fine hair drawn back in a fairly modest fashion, presumably prepared to obey the dictums of nineteenth-century society and patiently await the arrival of a suitable husband. Yet Glaspell rebelled against Victorian morality and mores: she dreamed of going to college, and meanwhile, challenging male control of the media, started writing up the social life of her town for the local *Weekly Outlook*. Some years later, she would be one of the first women among the Greenwich Village bohemians to bob her hair, and photographs and portraits from this period depict her deep in thought, mysterious and distant, and undoubtedly modern.

Glaspell was born in the American Midwest to parents who preferred church activities to the cultural and social scene of their town and desired a happy, fruitful marriage for their daughter. Although she disappointed them on that score, they supported her literary ambitions as she wrought for herself a more modern life, becoming a prolific short-story writer, a best-selling novelist, and an experimental playwright who would be awarded Broadway's Pulitzer Prize for drama in 1931. Glaspell also co-founded America's most influential little theater,[1] the Provincetown Players, with the express aim of giving American dramatists a stage of their own. In spite of such achievements, the professionalization of literature as identified by Paul Lauter (Lauter 1983) and the general silencing of women's voices caused her whole oeuvre to be ignored from the late 1930s to the early 1980s, when the women's movement recovered her story "A Jury of Her Peers" (1917). This version of the play *Trifles* (1916) was recognized as a perfectly composed example of how the bonding between women can combat injustice and domestic violence, and of the different spheres and languages that separate men and women.[2]

The slow recognition of Glaspell's stature as a playwright was set in motion in 1981, when the feminist theater scholar Judith

1.1 Susan Glaspell *c.* 1916. Photograph reproduced by courtesy of the Billy Rose Theatre Division, the New York Public Library for the Performing Arts, Astor, Lenox and Tilden Foundations

Barlow included *Trifles* in an anthology of plays by women, *Plays by American Women: The Early Years: 1900–1930*.[3] The following year, the British scholar of American theater, Chris Bigsby, gave Glaspell a small section in his *Critical Introduction to Twentieth-Century American Drama*, and in 1987 he edited a collection of her plays for Cambridge University Press. Thus *Trifles*, first performed and published in 1916, became once again readily available; it has slowly supplanted "A Jury of Her Peers" in recent anthologies of women's writing or of American literature and is now widely taught (see Chapter 4). Glaspell's other plays, even those included in Bigsby's volume – *The Outside, The Verge*, and *Inheritors* – have rarely made it into the classroom or lecture hall, although *The Verge* and *Inheritors* have been performed recently, as is indicated in later chapters of this book, and academic criticism is showing more interest – as witnessed by the numerous critical studies and essays published recently (Gainor 2001, Carpentier 2006, and Carpentier and Ozieblo 2006), and by the forthcoming *Complete Plays*.[4]

Glaspell wrote her early plays for performance by the amateur little theaters of Greenwich Village and for an audience of friends who shared her rejection of "patterned" Broadway plays that "didn't ask much of *you*" (Glaspell 1927: 248), as well as her convictions on politics, feminism, and other contemporary developments, such as psychoanalysis. Reviewers on both sides of the Atlantic received most of her plays with glowing praise, comparing her to Strindberg, Chekhov, Ibsen, or Shaw, although some did object to what they experienced as "verbose passages" (Atkinson 1927: 1), "literary quality" (Anon. 1920a: 383), and lack of exciting "dramatic action" on stage (Zatkin 1927: 56). Frank Shay, writing for the *Greenwich Villager* in 1921, boldly claimed that "*The Verge* definitely places Susan Glaspell alongside Strindberg, Tchekoff and about three notches above Shaw" (Shay 1921: 7). His claim was endorsed in 1924 by the British critic for the *Daily Telegraph*, A. D. Peters, who wrote that Glaspell belonged to:

> the purely intellectual school of American drama, if one may be permitted to label her work with a word so much feared

and so often misunderstood. . . . She follows directly in the Ibsen tradition, and may justly be described, I think, as his spiritual descendant in America. In fact, she is very much more nearly related to him than Shaw ever was or will be. . . . She is the most important of the contemporary American dramatists, and in the opinion of almost all she vies for the first place with Eugene O'Neill.

(Peters 1924)

Glaspell's "originality" was frequently remarked on by reviewers (see, for example, Anon. 1925b: 295), as was her need to examine the workings of her characters' minds; for one critic she was "a dramatist of the Ego – not so flamboyant as [Ernst] Toller, and with the ironic pity of [John] Galsworthy" (Malone 1924: 107). On the other hand, the underlying social comedy of Glaspell's plays, which she adroitly allowed to come to the fore in *Chains of Dew*, today invites comparison with Noel Coward (Ozieblo 2006b: 21), while J. Ellen Gainor notes that J. B. Priestley's "work resonated with Glaspell's" (Gainor 2001: 247), particularly with the unpublished and unperformed *Springs Eternal*.

Susan Glaspell and the Provincetown Players

The origin of the Provincetown Players should be ascribed to Susan Glaspell's short play *Suppressed Desires* (see Chapter 2), which she co-authored with her husband George Cram Cook and presented to the recently formed Washington Square Players. A skit on the newly fashionable faith in psychoanalysis, the play was rejected, as Glaspell tells us, because it was "too special" (Glaspell 1927: 250); Cook, indignant at the slight, organized a performance in a friend's home that summer, 1915, in Provincetown, Cape Cod. The following summer, with the manic zeal that characterized most of his activities, he announced a season of plays for July and August and converted a disused fish shed on a rickety wharf opposite their home in Provincetown into a makeshift theater. Among the plays performed that summer were

Glaspell's *Trifles* and Eugene O'Neill's *Bound East for Cardiff*. It was Glaspell who had convinced O'Neill to read his play to the future Players and her judgement was proved correct. She would later write that, after the performance:

> Then we knew what we were for. . . . I may see it through memories too emotional, but it seems to me I have never sat before a more moving production than our "Bound East for Cardiff," when Eugene O'Neill was produced for the first time on any stage. . . . It is not merely figurative language to say the old wharf shook with applause.
>
> (Glaspell 1927: 254)

Glaspell's part in the founding and success of the Provincetown Players is rarely given the significance her devotion to the venture merits, and is generally confined to her work as a dramatist. The reviewer John Corbin wrote as early as 1919 that "If the Provincetown Players had done nothing more than to give us the delicately humorous and sensitive plays of Susan Glaspell, they would have amply justified their existence" (Corbin 1919). And yet the more perceptive anonymous author of an article in the British *Time and Tide* asserted:

> She gave of her best to the Playwrights Theatre, working as hard for it as Lady Gregory has worked for the Irish theatre, and obtaining from it as her reward that opportunity for expression which is denied to the younger generation of English dramatists at the present time.
>
> (Anon. 1925b: 295)

The Provincetown Players initially performed eight or nine bills of three short plays every winter and only gradually took on the challenge of the full-length play. Thus Glaspell, who wrote eleven plays for the group, offered *Trifles, The Outside, Close the Book, Woman's Honor,* and *The People*, and co-authored *Suppressed Desires* and *Tickless Time* with her husband. In 1919, the Players performed *Bernice*, her first longer play, then the full-length *Inheritors* and *The Verge* in 1921, and *Chains of Dew* (written in 1920) in 1922. The Players ended their activities in 1922, when Glaspell and Cook, weary of the company's internal power struggles, decided to travel to Greece.

After her return from Greece – alone, as her husband had died there in 1924 – Glaspell, finding no support from the old friends who had usurped the theater she and Cook had created, returned to fiction. She did co-write *The Comic Artist* with her companion Norman Matson, but disowned the play when the relationship with Matson ended. Her one theatrical success after the Provincetown Players period was *Alison's House*, performed in 1930. This was awarded the Pulitzer Prize in 1931, and although critics believed that her work as a whole merited the prize, they did not all consider *Alison's House* to be her best play (see Chapter 3). The last play Glaspell wrote, *Springs Eternal*, was neither performed nor published; the manuscript is in the Glaspell papers at the New York Public Library. Except for this play and *Chains of Dew* (copyrighted in 1921 but never published), Glaspell's plays were available to her contemporaries both in the United States (published by Frank Shay) and in the United Kingdom (published by Ernest Benn), where they were successfully performed by avant-garde groups such as Edith Craig's the Pioneer Players, the People's National Theatre, the Gate Theatre, and the Lena Ashwell Players.

Susan Glaspell's life

Susan Glaspell was born in Davenport, Iowa in 1876.[5] Her father's family had owned land, but it was gradually sold off, so that her father, Elmer Glaspell, inherited only a small-holding that was, quite literally, on the wrong side of the railway tracks. Susan's mother, Alice Keating, came from a family that looked down on Elmer's attempts to keep himself employed. The Davenport register has him as a contractor, building sewers and drains for the growing town. As a young girl and adolescent, Susan Glaspell longed to be a part of Davenport society; her earliest known writing is for the Davenport *Weekly Outlook*, reporting on the comings and goings of precisely those people she then admired. It was by her writing that she eventually won their acceptance and recognition: once she started publishing short stories in magazines such as *Harper's* and *Youth's Companion*, and had won the *Black Cat* Prize for a story in 1904, Alice French (a.k.a. Octave Thanet), of best Davenport stock and author of numerous novels and stories, took the young Susan under her wing. Glaspell then joined a staid Davenport literary society, the Tuesday Club, and, after the publication of her first novel, *The Glory of the Conquered* (1909), and a lengthy sojourn in Paris, was invited to lecture on topics such as the novel and European literature.

Although Glaspell had coveted such recognition, by the time it came she had developed in other directions. The discipline and influence of her home atmosphere, particularly her parents' commitment to the Church and its missionary activities, had paled when confronted with the independence that a couple of years of study at Drake University in Des Moines brought her. After completing the requirements for her degree in 1899, she worked for the *Des Moines Daily News*, but, in 1901, decided to return to Davenport in order to devote her time entirely to the writing of fiction. Of the cases she covered as a reporter, the best known is the story of the murder of Mr. Hossack by, presumably, his wife. Fifteen years later, she converted this into *Trifles* (see Chapter 4), her best-known play.

The independence she had acquired while away from her family gave Glaspell the courage to join the radicals and non-conformists of Davenport who were led by George Cram Cook, known as Jig, and a very young, committed socialist, Floyd Dell – journalist and future novelist – who had only recently come to town.[6] Davenport, founded in 1836, was sufficiently small and Midwestern to be shocked by the behavior of Cook, scion of one of its best families, but also sufficiently marked by the experience of European immigrants, particularly the Hungarian revolutionaries, to sponsor a lively artistic, musical, and intellectual cultural life. As for Cook, he had recently abandoned a lectureship at Stanford University in order to become a truck farmer on his family's land, selling his produce at the town market and writing and philosophizing in the long winter evenings. This lifestyle had precipitated a separation from his first wife, and Cook was now fighting for a divorce in order to marry the much younger and very pretty Mollie Price, who, in the meantime, was working on anarchist Emma Goldman's magazine *Mother Earth* in New York. It was at this point that Glaspell met Cook and the two fell in love. But they would not marry until 1913, after Cook's divorce from Mollie, by which time he had had two children by her.

Glaspell joined the Monist Society that Cook and Dell founded in 1907 for, as Cook breezily put it, "the propagation of our philosophy in the guise of religion, or religion in the guise of philosophy" (Glaspell 1927: 191). American Monism had its roots in Emersonian Transcendentalism and came to life under the influence of Ernst Haeckel's *The Riddle of the Universe*, an account of his philosophy that was highly popular at the time (see Murphy 2005: 26–29). Years later, Glaspell would recover Cook's lecture on Monism and include it in *The Road to the Temple*, the biography she published of her husband in 1927, admitting that his conception of continuity and unity of all things in time and nature had affected her deeply. Discussions at the Monist Society stimulated her to sharpen her idealism and to penetrate deeper into the thought of the German philosophers she had read at college. Floyd Dell had suggested the name for their society, which he took from the German Monist League that Haeckel had founded in 1905 in order to spread his "holistic philosophy (a kind of scientific pantheism) that attempted to reconcile the contemporary knowledge of the origin of the species and the evolution of man with the need for religion" (Hinz-Bode 2006b: 93). As a young woman, Glaspell clearly delighted at shocking her parents and the more traditional members of Davenport society: she tells us in *The Road to the Temple* that she would "Declin[e] to go to church with my parents in the morning" and then "ostentatiously set out for the Monist Society in the afternoon" (Glaspell 1927: 191). As we will see, Monism permeated her thought and ideologically dominates *Inheritors* and *The Verge*; however, fiction allowed her the space necessary to develop Haeckel's thought more fully, as she does in *Norma Ashe* (1942) and *Judd Rankin's Daughter* (1945), where "Glaspell repeatedly interrogates Haeckel's . . . theory of monism as well as other complementary theories of the spiritual in human life and reinvests the best from these philosophies with her own celebration of impressionistic epistemology" (Papke 2006: 8). Darwin's theory of evolution, still highly controversial in many circles at the beginning of the twentieth century, also finds its way into much of her writing, especially *The Verge*.

Glaspell, anxious to escape from the small-town constrictions imposed by Davenport, moved in 1911 to New York, where she settled in Greenwich Village, the traditional refuge of bohemian, innovative spirits of all stripes. The summers were spent in Provincetown, Cape Cod, and it was there that Glaspell and George Cram Cook bought a house, number 564 on Commercial Street, which would be Glaspell's home until her death in 1948 from viral pneumonia.

In 1922 Glaspell traveled to Greece with her husband. Cook had dreamed of living in Greece all his life, and now, disappointed by the squabbling Provincetown Players, he seized his opportunity to get to know the very cradle of the classicism he so admired. Glaspell went with him joyfully, also eager for the experience of further travel. After spending time in Athens, they went on to Delphos, site of the Sacred Oracle, where they settled, renting a house overlooking the vineyards and the coast, with Mt. Parnassus – its pasture lands the refuge of shepherds and its forests the hideout of bandits – above them. In the summer, they moved onto its slopes with the shepherds, camping there under the huge pines.

This seemingly idyllic life was brought to an end by Cook's death, in January 1924.[7] On returning to New York, Glaspell found herself without a theater to write for, and, after reconstructing her husband's life into the hagio-biography *The Road to the Temple* (1927), she returned to fiction, the genre that had first captured her interest. Some of her best writing comes from this period. As Martha Carpentier has pointed out, Glaspell's exposure to the bohemian art crowd of Greenwich Village, the discipline of playwriting and the close contact with Greek culture, past and present, "expanded her skills as a writer" so that the novels written on her return to America "gain in psychological and artistic complexity because they reflect the ferment of the modernist period – its burgeoning feminism, its preoccupation with psychoanalysis and mythology, and its experimental expressionistic techniques" (Carpentier 2001: 8, 9).

Glaspell returned to the theater when Hallie Flanagan appointed her the director of the Federal Theatre's Midwest Play Bureau in 1936.[8] She moved to Chicago for the few years that the Federal Theatre existed, and her role there was to seek out and promote the writing of plays by Midwesterners, a task that echoed with the original aim of the Provincetown Players that she had co-founded: to offer a stage for aspiring American playwrights. Among the successes of Glaspell's work for the Federal Theatre was Arnold Sundgaard's living newspaper on syphilis, *Spirochete*, which she encouraged him to write and which was performed in numerous towns in 1938. Glaspell withdrew from the Play Bureau in protest over the mounting paperwork and increasing censorship a few months before Congress closed down the Federal Theatre in 1939.

Themes in Susan Glaspell's writing

Among the recurrent themes in Glaspell's fiction are motherhood, particularly frustrated motherhood, and orphaned children, and her novels portray "her deep understanding of the empowering ties between women and their origin in the pre-oedipal mother–daughter relationship, as well as her innovative use of a female semiotic" (Carpentier 2001: 1–2). These themes are explored in *Brook Evans* (1928), *Fugitive's Return* (1929) and *The Morning Is Near Us* (1939). Although Glaspell did not have children of her own, she reveals in *The Road to the Temple* that her desire to experience motherhood was frustrated a number of times (Glaspell 1927: 239); Cook's two children by his previous marriage, Nilla and Harl, spent the summers with them in Provincetown under Glaspell's charge, and both remained close to her after their father's death, as did Nilla's son, Sirius Cook.

The theme of motherhood also appears in Glaspell's plays but, as we shall see, during the Provincetown period she was more involved in issues that sprang from current affairs, such as the closing of a newspaper (*The People*), the Espionage and Sedition

Acts (*Inheritors*) or freedom of information and birth control (*Chains of Dew*). A theme that runs through all her work is that of individual freedom and its limitations: the protagonist of an early story, "The Rules of the Institution," recognizes that "affection and obligation were agents holding one to one's place" and yet decides that "she owed no allegiance to an order that held life in chains" (Glaspell 1914: 208). But in the later play *Chains of Dew* and the novel *Ambrose Holt and Family* Glaspell's protagonists decide that their "affections and obligations" cannot be so easily dropped and accept that they must sacrifice themselves to make another happy. In the novel Blossom wonders "how much you had the right to change yourself, or rather, to become yourself, when it changed things for those near you" (Glaspell 1931: 224).

The interaction of the artist with society and the artist's duty to him/herself and society are issues that also pervade Glaspell's work: they dominated her first novel, *The Glory of the Conquered* (1909), and are significant in *Chains of Dew*, and, in particular, in *Alison's House*, as also in *The Comic Artist* (1927), the play she co-wrote with Norman Matson while they lived together after her return from Greece. Kristina Hinz-Bode usefully summarizes the wide breadth of themes and forms that we find in Glaspell's novels and plays:

> In all her writings Glaspell acknowledged the wide range of artistic answers to the modern experience of doubt and disorder: the realists' project of enacting stories of self-empowerment, the determinist stance of naturalism, the ecstatic insistence on a truth beyond surface reality that drives the works of German expressionism, the retreat into the individual consciousness evident in modernist aestheticism, the socialist and Marxist explanations of the world, and the intellectual and philosophical position that must fall silent in the atrocities of modern warfare and terror.
>
> (Hinz-Bode 2006b: 90)

2 The short plays

Although the Provincetown Players originated in George Cram Cook's ardent yearning to return to the Greek Dionysian roots of theater and so to create a new communal spirit in America, he also aspired to give American playwrights an opportunity to stage their plays. And yet, the prevailing opinion on the work of the Players, based largely on the autobiography of one of their members, Hutchins Hapgood – a journalist and close friend of Glaspell and Cook – has tended to foreground their "amateurish, rebellious and informal spirit" (Sarlós 1982: 6). Hapgood saw their beginnings as a response to the "negative forces" of the First World War, and also as a conscious attempt to solve the larger social problems through a refreshingly idealistic conviction that self-understanding and honesty will lead to the "deeper culture" necessary for true progress (Hapgood 1939: 393). Robert Károly Sarlós, whose 1982 study of the Players is still the most complete history of their adventure, admits that "the plays were first thought of as a profoundly therapeutic party-game for a small, close-knit group," but he hastens to add that "the idea no sooner emerged than it materialized in the form of scripts" (Sarlós 1982: 14). Indeed, the first two plays, Glaspell and Cook's *Suppressed Desires* and Neith Boyce's *Constancy*, deal with ideas and incidents that formed parts of the everyday lives of the group. The later plays also served to release tensions through comedy or drama but, at the same time, they were frequently the work of writers fully committed to their craft, as was Susan Glaspell.

By the time Glaspell turned to the stage, she was a mature, established author of novels and short stories. She had published *The Glory of the Conquered* (1909), *The Visioning* (1911) and *Fidelity* (1915) and countless short stories in prestigious magazines, such as *Harper's, Munsey's, Booklovers, The American* and *Black Cat*. Although, as she assures her readers in *The Road to the Temple*, she had never "studied" playwriting (Glaspell 1927: 255), she had helped create the ideal learning environment and space for a dramatist: a stage of her own. The Provincetown Players and their Playwrights' Theater on Macdougal Street guaranteed her a stage, however small and meagerly equipped, an avid audience, and an inexperienced group of amateur actors who quickly acquired the essential skills necessary for a successful performance: thus, she learned economy of means, of space and of time, and how to form concentrated images that encapsulated the ideas she wanted to put across, relying more on her words than on the actors at her disposal. The issues she had already raised in her fiction reappear in her plays, with the most significant of these undoubtedly a sincere questioning of the role of the individual in society; Glaspell's exploration of how the restrictions imposed by society affect us, how human beings interact, how the exercise of free will inevitably clashes even with freely assumed obligation to others, is framed by her deep Darwinian conviction that evolution is desirable because it will eventually fashion a better world. This conviction is overlaid by a Nietzschean faith in the will of mankind to overcome, converted into a feminist tenet, for Glaspell quietly adopted Zarathustra's "I will" for women (Nietzsche 1883: 92). The principal cause that Glaspell espoused in her plays, as in her novels, was what she perceived as the inequitable situation of women who had been robbed of their independence by social mores; she railed particularly at the conventional concept of marriage that chained women to burdens that education and an acute sense of responsibility made it virtually impossible to evade. She also believed that the improvement of the race could be brought about – or at least hastened – by Art: that is, through her writing and through the theater. The melodramas of Broadway bored her; her denunciation of its productions in *The Road to the*

Temple (Glaspell 1927: 248) could have come from renowned European theater practitioners such as Bertolt Brecht or Antonin Artaud, who sought reform by awakening the spectator to the injustices of society. In order to combat the stagnation of Broadway, Glaspell sought new ways of theatrical expression more in accord with the modernism she had absorbed during her year in Paris and with which she had begun to experiment in her fiction.

Suppressed Desires

Glaspell wrote her first play, *Suppressed Desires: A Freudian Comedy*, with her husband, George Cram Cook.[1] It was performed in July 1915 (probably on the 15th) in the Provincetown home of fellow Greenwich Villagers Hutchins Hapgood and Neith Boyce, together with Boyce's *Constancy*. The evening acquired legendary status among the Provincetowners: the setting was improvised by Robert Edmond Jones, who had just returned from a year's study in Europe with the German director Max Reinhardt and was later to become a leading American stage designer. He rearranged cushions and lamps to create the desired effect and physically implicated the audience in the production by using "the verandah with the ocean behind for the first play [*Constancy*], and, by the simple expedient of asking the audience to turn its chairs about, the broad doorway at the opposite end of the room for the second [*Suppressed Desires*]" (Deutsch and Hanau 1931: 7).

A number of performances for friends followed, and in November 1916 *Suppressed Desires* was included in the second bill of the recently created Provincetown Players in their New York theater. In 1918, this brief satire on psychoanalysis was performed at the Comedy Theatre by the Washington Square Players – who now preferred to forget that they had refused the play three years previously, thus goading its authors to create their own theater. One reviewer declared it to be "keenly written and a joy throughout," while the unsteady acting of the company was saved by the "sheer brilliance of line" (Anon 1918a: 7). The play proved to be a huge success: as Glaspell would write later, it was "given by every little theater, and almost every Methodist church; golf clubs in Honolulu, colleges in Constantinople; in Paris and China and every rural route in America" (Glaspell 1927: 250).

Suppressed Desires is an engaging response to the craze for psychoanalysis that was then sweeping through Greenwich Village (see Sievers 1955); in *The Road to the Temple* Glaspell dryly complains, "You could not go out to buy a bun without hearing of some one's complex" (Glaspell 1927: 250). It is impossible to say how much of *Suppressed Desires* should be attributed to either Glaspell or Cook. But the play certainly shows the light, satirical, comedic touch that Glaspell would bring to later plays and which is totally lacking in Cook's writing. She and Cook

> thought [psychoanalysis] would be amusing in a play, so we had a good time writing "Suppressed Desires." Before the grate in Milligan Place we tossed the lines back and forth at one another, and wondered if any one else would ever have as much fun with it as we were having.
>
> (*ibid.*: 250)

The audience of friends invited to the first performances of *Suppressed Desires* would have delighted in all the allusions both to current trends and to the marital problems and misdemeanors of common acquaintances. Nonetheless, today the play is still amusing and wholly comprehensible to an audience ignorant of the ins and outs of the human relationships of that specific group of people vacationing on the Cape in 1915.

A popularized American version of Freud's evolving methods of psychoanalysis widely prevalent in the second decade of the twentieth century is at the core of *Suppressed Desires*. Henrietta enlightens her less sophisticated sister Mabel as to the effects of any "forbidden impulse" that is allowed to "fester" (Glaspell 1916: 38) in the unconscious mind, assuring her that "In extreme cases it drives you insane" (*ibid.*: 38). Henrietta convinces both her husband Stephen and her sister to visit Dr. Russell, only then to dismiss psychoanalysis when she learns that her revered specialist has interpreted their dreams to mean that Stephen wants to leave her and that Mabel desires Stephen. The play ends with Mabel's fretful question: "What am I to do with my suppressed desire?" and Henrietta's blithe response: "Mabel, you just keep right on suppressing it" (*ibid.*: 51).

The realistic, though simple, setting of the play reflects the characters and their preoccupations. The single set is a room used for dining and working: the Brewsters clearly share the big work table at which Stephen designs homes and Henrietta writes scientific essays on psychoanalysis for serious publications. Through the window, we see street lights and the top of the arch at the other side of Washington Square, an obvious allusion to the radical yet bourgeois friends whom Glaspell mocks in her play and who all lived in the area. Glaspell took care with the settings of her plays and designed them consciously as a symbolic or even expressionistic means of transmitting information about the characters as much as a general mood, thus allowing her to economize on preliminary exposition. She would use the same technique in her next play, *Trifles* (see Chapter 4), where the interior setting becomes pregnant with meaning.

The People

The People, directed by Nina Moise, the first professional to join the Players, was performed in March 1917 at the Playwrights' Theater in the eighth bill of that season. In this play the action takes place in the "*inner*" office of a publication "*which is radical and poor*" (Glaspell 1926b: 29). The stage is almost unfurnished, indicative of the bare space in which the journal is brought to life, distant from those it wishes to touch and transform. As editor Ed laments on his return from an unsuccessful and frustrating fund-raising trip across the country: "You can't keep vision in this office. It's easy enough to have a beautiful feeling about the human race when none of it is around" (*ibid.*: 37). And yet it is members of the human race, representatives not of the intellectuals, the bourgeois "pigs" (*ibid.*: 33) that the Firebrand denounces, but of the "people," who eventually bring hope to the editors of the publication. The suggestions of a group of allegorical characters – the Earnest Approach, the Light Touch, the Firebrand, the Philosopher and the Artist – for keeping the journal afloat have the righteous implications of a medieval morality play. At the same time, the speed with which they are offered, coupled with their conflicting import, not only render them incongruous but confer a surreal, nightmarish quality to the scene, reminiscent of Strindberg's *A Dream Play*. At one point, Ed cries out: "Dear God! There are things it seems to me I can *not* bear" (*ibid*.: 33). They are interrupted by the Boy from Georgia, the Man from the Cape and the Woman from Idaho, all of whom have come from their distant homes in a Whitmanesque trance to thank the editors of the paper for bringing them "to life" (*ibid*.: 39) and to offer their services. As the Woman from Idaho, acted by Glaspell in the Provincetown production of 1917, explains, "we've come because you made us want something we didn't have, made us want it so much we had to move the way we thought was toward it – before the sun goes down" (*ibid*.: 39). The idealism of these simple folks, representatives of the "people" that Ed and his staff have been trying to reach, overcomes their dejection and will, Glaspell allows us to hope, spur them on to further efforts.

The People shows Glaspell's skill in transforming a real-life situation into a theatrically valid moment; applying her Darwinian idealism, she confers on the everyday problems of the socialist magazine *The Masses* (see Fishbein 1982) the dramatic tension necessary to provoke an audience to consider the need to evolve and so to improve humanity. Glaspell used the ideological and functional problems of the magazine, edited by fellow-villagers Max Eastman and Floyd Dell, to discuss the aims of the publication and its desire to reach the people. She gave the Woman from Idaho words that conveyed her own evolutionary, idealistic beliefs: "Let life become what it may become! – so beautiful that everything that is back of us is worth everything it cost" (Glaspell 1926b: 43). Although the Provincetown Players initially refused to invite the press or to publicize their little theater, some critics did brave the uncomfortable seating arrangements and the frequently long waits between plays. Heywood Broun, who wrote for the *New York Tribune*, was one of the first to review a Provincetown performance, and after seeing *The People* he wrote: "Susan Glaspell has done more for American drama than any playwright of the year. . . . [*The People*] is built upon a gorgeous plan and developed with humor and telling eloquence, despite a trace of an intrusive literary quality" (Broun 1917).

Close the Book

The bill that opened the Provincetown Players' second New York season on 2 November 1917 included Glaspell's *Close the Book*. This play is in the spirit of *Suppressed Desires*, *The People*, and *Woman's Honor*, which she would offer the Players the following year, all light comedies that abandon the melodrama that delighted American audiences on Broadway for the more sophisticated British tradition of G. B. Shaw, and anticipate the plays of Noel Coward or J. B. Priestley. Glaspell astutely mocks social trends and obsessions while at the same time transmitting a deeper social message. *Close the Book* urges us to reconsider our attitudes to those who are in some way different, therefore regarded as alien and thus inferior – or superior, depending on one's perceived position. It is Glaspell's earliest theatrical statement on racial difference and she makes her young protagonist Jhansi into an orphan who is convinced that she is a gypsy. Jhansi also believes that the nomadic life of her supposed gypsy forebears, which is the life she desires, is infinitely superior to the staid, traditional, non-questioning lives of the family into which she is about to marry. Moments before a family dinner to celebrate her engagement to Peyton, an instructor at the university, she airily insists: "I should take you by the hand and you and I should walk together down the open road" (Glaspell 1926a: 49). Peyton promises they will one day do this but he recognizes that "It's easier to be free when there's nobody who minds" (*ibid.*: 48). Words such as these are repeated throughout Glaspell's oeuvre as her protagonists struggle with their desire for freedom, which is generally equated with self-realization, Darwinian evolution and Nietzschean overcoming. This is the only time, however, when the realization that real self-sacrifice may be necessary in order not to hurt others is attributed to a male character.[2]

In this realistic play, Glaspell attacks the institutions of marriage and of learning by ridiculing the reactionary attitudes of its most distinguished representatives: Uncle George, president of the board of regents of the university, wishes that his nephew Peyton would "sow [his wild oats] in less intellectual fields" (*ibid*.: 52) and considers Jhansi to be a "bad influence. She's leading our young people to criticize the society their fathers have builded up" (*ibid*.: 53). Peyton's mother, one of the town's first ladies, has tart Shavian lines that must have raised conspiratorial laughs among the Provincetown audience – as they would certainly do today:

> MRS. ROOT: She [Jhansi] won't be in a position to say so much about freedom after she is married.
> UNCLE GEORGE: But they say she's a gypsy.
> MRS. ROOT: She won't be a gypsy after she's Peyton's wife. She'll be a married woman.
> UNCLE GEORGE: Yes, but in the meantime we will have swallowed a gypsy.
>
> (*ibid*.: 52)

Glaspell, who played Mrs. Root, here recognizes that marriage obliterates a woman's identity and individuality, literally swallowing up not only her possible racial differences but all her aspirations. As it turns out, Jhansi is not a gypsy, merely an orphan of simple folks who was brought up by a family that hid her origins from her. On the other hand, the same book – *Iowa Descendants of New England Families* – that reveals the truth of Jhansi's birth also reveals the past sins of Peyton's family, whose fortunes were founded on selling firearms to the Indians. Before more can be revealed, Grandmother orders Peyton to "Close the book!" (*ibid*.: 65). As always, Glaspell makes good use of the constrictions imposed by the small Provincetown stage. The play is set in one room which reveals all we need to know of the characters: it is the library of people who are *"important in their community, a university town, and who think of themselves as people of culture"* (*ibid.*: 47). Their pride in their status in the town, just as Jhansi's pride in being an "outsider," is mercilessly torn apart as their reactions to the truth of their origins reveal their superficiality and self-interest.

The Outside

Glaspell's next play, *The Outside*, opened at the Playwrights' Theater on 28 December 1917. For the setting, she used the dangerous outer coast of the curve of Cape Cod she knew well, and built the plot around the metaphor of the line where the sand dunes and the woods meet. As she admitted in *The Road to the Temple*:

> I loved [the line] where the woods sent out the life that can meet the sand, and the sand in turn tries to cover the woods – a fighting-line, the front line. It seemed to us a valiant, a dramatic line and we seldom passed without noticing, as in tribute.
>
> (Glaspell 1927: 287)

The area was dotted with life-saving stations, many fallen into disuse and bought up for summer residences by the Greenwich Villagers.[3] The lost struggle for survival embodied in the abandoned life-saving station and the ongoing struggle of the vegetation fighting to overcome the sand is reproduced by the action of the play. The Captain and his men have recovered a body from the ocean and brought it to the disused life-saving station that had once been theirs; however, they are unable to bring the corpse back to life. The women living in the station – Mrs. Patrick and her servant, Allie Mayo – observe the hopeless struggle to save the drowned man's life and, in an epiphanic moment that opens into understanding, accept that nature should serve as their example.

The Outside focuses on these two women who have lost their husbands: Mrs. Patrick, having lost hers to another woman, secludes herself in the desolate life-saving station with Allie

Mayo, whose husband never returned from a whaling expedition. Allie's grief is known in the town. As one of the life-savers explains: "Allie Mayo has got a prejudice against words. . . . She's not spoke an unnecessary word for twenty years" (Glaspell 1920b: 51). Both women, seeing themselves "outside" a society that is built on couples and families, take refuge in themselves and, knowing that society will make exiles of them, create their own exile in silence and solitude. But it is Allie who, roused by the life-savers' futile attempts to restore life, turns to nature, and returns to the promise of human communication as she tries to convince Mrs. Patrick that her words are now necessary to save them both:

> ALLIE MAYO: When you keep still for twenty years you know – things you didn't know you knew. I know why you're doing that. [*Mrs Patrick is pushing sand on half buried grass*] . . . Don't bury the only thing that will grow. Let it grow. (*[Mrs. Patrick] still crying under her breath turns abruptly and starts toward the line where dunes and woods meet.*) I know where you're going! . . . What you'll try to do. Over there . . . Bury it. The life in you. Bury it – watching the sand bury the woods. But I'll tell you something! *They* fight too. The woods! They fight for life the way that captain fought for life in there!
> MRS. PATRICK: (*with a strange exultation*) And lose the way he lost in there!
> ALLIE MAYO: (*sure, somber*) They don't lose.
>
> (*ibid.*: 52–53)

Glaspell played Allie Mayo in the first production and so publicly gave voice to her Monist and Darwinian convictions of the oneness, interaction and evolution of all living beings (see Chapter 1). The theme that she would explore in greater depth in *The Verge* – that it is possible to overcome the stifling old patterns – is present in Allie's cry: "And life grows over buried life! . . . It will. And Springs will come when you will want to know that it is Spring" (*ibid.*: 54).

Silence, and therefore lack of interaction with others, is a theme that Glaspell returns to frequently in her novels and plays (see Ozieblo 2006a: 148–50). In *Trifles* and *Bernice*, as we will see, she creates an absent, and therefore silenced, protagonist; in *The Outside*, however, the women are present on stage, but they have decided not to speak, and so not to participate in society, their choice giving them a sense of power. In Glaspell's novel *Fugitive's Return* (1929), the protagonist Irma is empowered by her chosen silence and retreat from Cape Cod society to the more primitive life of Delphos, a remote village in Greece. However, in both the novel and the short story "A Rose in the Sand: The Salvation of a Lonely Soul" (published in the magazine *Pall Mall* in 1927), a reworking of *The Outside*, nature is no longer invoked as a life-giving force: it is substituted by a child and by the protagonist's nurturing instinct.

Although it ends on a note of optimism as Allie persuades Mrs. Patrick to ally herself with nature, *The Outside* is a somber play. It is the only piece of this period, apart from *Trifles*, that totally lacks the veneer of comedy with which Glaspell generally invested her pieces, although one reviewer would assert in 1920 that all Glaspell's plays are "deliciously and slyly humorous" (Anon 1920b). *The Outside* has not received much critical attention from scholars (of the shorter plays, only *Trifles* has been written about at length) and yet it has excited some controversy as to the interpretation put forward by feminist critics, for whom: "Unobtrusively, Glaspell points to the irony of the talkative, sociable men fighting for life and losing, while the silent women, who have rejected traditional social customs, learn from nature and win through to a deeper intuition of life (Ozieblo 2006a: 149). Kristina Hinz-Bode, in a recent study of the language and location of Glaspell's dramatic work rejects this "struggle between the sexes" (Gainor 2001: 75) approach and, basing her argument on a detailed study of the language of the play, considers that it is the men's "dogged refusal to accept death's victory" (Hinz-Bode 2006a: 90) that inspires Allie to recognize the need to live within a community.

The set of *The Outside*, as already indicated, is highly realistic in that it uses an actual space, and Glaspell challenges any designer with her stage directions:

> *About two thirds of the back wall is open, because of the big sliding door, of the type of barn door, and through this open door are seen the sand dunes, and beyond them the woods . . . through the open door the sea also is seen.*
>
> (Glaspell 1920b: 48)

There is also another door in a wall that slants across the stage, and through this we see the life-savers at work. How the anonymous designer resolved these directions in the small space of the Provincetown stage is difficult to imagine, and there are no photographs to help. Glaspell paints a vivid expressionistic picture for the viewer, presumably achieved by resourceful use of lighting and minimalist decor: the drab gray walls of the life-station, the "*bleak*" (*ibid*.: 50), silent women, the dejected life-savers and the studied movements of all the characters gain meaning when contrasted with the victorious struggle for survival of nature going on outside. In this way, through the use of symbolism and expressionism, Glaspell accomplishes what Gainor has identified as the "holistic artistry in production (*Gesamtkunstwerk*) that critics associate with the calculated theatrical experiments of the modern era" (Gainor 2001: 75).

Woman's Honor

Woman's Honor, performed in the last bill of that same season, in April 1918, returns to the light satire in which Glaspell excelled. She co-directed the play with Nina Moise and acted the role of the Cheated One. Whereas in *The Outside* Glaspell had examined two women's reactions to the exclusion of single women from social life, in *Woman's Honor* she turns to a social myth that affects all women, that of their reputation. As Gainor has indicated, although not generally applied, laws regulating women's behavior still exist in the United States: for example, the 1909 "Slander of Woman" statute came under discussion in January 2005 in the Washington State legislature (Gainor 2006: 66).

In *Woman's Honor*, Gordon Wallace is charged with murder but refuses to give his alibi: he had spent the night the murder was committed with a woman and, true to ideals that even his lawyer, Mr. Foster, finds old fashioned, does not want to defile her honor by giving her name. Wallace rebukes his lawyer:

> Mr. Foster, I tell you again, I dislike your attitude toward women! Laugh at me if you will, but I have respect and reverence for women. I believe that it is perfectly true that men must guard them. Call me a romantic young fool if it pleases you, but I have had a mother – a sister – sweetheart. Yes, I am ready to die to shield a woman's honor!
>
> (Glaspell 1920d: 84)

Foster leaks this to the press and as a result uncountable numbers of women arrive to swear that they were with Wallace on the night of the murder, prepared, for many different reasons, to lose their "honor," which they all see as an unnecessary fiction and a burden. Glaspell achieves comedy by the quick repetition of the women's depositions as they arrive one by one, confounding the lawyer and so agitating the prisoner that he prefers to plead guilty rather than listen to more false confessions from desperate women he does not know. The women in *Woman's Honor* – as was the case with the characters of *The People* – are allegorical types, identified by their main characteristic: the Shielded One, the Motherly One, the Scornful One, the Silly One, the Mercenary One and the Cheated One symbolize the stereotypical roles that society has thrust upon women.

All the women who speak – and there are others waiting in the adjoining room who are not allowed to enter the confined space where the prisoner is being held – consider it crucial that they be chosen to represent the fallen woman. For the Motherly One, a nurse by profession, it is simply a matter of saving Wallace's life – although she empathizes with the woman who presumably loves the young man and is "some nice girl afraid of her mother" (*ibid.*: 91). The Shielded One's motives are more far-reaching and add a note of bitter comedy:

> I speak for all the women of my – (*hesitates*) under-world, all those others smothered under men's lofty sentiments toward

them! I wish I could paint for you the horrors of the shielded
life. (*Says "shielded" as if it were "shameful."*) I know you
would feel something must be done to save us.

(*ibid.*: 97)

Her reforming zeal contrasts with the Silly One's romantic
notions of love and with the Scornful and Cheated Ones' more
personal motives of revenge. These women, who all realize that
they have suffered from the impositions of so-called woman's
honor, are prevented from reaching an agreement as to how they
can best expose the concept as false, and in the process save
Wallace's life, by the young man's decision to plead guilty rather
than face so many victims of this misconception of virtue that
society has forced on them.

The Motherly One is the prototype of the calm, wise, older
woman who appears in many of Glaspell's later works and who
is most aware of the workings of society; she voices Glaspell's
contradictory feelings about individuality and evolution in
traditional society when she says: "You get made into one thing
and then it's not easy to be another" (*ibid.*: 95). To the Scornful
One's observation that "woman's honor would have died out
long ago if it hadn't been for men's talk about it," the Motherly
One soberly answers: "I suppose it really has to be kept up, as
long as it gives men such noble feelings" (*ibid.*: 93).[4] It is the
Scornful One who attempts to define woman's honor: "Did it
ever strike you as funny that woman's honor is only about one
thing, and that man's honor is about everything but that thing?"
(*ibid.*: 90). A disconcertingly comic moment is introduced with
the entrance of the Mercenary One, who is taken to be a prostitute by the other women – but turns out to be applying for a
stenographer's job. The lightness of touch in this play makes it
possible for audiences to laugh at what Glaspell considers a
manifestation of the social hypocrisy regarding women that she
parodies and leaves before us to reconsider.

Curiously, the reviewers of *Woman's Honor* all emphasized
the young man's desire to sacrifice himself for the woman he
loves, but none of them dwell on the reasons why so many women
wanted to save him, thus sacrificing their so-called honor.[5] The

piece was revived by the Players in April 1919, when it was reviewed by Rebecca Drucker for the *New York Times*, and she too failed to understand the import of the women's project. For her, they are merely "altruistically ready to part with theirs [their honor] to save the young man from his old-fashioned wrongheadedness" (Drucker 1919). But Drucker does give us a feeling of the impression the play left on the audience when she tells us:

> The deft satiric dialogue sparkles and sparkles, it lets in light and air on a topic that is usually treated with a stuffy and stilted romanticism. . . . [Glaspell] is a fresh and original genius in the theatre – shrewdly aware of human values, satiric and sensitive.
>
> (*ibid.*)

Tickless Time

The last of Glaspell's short plays, *Tickless Time*, was performed in December 1918. Co-written and co-directed with her husband, it is one of her few pieces in which Glaspell did not act. Another exploration of the quirks of behavior and obsessions of the Provincetowners, it bears the imprint of her control of comic dialogue and concern with the individual in society. Here, Ian Joyce has made a sundial (as Cook had done) and has discovered that clocks do not keep "true time": they symbolize "the whole standardization of our lives" (Glaspell 1928b: 126). Ian and his wife Eloise decide to bury their clocks and live by "true" time, until he, in his search for truth, reveals that, given the irregularities of the sun, it shows the "right" time only four days in the year (*ibid.*: 137). Eloise cannot accept that the sun is not "correct"; she wants an absolute truth that will replace the standardization imposed by clocks. Their friends, with a total lack of understanding of the importance of this search for truth, are offended that their wedding gift, a cuckoo clock, has been buried along with the other clocks, and ask: "what difference does it make if we're wrong, if we're all wrong together?" (*ibid.*: 134), so rejecting the right to freedom of thought and opinion. And the cook, Annie, threatens to leave because "You can't cook without a clock" (*ibid*.: 135), finding the dial insufficiently exact to calculate the three minutes required to fry onions. As Marcia Noe and Robert Marlowe (2006) show, Cook and Glaspell were motivated in this play by current discussions of relativity; however, the concern with the need to comply and follow the leader that *Tickless Time* parodies at a time of increased censorship and control during the last months of the First World War also inspires this seemingly light burlesque on standardization.

Tickless Time is placed in a garden symbolically dominated by a tree, sunflowers growing against a fence, and a sundial. However, the setting does not reflect the characters as it did in Glaspell's previous work, but rather the argument over sun time. Glaspell refines her earlier experiments with allegory and creates stereotypical characters in *Tickless Time*, which could be played with the exaggerated movements of pantomime. There is no prefatory scene to introduce the characters comparable to the talk of the life-savers at the opening of *The Outside*. All we know of Ian and Eloise we learn from their words and gestures and from the essentialized descriptions provided in the *dramatis personae*: Ian Joyce "Has Made a Sundial" while his wife is "Wedded to the Sundial"; the neighbors are "a Standardized Mind" and a "Standardized Wife" (Glaspell 1928b: 122).[6] Glaspell's stage directions for their movements – intense, wild, exulted, and frequently childlike, as when Eloise holds "the clock with both hands and places it against her left ear" (*ibid*.: 129) – reinforce the parodic quality of the play. This departure from the realistic, even naturalistic, setting and action of *Trifles*, *Close the Book* and *The Outside* allowed Glaspell to explore the possibilities of political commentary through the mode of surreal, dream-like pantomime designed to uncover and ridicule an audience's obsessions.

The anthology *Ten Modern Plays* – which includes *Tickless Time* – comes with acting notes that consider the play to be a "sophisticated comedy" requiring "more finished" acting than do other comedies in the anthology, for it is "self-conscious, posed, intellectual, a kind of comedy of manners – and may be caviar to some audiences." The author appreciates the "farcical touches" of *Tickless Time* but worries over the casting of Ian and Eloise: "These two players must be able to appreciate and portray the simple-mindedness which marks them both, as well as Ian's muddled rhapsodic idealism and his wife's muddled attempts to follow him." He ends by advising actors and producers to read Glaspell's later, full-length *Inheritors* and *Bernice*, "for in *Tickless Time* Miss Glaspell seems to be deliberately making fun of her own serious work" (Hampden 1928: 243), thus recognizing the intratextuality of Glaspell's oeuvre.

In her early, short plays Glaspell experimented with stage conventions and holistic theatrical expression in preparation for the full-length works upon which she now embarked. Her education had given her a good grounding in the classics and philosophy, and her European trip had exposed her to the innovations of modernism in all the arts: pictures by Matisse, Braque, Picasso at the leading galleries, and plays by Ibsen, Strindberg and Maeterlinck in the experimental theaters. With the Provincetown Players she learned to apply her literary gifts to the theater and to move fluidly between genres. These early plays are the antecedents of later stories, full-length plays or novels, in which, able to go beyond the condensation required in a short play, she could explore her characters and their motives further. The plays are gems of conciseness, control of characters, plot, comedy, staging and histrionic devices, and experiment with the myriad means and modes of the modernist theater.

3   The full-length plays

The short plays that Glaspell wrote during the first years of the Provincetown Players provided her with valuable experience in dramatic writing and production. Although one of the early tenets of the Players had been that authors should direct their own plays, Glaspell preferred to act rather than direct. She took a part in almost all her early plays and merited the praise of the French director Jacques Copeau for the authenticity and purity of her interpretation of the Woman of Idaho in *The People* (Ozieblo 2000: 110). In *Bernice* she played the part of Abbie and was declared "not technically adept" by the reviewer Heywood Broun, who, however, admitted that "she plays with convincing spirit and feeling" (Broun 1919). In the early plays, Glaspell experimented with the trends of modernist European drama as she forged a style of her own with the express design to move her audiences to rethink their conventional attitudes. In *Bernice* (1919), her first three-act play, Glaspell continues her discussion of the relationships between men and women on which she had embarked, more covertly, in *The Outside*, but in this play it is the husband, Craig, who is clearly "outside" the women's community she has created.

Bernice

Directed by James Ballantine, *Bernice* was performed by the Provincetown Players from 21 to 27 March in 1919 as part of the fifth bill of the third season at the Playwrights' Theater on

Macdougal Street; it has been revived only once, by the London Gate Theatre in October 1925. It is a "penetrating study of the power games people play" (Ozieblo 2000: 142), and was defined as "a mystery play" by Edna Kenton (1997: 99). Like *Trifles*, it boasts an absent protagonist and is a detective play that through moments of clarifying vision uncovers the enigma of personal motives. As the reviewer of the *New York Herald* perceived, it is a play "of the Ibsen type" although "much more modern than the work of the Norwegian" (Anon. 1919). Ibsen's *The Master Builder* is a study of the erotic, almost demonic power of women and their desire to manipulate men; Hilde Wangel is seen as a negative force and Halvard Solness's reaction, his refusal to recognize his limits, can only lead to his destruction. Glaspell's Bernice, who is dead when the play opens, also stage-manages the life of the man she loves, her husband Craig, but she does this from beyond the grave. On her death-bed, knowing that such knowledge will boost Craig's sapless ego, she extracts a promise from her servant Abbie to tell him that she had committed suicide. By making him feel he had influenced her decision, she manipulates Craig into a positive mood of possible accomplishment rather than toward a lethal desire of over-achievement, as Hilde had done with Solness. Craig had always complained that he had never "*had* Bernice," that she had never allowed him to "dominate" (Glaspell 1919: 27) or "reshape" her (*ibid.*: 17) and now, believing that his infidelities had led her to commit suicide, he can cry out: "You never *knew* Bernice. You thought she didn't love me. You think I didn't matter. But Bernice *killed* herself because she loved me so!" (*ibid.*: 18). Disconcerting for a feminist reading of the play, however, is the fact that Bernice's power lies in her death; in life she had been aloof, leading an independent life that Craig had interpreted as a belittling of his virility.

The pivot of the play is the deep bond between Bernice and Margaret Pierce, who, on arriving to nurse her ill friend, learns that she has already died. Although contemporary reviewers generally focused on Craig (see Gainor 2001: 108–11) and recent work on Glaspell has questioned her commitment to women's friendships (see Fletcher 2006), Bernice, Margaret and even Abbie are clearly women who understand and support one another while Craig is portrayed as an outsider; Glaspell subverts not only the conventional triangular relationships of two women and a man but the very sense of women being on "the outside" that Glaspell had created in the play of that title. Thus a community of women is created and, as Cheryl Black argues, "barring heterocentric assumptions, there is as much evidence in the play to suggest a sexual relationship between Margaret and Bernice as there is between Craig and Bernice" (Black 2005: 56). However, the sexual activity of the characters is not dwelt upon: even Craig's infidelities are glossed over as basically irrelevant to the action of the play. Our attention is held by Margaret's desire to understand her friend's decision to promote the lie of suicide. Craig shares Abbie's disclosure with Margaret but, as we had been warned by Craig and by Bernice's father, "Margaret sees everything" (Glaspell 1919: 10) and is able to unravel the mystery her friend had fashioned.

Dramatically, the play is structured around Margaret's piercing moments of perception or *anagnorisis*, the classical device of Greek tragedy that leads to the denouement when the unsuspected motives that rule the plot are finally uncovered. Glaspell skillfully builds tension from the start of the play by emphasizing Abbie's apprehension at the arrival of Margaret. Tension is maintained by partial disclosures of the "truth" which result from Margaret's deepening understanding of her friend and her intense and painful approximation to Bernice's purpose in bidding Abbie tell Craig that she had committed suicide. As Bernice had predicted, and as Margaret comes to understand, Craig, confident in his egotistic interpretation of the information disclosed by Abbie, now believes that, however unknowingly, he had in fact exerted power over her, had been able to "destroy" and "reshape" her life (*ibid.*: 17) and so he can now recognize his manhood. Ironically, Craig's newly acquired – and totally misconstrued – sense of virile power is based on a fiction while our impression of Bernice, her character and her death, has been construed and re-construed before us by those who knew her into a multiplicity of images so that we are "left to sort out the conflicting meanings that emerge" (Friedman 1995: 156).

As in all her previous works, Glaspell makes the set into a vital part of the holistic impression that the action leaves on its audience. In the stage directions, she anthropomorphizes the house: "*You feel yourself in the house of a woman you would like to know, a woman of sure and beautiful instincts, who lives simply*" (Glaspell 1919: 9). The small transformations – a chair, a table, and a vase moved from one spot to the other at the beginning and end of the play – reflect the action: Bernice's will prevails and she has been understood by those who loved her, albeit differently by each one. Throughout the play, the door to the room where Bernice is laid out remains closed, an intractable barrier to comprehension and communication. In *The Outside*, Mrs. Patrick and Allie Mayo had refused language; in *Bernice*, the protagonist can no longer speak and her past words and actions must be interpreted by those who remain. None of the characters feel they can face her in death until they have solved for themselves the mystery she has imposed on them. Finally, Margaret, after communing with the spirit of Bernice in the closed room, comes out "*leaving the door wide open behind her*" (*ibid.*: 54) and, turning to Abbie, exclaims, "Power. Oh, how strange" (*ibid.*: 55).

Margaret's mode of expression prefigures the language that Glaspell would use so successfully in *The Verge*, a language bordering on the poetic that is highly expressive of her inner self. Nonetheless, Heywood Broun chose to defend the play as realistic, arguing that *Bernice* "bears eloquent testimony that a realistic play need by no means be humdrum and prosy." He substantiates his praise of realism on the grounds that "There is no finer adventure in the world, or in the theatre, than the search for truth, and no triumph so complete as its discovery" (Broun 1919) thus denying the subjectivity that Glaspell subtly poses in the different interpretations of Bernice's death. Another reviewer, John Corbin, was also delighted by *Bernice*, recognizing it as:

quite beautifully simple and deft, perfect in each of its several characterizations as in the great central personality of Bernice. It is a play after Maeterlinck's own heart, and (though it bears no trace of its author's abundant humor) it is tender and heart-wise as Barrie at his best.

(Corbin 1919)

Chains of Dew

Susan Glaspell's next play, *Chains of Dew*, although written in 1919, was not performed by the Players until 1922, when it was directed by Ralph Stewart with sets by Cleon Throckmorton. Because of the circumstances of its production – indiscriminate cutting, bad casting, and the absence of the author during rehearsals – it has frequently been regarded as unfinished and has never been published.[1] However, Glaspell, ambitious for recognition beyond Greenwich Village, had submitted it to a number of Broadway directors in 1920, and she agreed to a production at her own theater only when it became clear that the Players did not have a play to complete the 1921–22 season (see Ozieblo 2000: 155–66 and Ozieblo 2006b). By the time *Chains of Dew* went into rehearsal, Glaspell had left for Greece with her husband for a long-planned and desired sojourn in the cradle of classical theater. The play opened at the end of April 1922, played for eighteen days, and has never been revived.[2]

Chains of Dew, like *Bernice*, is a realistic play in its setting and in how it portrays the struggle of Diantha (called Dotty by her husband) and her mother-in-law to reach an understanding of the behavior of Seymore, Diantha's husband, and of their responsibility toward him. As in so many of her plays, novels and stories, Glaspell is querying the right to individual and artistic freedom and development in the context of society: the small family group but also the larger community of a Midwestern town. The social issue that she raises in *Chains of Dew* is the campaign to legalize birth control. Although educated and upper-middle-class women did have some knowledge of birth control by the early twentieth century, under the 1873 Comstock Laws it was illegal for such information to circulate.[3] In *Chains of Dew*, set in the Midwest in the early 1900s, Diantha is very quickly convinced by Nora, a birth-control worker who has arrived unexpectedly from New York, to join the effort to legalize contraception. Nora – whose name is clearly a nod in the direction of Ibsen's *A Doll's House* – is a friend of her husband. Seymore's mother joins in most eagerly too, even though – or perhaps because – she has had seven children. The last of these, who, as he reminds her in Act II, would not exist if there had been birth control some thirty years previously, is Diantha's husband, the director of a bank but also a poet who, according to his New York friends, just falls short of being a great poet.

As the plot develops, we realize that Diantha is not the semi-invalid that Seymore makes her out to be, but an intelligent, lively woman who, although greatly in love with her husband, is beginning to resent his manipulative behavior and is looking for ways to convert her marriage into a more companionate relationship, as advocated by turn-of-the-century progressivism. During his absence she attempts to transform herself into what she thinks a wife should be: an intellectual companion for her husband and not merely a pretty doll. Nora's arrival helps her in this process, and she even bobs her hair to emulate the model of the New Woman that Nora represents. However, Seymore is not happy at this transformation in his own home; like Craig in *Bernice*, he too needs to believe that his wife (and mother) depend on him for all their needs and satisfactions. Finally, in a sorry reversal of feminist expectations,[4] Mother and Diantha give up their new-found freedom, Nora departs just as suddenly as she had arrived, and Seymore can continue complaining about the chains and obligations of marriage and society life that bite into his writing time.

Possibly the most interesting role in *Chains of Dew* is that of the Mother, who makes artistic rag dolls to fill her time and symbolically express her frustrations within the gilded prison that Seymore has built for himself and his family. The process of her realization of Seymore's psychological need of familial "chains" is carefully staged, as is her gradual recognition of a Freudian, maternal guilt – "Oh my dear – it's hard to be a mother" (Glaspell 1920a: III, 29) – that leads to the Hegelian question: "Would it be possible to think highly enough of personal liberty to feel a man had a right to keep himself in bondage if he wanted to?" (*ibid.*).

Although Glaspell wrote *Chains of Dew* as a comedy for Broadway – where audiences wanted to be entertained but not enlightened – she found it impossible to maintain the blithe spirit of a Noel Coward play; true to herself, she introduced a Shavian critique of the social fabric, a discussion of the artist in society, and an exploration of the "essential significance of *connection* in human existence" in its struggle with the "notion of self as a separate and independent entity" (Hinz-Bode 2006a: 140). Whereas Rachel Crothers, Glaspell's contemporary and one of the few women playwrights who made a living on Broadway, sustained the comedy in, for example, *Susan and God*, where the protagonist also breaks loose only to return into the fold of society, Glaspell brought in a dark, tragic element in Diantha's acceptance to take on the "greatest [sacrifice] of all," that is, to "let [herself] be sacrificed for" (Glaspell 1920a: III, 31).

Reviewers were disconcerted by the sub-standard production at the Playwrights' Theater: Alison Smith, writing for the *New York Evening Globe*, saw Glaspell as "wabbling dangerously" between "hilarious satire" and "grim sincerity" (Smith 1922). Other critics realized the play's Broadway possibilities: an anonymous reviewer thought Glaspell was merely criticizing her own set, the Greenwich Village radicals, and that the play "could be enjoyed by many of those living above that spiritual dead line of Washington Square which these players seem to have drawn for themselves" (Anon. 1922). Alexander Woollcott, who recognized the "somewhat anachronistic aspect" of *Chains of Dew*, could praise it as "touched . . . with charming fancy, lighted . . . by gleams of the shrewdest and most subtle humor" while astutely "put[ting his] finger right on the weak spot" (Woollcott 1922). The weak spot is the husband, the banker–poet Seymore, who would have to be a Clark Gable in order to be convincing.[5] The play hinges on Diantha and the audience believing that he is not a "conceited prig" (Hinz-Bode 2006a: 136) and a bad poet to boot, but a truly loveable man. Diantha defends him to both Mother and Nora with these words: "You haven't said anything about the nice things – the delightful things, and the *great* things. Everyone knows Seymore is a poet. Well, certain peculiarities – go with gifts. And if a man has the soul of a poet, he does have a

– a sadness – it's *part* of being a poet" (Glaspell 1920a: III, 34). Such a defense is reminiscent of Glaspell's attitude to her husband George Cram Cook in the biography with which she honored him, *The Road to the Temple*.

Inheritors

Glaspell's next play, *Inheritors*, her most frequently revived piece, was recognized as a "lost gem" (Gluck 2005) after the 2005 production at the Metropolitan Playhouse in New York. It was first performed in March 1921 by the Provincetown Players, directed by Jasper Deeter. In Britain, *Inheritors* was performed in Liverpool and London in 1925 and by the Orange Tree Theatre, Richmond, in 1997; and it was revived by the Civic Repertory Company in New York in 1927 and by the Mirror Theater in 1983. Deeter was so taken by the play that he would stage *Inheritors* almost every year from 1923 to 1954 at the Hedgerow Theatre in Moylan, Pennsylvania.[6]

Glaspell wrote *Inheritors* for the Players' subscription audience of like-minded Greenwich Village bohemians she knew so well and, as J. Ellen Gainor indicates, for once she openly "joined her colleagues in political activism, directly challenging governmental repression and risking prosecution for her writing" (Gainor 2001: 115). The overt theme of the play was the impact of the First World War on American values – the resulting restrictions on freedom of speech, the xenophobia, and the isolationism justified by a need to make democracy safe. The Espionage and Sedition Acts of 1917 and 1918 were still in force when Glaspell wrote and she knew well their effects: both *The Masses* and Emma Goldman's *Mother Earth*, magazines whose editors and contributors she knew, had been shut down, accused of promoting pacifism.

Rather than place *Inheritors* in a magazine office, as she had done in *The People* and Act I of *Chains of Dew*, Glaspell preferred to revisit her roots and set the play in a realistic Midwestern farming town. Using a four-act structure, she made the first act into a prologue that takes the audience back to 1879, forty years prior to the main action of the play. Here,

Glaspell retells the history of America: pioneers settling in the Midwest, Native Indians despoiled of their land and heritage, immigrants from Old Europe bringing their culture and knowledge to their new home. The remaining three acts tell the story of a young woman, descended from those very pioneers, who, in 1920, cannot countenance how America is treating a group of students from India who are protesting British rule. Glaspell draws a clear parallel between the Indians that are to be imprisoned and then deported under the Espionage Act and the displacement of Native Indians in the nineteenth century. The "scope, sweep, and political force of Glaspell's writing in this play," as Gainor argues, has been equaled only by Tony Kushner's *Angels in America* (Gainor 2001: 141). The vision that Glaspell offers of America has never lost its validity, as the numerous revivals attest. Productions in Britain garnered enthusiastic reviews, although some critics rejected outright that the problems addressed in the play could have anything to do with the British (Anon. 1925a and Anon. 1925c). A reviewer of the 1997 production at the Orange Tree Theatre considered *Inheritors* to be "remarkable for its radicalism and its date" (Hewison 1997).

Glaspell returns to the theme of personal freedom versus obligations to family and society in *Inheritors* – a theme that she had been developing in earlier stories and novels as well as in *Bernice* and *Chains of Dew*. However, in *Inheritors*, which is "enormously resonant philosophically" (Denton 2005), Glaspell complicates her argument by implicating the state and questioning not only what it means to be a good daughter, but what it means to be a good American; as Marie Molnar has pointed out, Glaspell "uses Sophocles' *Antigone* as a subtext and a basis for the structure of her play" (Molnar 2006: 38). In the second act of *Inheritors*, in 1920, the college that Silas Morton, son of pioneers, and Felix Fejevary, a Hungarian refugee, had founded in 1879 on Morton's hill overlooking the town needs money to expand. In order to convince the government to come up with funding, Felix Fejevary Jr., trustee of the college his father had founded, must coerce a professor to give up his radical stance on conscientious objection to the war, and expel the Indian students who are protesting on his campus. Echoing Diantha in the earlier play, Fejevary argues:

> No one is entirely free. That's naïve. It's rather egotistical to want to be. We're held by our relations to others – by our obligations to the (*vaguely*) – the ultimate thing. . . . You'd like, of course, to be just what you want to be – but isn't there something selfish in that satisfaction?
>
> (Glaspell 1921: 135, 136)

The hill on which the campus stands is the governing metaphor of the play, and the Metropolitan Playhouse production made good use of it in the minimalist set, on their small stage. It stands firm in the background, bathed in a bright orange-yellow glow.[7]

While in *Chains of Dew*, hoping to entertain a Broadway audience, Glaspell employed her gifts for comedy and wrote in a flippant, satirical tone, in *Inheritors* she is much more sober. At the end of the play, her young heroine, Madeline Morton Fejevary – a "part of Ibsenesque proportion" (Hewison 1997) – departs for prison; in her attempt to intercede between the protesting Indian students and the police, she had clubbed a policeman with her tennis racquet, the only weapon available to her – a symbol of her love of free movement and youthful fun. Now she must appear before the judge, and under the Espionage and Sedition Acts she will be sentenced to prison; she has refused to seek her uncle Fejevary's aid, to retract, as he demands, and be "just a girl [who] didn't know what she was saying" (Glaspell 1921: 145). Previously, in a scene of stark emotion, Madeline had chalked out on the floor of her father's kitchen the area of the cell in which a friend was being held. Fred had protested at war because he "couldn't be a part of nations of men killing each other" (*ibid.*: 152). Madeline goes into the chalked cell and feels its walls closing in on her; the stage directions tell us that, for a moment, "*she is all the people who are in those cells*" (*ibid.*: 144).

Although quite unwittingly, it is Madeline's father who convinces her to stand by her convictions. Ira Morton takes great pride in the strain of corn he has developed and, in speeches that reflect a discussion of Darwin's theories of evolution in Act I,[8] but also Claire's attempts in *The Verge* to create new plant life, he tells of his ambition to improve the land his father left him, land that had been taken from the Indians. He explains how the corn, through the process of pollination and aided by his watchful care, had improved: "the pollen blows from corn to corn like a . . . gift" (*ibid.*: 155). So that now Madeline, even though she is deserting the father who needs her and preferring her own moral satisfaction to her daughterly obligation, converts his ambition into a metaphor that justifies her decision: "But father has been telling me about the corn. It gives itself away all the time – the best corn a gift to other corn. What you are – that doesn't stay with you. Then . . . be the most you can be, so life will be more because you were" (*ibid.*: 156).

Bernice in the play of that title and Claire in *The Verge* are women who also prefer to be "the most you can be" rather than fulfill the obligations that family and society impose on them. For Madeline's aunt Isabel, life is "Sacrificing for one another," to which Madeline impulsively responds, "I hope I never have a family" (*ibid.*: 148). Diantha in *Chains of Dew* and Alison in *Alison's House* stand out in Glaspell's dramatic oeuvre as heroines who sacrifice their aspirations in obeying the dictates of society. Madeline realizes "It's love that – brings life along, and then it's love – holds life back" (*ibid.*: 153), so commenting on the romantic notions of love that entrap women which Glaspell is frequently suspected of endorsing and yet critiques in all her writing, as a careful reading shows.[9]

The Comic Artist

Although on her return from Greece in 1924 after Cook's death Glaspell found herself without a theater to write for (see Ozieblo 2000: 227–34), she did not forsake the stage completely. She devoted most of her time and energies to the biography of her deceased husband and then returned to fiction, but it seems she did find time to co-write two plays with her new companion, Norman Matson: *The Comic Artist*, which was published and eventually performed; and *The Good Bozo*, mentioned in their letters although no script has been found.[10] How much of the inspiration and writing were hers is impossible to establish, but Glaspell disowned *The Comic Artist* after her relationship with Matson had dissolved. Nonetheless, as Gainor has pointed out, Glaspell's "dialogic patterns and diction" can be identified at specific moments (Gainor 2001: 212). This play on the rivalry of two brothers for the love of Nina maintains the realism of setting and psychological enquiry that Glaspell had used in *Bernice* but does not continue the exploration of theatrical innovation that *The Verge* surely led critics to expect.

In spite of Glaspell's initial efforts, *The Comic Artist*, which had premiered in London on 24 June 1928 in a private performance by the Play Actors at the Strand, did not reach Broadway until 1933, when it was performed at the Morosco Theatre. Glaspell did not supervise the production, which offered an alternate, happy ending to that which appears in the published version of 1927, where Karl, the comic artist, drowns. Themes such as personal relationships and the role of the artist in society, which appear in Glaspell's other writing, are present in this play. Gainor sees it as exploring "both theatrical modernism and related issues of high versus mass culture" (Gainor 2001: 200). If we concentrate on the family issues that the play examines, we can relate it to Neith Boyce's *The Two Sons*, a short play performed by the Provincetown Players in 1917, which may well have influenced Eugene O'Neill's *Beyond the Horizon*, performed in 1920 (see Ozieblo 2000: 102).

Alison's House

Alison's House, first performed in December 1930 by Eva Le Gallienne's Civic Repertory Company, is also closer to *Bernice* than to *The Verge*. As with most of Susan Glaspell's plays, it is a family drama. However, like *Chains of Dew*, it was not written for the Provincetown Players and so eschews experimental techniques in favor of a quiet realism. Although there are moments of biting humor, *Alison's House* is reminiscent of *Bernice* in its sober setting and psychological unraveling of the mysteries of family relationships. It is set in the old Stanhope family homestead, on the last day of the nineteenth century, and exudes a

Chekhovian nostalgia that is, however, given an optimistic turn as the play ends and *"distant bells ring in the new century"* (Glaspell 1930: 155). But Glaspell's nostalgia is made ambivalent by her Shavian critique of Victorian mores, delicately balanced by a happy resolution that points toward the greater freedoms of the twentieth century. According to one critic, it is "a drama of intense realism, a realism which somehow exudes the spirit of a real America, an America which still bears herself with dignity and reverence" (Blon 1933). Although the play pays homage to the values of the past, it also makes apparent the suffering they inflict on the members of the *"family of traditions and culti- vation"* (Glaspell 1930: 3) who inhabit the old homestead that is about to be sold. The two rooms of the set reflect the values of this family, and Glaspell carefully specifies both the furnishings and the feel of the place, much as she had done for *Bernice*. The house had been the home of the reclusive poet Alison Stanhope, who had died eighteen years previously, leaving behind her poetry, which the family had published. Now, as they are prepar- ing to leave the house to others, they find more poems.

As all contemporary reviewers indicated, there are clear allu- sions to Emily Dickinson in *Alison's House* (see Rodier 1995). However, the legend that the Dickinson family prohibited Glaspell's original design, an openly biographical play, using the Dickinson name and quoting the poetry, has not been docu- mented (see Ozieblo 2000: 238–44). Linda Ben-Zvi believes that Glaspell changed the location and the names "lest the play be seen as a direct biographical study of the poet and not be judged on its own merit" (Ben-Zvi 2005: 335). However, we know that Glaspell had been attracted to Dickinson's poetry as a young woman: in her first novel, *The Glory of the Conquered* (1909), she quotes a Dickinson poem that had been published anonymously in 1878, and we can assume that the rumors of Dickinson's secret love for a married man that Martha Dickinson Bianchi's *The Life and Letters of Emily Dickinson* (1924) had brought before the public had established a "more personal bond: she [Glaspell] identified with the poet, seeing in her a victim of society's stranglehold on women" (Ozieblo 2000: 240). Glaspell supported such an assumption when she told a *New*

York Times reporter that the play "grew out of a feeling for her [Dickinson's] work and character" (quoted in Ben-Zvi 2005: 335). Nevertheless, the opening of *Alison's House* on 1 December 1930, coinciding almost exactly with the centenary of Dickinson's birth, must have ratified the rumors. Although reviews were mixed, the play won the 1931 Pulitzer Prize and was, as Eva Le Gallienne remembers in her autobiography, "well-received by the public" (Le Gallienne 1934: 231).[11]

As in her earlier plays, Glaspell once again explores the concept of freedom within a setting of relationships essential to survival: family and society. Yet again she creates a complex image of a dead woman, the poet Alison, through the memories and conjectures of others, and prevents simplistic conclusions and judgements by presenting multiple viewpoints (see *Trifles* and *Bernice*). All the adult members of the Stanhope family have been tempted to abandon social strictures and risk scandal, but only one, Elsa, of the younger generation, had succumbed and "ran away with a married man – living in shame and leaving misery behind" her (Glaspell 1930: 146). Her aunt Alison, long dead when the play opens, had rejected a married lover and quite literally shut herself in her room, where she wrote poems that were never published. The passing of old values with the turn of the century is embodied in the different attitude to adulterous love that the family exemplifies: Eben, Elsa's brother, accepts her decision and is in fact toying with the possibility of abandoning his own wife, whom he no longer loves. Mr. Stanhope, Alison's brother, had been instrumental in Alison's decision not to "run away" with the man she loved, although he too had a secret love, a woman he had given up so as not to break up two families. Stanhope does not want the love poems his sister wrote "going into your vulgar world" (*ibid.*: 145), as he tells his youngest son Ted, whereas Elsa and Eben are adamant that the poems were written for the world. Elsa in particular feels they were written for her – but also for all women to tell the story of women's desire and loneliness when they adhere strictly to the moral codes society imposes on them.

The relationship of art and society is crucial to the play, and Glaspell treats it here with less ambiguity than she had done in

Chains of Dew, where the comments of Seymore's friends and the two poems that we hear can only make us doubt his poetic gifts. But Alison is definitely portrayed as a great poet, and, as the audience is not exposed to her poetry, it accepts the other characters' exalted reactions to poems contained in a portfolio that Alison's sister, Aunt Agatha, with her dying breath, gives to Elsa. Throughout the play, Glaspell has been building up the audience's trust in the Stanhope family, so that when, on reading the poems, they reverently whisper, "Alison – at her best" (*ibid.*: 136), the spectator has no trouble accepting their opinion.

Springs Eternal

The last play that Susan Glaspell wrote, *Springs Eternal*, is available only in typescript.[12] It was written during the Second World War, after the Japanese attack on Pearl Harbor, and Glaspell later reworked its ideas into her 1945 novel, *Judd Rankin's Daughter*. As with *Chains of Dew* and *The Verge*, this play starts out as a light social comedy but it does not progress to the tragic end of her earlier works. *Springs Eternal*, as a comedy should, ends in marriage, but the entertainment is deflected by "talky" dialogues on the themes that recur in all Glaspell's writing: that is, the individual's responsibility to society and the significance of artistic creation. Glaspell also builds in the generational conflict that had appeared in *Alison's House*, making it into a key issue; she explores the older generation's responsibility for the war and the world they are handing over to their children, and how the two generations can reach an understanding through art. Although too long, possibly unfinished, and not successful in its dramatization of the Higgenbothem family dilemmas, Gainor affirms that, in spite of its flaws, *Springs Eternal* "confirms Glaspell's position as an important American playwright" (Gainor 2001: 261).

4 Key plays I
Trifles

The one-act play *Trifles* was described by Ines Haynes Irwin, Susan Glaspell's militant feminist friend, as "the grimmest, tensest half-hour of tragedy ever produced: a very arrow-flight of poignancy" (Irwin 1922). It was Glaspell's first solo incursion into drama, and the experience convinced her that the medium of the theater was well suited to her Shavian desire to subvert given opinions and behaviors. Assured of a stage for her plays, she devoted the following seven years to drama. *Trifles*, first published by Frank Shay in 1916, is her most frequently anthologized piece and as such is her best-known and most taught play, although, as should be clear by now, the rest of her dramatic oeuvre merits attention for the ways in which she went beyond this initiating experiment which, according to the contemporary drama critic Ludwig Lewisohn, "sums up . . . all the qualities and trends of those early years [of the beginnings of the American theater]" (Lewisohn 1931: 393). In 1917, Glaspell reworked *Trifles* into a short story, "A Jury of Her Peers," which she published in the magazine *Everyweek* (March 1917) and which has been better known and more frequently anthologized than the original play till quite recently.

Trifles was first performed on the Provincetown wharf on 8 August 1916 – during the legendary summer that gave birth to the Provincetown Players. Glaspell then sold the rights to the Washington Square Players, who performed it in November of that year in New York, thus giving the play the publicity it deserved. True to their commitment to the non-commercial

theater, the Provincetown Players refused to give critics compli-
mentary tickets until, in May 1918, the *New York Times* credited
their Washington Square colleagues with discovering Glaspell
(Corbin 1918), thus forcing them to change their policy if their
contribution to American drama was to be acknowledged. There
are no reviews or photographs of the first Provincetown performance, but both Heywood Broun and Arthur Hornblow, who
reviewed the Washington Square production for the *New York
Tribune* and *Theatre* magazine, respectively, praised the play.
Broun was struck by the "most uncommon method" Glaspell
had hit upon and he admitted that *Trifles* "shows that indirection
need not be denied to the playwright if only he is clever enough
to handle this most difficult manner of telling a story for the
stage" (Broun 1916). Glaspell indeed carried the possibilities of
"indirection" to their extreme when she made Minnie Foster
Wright, suspected of murder and held in prison, the first of her
absent protagonists. *Trifles* is also her first play to use the model
of the detective story, which she transforms into a vehicle to
question a given "truth" through the words of those who knew
the absent woman. She would use a similar model in *Bernice*
(1919) and in *Alison's House* (1930), and, later, in the novel *The
Morning Is Near Us* (1939).

The one historical photograph that we have of *Trifles*, is of the
November 1916 Washington Square Players' production.[1] We see
the gloomy interior of a bare kitchen dominated by a plain table
and an empty rocking chair. Dirtied white towels hang on rails
placed somewhat incongruously on the back wall between two
high windows, thus producing smudges of light that oddly reproduce the patches of winter sunlight in the windows. The County
Attorney, notebook in hand, stands closest to the stove. In spite
of his obvious youth, he is the highest authority present, and the
Sheriff's pose transmits his indignation at having his decisions
questioned by the younger man. The farmer, Mr. Hale, occupies
a central position by the rocking chair and is elaborating on his
encounter of the previous day with Minnie Foster Wright. In spite
of the inner tensions that are apparent among the three men and
their different social and hierarchical status, they are united by
their common pursuit of the criminal – presumably a woman who

4.1 Trifles. Photograph reproduced by courtesy of the Billy Rose Theatre Division, the New York Library for the Performing Arts, Astor, Lenox and Tilden Foundations

has killed one of their number. The women, wives of the Sheriff and the farmer, have remained, as Glaspell specifies, by the door, side by side, silent, anguished onlookers from a different sphere of life. The scene is starkly realistic but static in the lack of inter-action between the two definitely separate groups of people.

In the original Provincetown production of *Trifles*, Glaspell took the role of Mrs. Hale (see Shaughnessy 2004) and her husband, George Cram Cook, played Mr. Hale. None of the other actors were professionals either, and Glaspell probably ceded her authorial privilege of directing to Cook. By all accounts, directing was worse than haphazard in the early productions of the Provincetown Players – until Nina Moise appeared in January 1917 to put some order into the chaotic, all-too-life-like movements of the actors on the stage (Sarlós 1982: 71–72).

The writing of *Trifles*

After completing her degree at Drake College in 1899, Glaspell had worked as a reporter for the *Des Moines Daily News* for a couple of years before she returned to Davenport to translate her experiences into short stories. However, the murder committed by Margaret Hossack, which she had covered for the *News*, eluded her and, although she tried a number of times, she was unable to find the right focus to convert her reports into fiction.[2] Hossack had been accused of bludgeoning her husband to death with an axe while he slept, and although there was no conclusive evidence, she was found guilty and sentenced to life imprisonment with hard labor. Glaspell's reports, especially after she had visited the Hossack farmhouse, had attempted to sway public opinion and build up support for the older woman who had suffered physical abuse from her husband. Two years later, a second jury, unconvinced by the evidence and taking into consideration Margaret Hossack's advanced age and health, ordered her to be released. The story had clearly continued to haunt Glaspell and, when her husband demanded she write a play for a summer season of theater that he had announced, the memory of the Hossack kitchen proved inspiring.

The image of that bleak kitchen was provoked by the make-shift stage her husband put up in the shed they had used the previous summer for a repeat performance of *Suppressed Desires* – thus corroborating Cook's conviction that American playwrights needed only a stage on which to see their plays performed for them to come into their own. Glaspell relived the process of writing *Trifles* in *The Road to the Temple*, where she tells us:

> So I went out on the wharf, sat alone on one of our wooden benches without a back, and looked a long time at that bare little stage. After a time the stage became a kitchen – a kitchen there all by itself. I saw just where the stove was, the table and the steps going upstairs. Then the door at the back opened, and people all bundled up came in – two or three men, I wasn't sure which, but sure enough about the two women, who hung back, reluctant to enter that kitchen.

When I was a newspaper reporter out in Iowa, I was sent down-state to do a murder trial, and I never forgot going into the kitchen of a woman locked up in town. I had meant to do it as a short story, but the stage took it for its own, so I hurried in from the wharf to write down what I had seen. Whenever I got stuck, I would run across the street to the old wharf, sit in that leaning little theater under which the sea sounded, until the play was ready to continue. Sometimes things written in my room would not form on the stage, and I must go home and cross them out.

(Glaspell 1927: 256)

This is one of the few descriptions of her writing process that Glaspell has given us and it is reinforced by later statements that indicate that in her fiction she also visualized her characters and listened to them, "experiencing particular pleasure when they surprised her by acquiring an identity and life of their own" (Ozieblo 2000: 274). J. Ellen Gainor compares Glaspell's process of artistic creation with that of Pirandello, but points out that Glaspell allows her characters more autonomy than the Italian playwright, and that she

emerges as a self-aware and critical conduit for character, action, and narrative. Her distance from her stage figures opens a space for resistance and critique more familiar to the discourses of reception theory than to statements about artistic production.

(Gainor 2001: 40)

It is precisely Glaspell's distance that gives her the space to step back and offer thought-provoking conclusions – and that allows for what has at times been considered a frustrating ambiguity in her writing, particularly as regards the situation of women in society and the means at their disposal of evading patriarchal oppression. The spectator or reader of *Trifles* will never know whether Minnie will be condemned or not, just as they will never be quite sure of Glaspell's opinion of the impromptu detectives she has created. Glaspell herself, in the writing of *Trifles*, felt "oppressed" in that, as she would later write in *The Road to the Temple*, Cook had insisted that she write a new play. Her protest that she had never "studied" playwriting was smothered by his peremptory "You've got a stage, haven't you?" (Glaspell 1927: 255). Cook's faith in his wife's talent was more than justified by *Trifles*, a play that has been considered exemplary in its concision and structure, and that in the 1980s and 1990s was seen as representative of feminist concerns albeit realistic in its plot and presentation.[3]

Trifles: concision and structure

As early reviewers rightly noted, in *Trifles* Glaspell worked through indirect implication in order to question what appears to be an obvious truth and so show other possible ways of interpreting the same facts. When the play opens, as audience we join Glaspell in her observation of two women, Mrs. Hale and Mrs. Peters, who enter a bleak, cold kitchen and instead of approaching the fire, huddle together by the door. They too are spectators, on the outside of the important mission entrusted to the Sheriff and the Attorney: the discovery of clues to the murder of John Wright. Yet it is precisely these two women who will solve the mystery by "reading" the clues that the men scorn – the trifles – that their close, penetrating scrutiny of the kitchen reveals. And as we gaze on these women they are transformed from observers to actors who assume the authority to decide what to do with the knowledge they have acquired, thus implying that a murder can be an act of "justifiable homicide by a battered woman" (Bryan 1997: 1296).[4]

The trifles Mrs. Hale and Mrs. Peters uncover belong to the world of women: a dreary kitchen, broken jars of preserves, a stove that does not work, unbaked bread, a shabby skirt, uneven stitching. Reading as women, they can interpret these as symbolic elements of the larger picture of a woman's life. As in all her plays, Glaspell skillfully creates an acting space that expresses the characters – in this case, the absent Minnie – so much so that although expressionism did not officially reach the Provincetown stage until a few years later with O'Neill's *The Emperor Jones* and Glaspell's *The Verge*, Linda Ben-Zvi has rightly discerned its influence in the setting of *Trifles*, a "powerful mise-en-scène that uses expressionistic touches to externalize Minnie's desperate state of mind" (Ben-Zvi 2005: 174). Concision is achieved by the tightly knit symbolism of the play, which makes wordy explanations unnecessary; indeed, as C. W. E. Bigsby has written: "Understatement has proved as effective a strategy for her [Glaspell] as it was to Hemingway" (Bigsby 1987: 12). This is particularly so in the use Glaspell makes of the dead canary: the women discover the bird and, as the stage directions indicate, "*Their eyes meet. A look of growing comprehension, of horror*" (Glaspell 1920c: 43) is all that passes between them as Mrs. Hale, with the complicity of Mrs. Peters, hides the bird from the men. The look and Mrs. Hale's action are sufficient for the audience to understand the link between the silenced, song-loving Minnie, the strangled canary and the morose John Wright. However, not all reviewers have appreciated the concision of *Trifles*: Lewisohn judged the writing to be too spare, "neither sufficient nor sufficiently direct," adequately to convey the inner meaning of the play, which he praised as "magnificent" and "inherently and intensely dramatic" (Lewisohn 1922: 104). Such a comment could, of course, be a reflection on the direction and the acting; Lewisohn is probably referring to the Washington Square Players' production of 1916.

The structure of *Trifles* is that of the popular detective story, in which, as in Edgar Allan Poe's "The Murders in the Rue Morgue" (1841), the official authority is supplanted by unofficial sleuths with the ability to see and interpret the clues (see Gainor 2001: 37–60). But here, these unofficial sleuths are women who, as wives in the 1910s, had no legal identity. Yet Glaspell, discreetly manipulating her audience, confers presence and identity on these women, the insignificant wives of those in authority. Apart from the opening scene, when they usurp women's traditional place by the kitchen stove in order to get warm, the men troop back and forth, throwing out patronizing comments, as they go from the bedroom to the barn searching for clues. Our attention converges on Mrs. Hale and Mrs. Peters, who can now occupy center-stage in the unwelcoming kitchen, as Glaspell reveals Minnie's story through them. She allows us to share their process of understanding that throws new light on the case and highlights the juxtaposition of man-made law and women's experiences (see Bryan 1997). The very distance that Glaspell creates between her characters and her audience by recognizing their autonomy of movement works to enable our recognition of the situation: the loneliness of the farmhouse and the slow process of perception and coming together that the women undergo as they identify with Minnie. Because we have been observing their development and their struggle, we are more likely to believe them than the men, who strike us as absurd in their self-important and futile quest. Thus the Attorney's convic-tion that "it's all perfectly clear except a reason for doing it" (Glaspell 1920c: 44) has been deconstructed for us: the reason is indeed amply clear but an all-male jury will never recognize it as evidence to condemn or justify Minnie's act of violence.

Trifles: feminist interpretations

Although both *Trifles* and "A Jury of Her Peers" had been avail-able in anthologies, they were rediscovered in the late seventies by feminist literary critics intent on recovering and re-reading texts by women.[5] The short story follows the play faithfully but gives narrative detail that in the play must be transmitted through the acting – thus most comments made on one can be applied to the other, especially those on the feminism of the pieces. Such criticism, as Gainor rightly points out (Gainor 2001: 43), concentrated on the feminist message and not on the form. Kristina Hinz-Bode has divided this early criticism into two camps: that which reads the play as a document advocating the empowerment of women through bonding; and that which reads it as an example of the lack of comprehension between men and women:

> With the help of [Luce] Irigaray and [Hélène] Cixous, for example, *Trifles* can be read as supporting the idea of a pre-existing female nature in need of empowerment within the patriarchal Symbolic Order. In contrast, in connection to

[Carol] Gilligan's and [Deborah] Tannen's research it can also be understood as thematizing the result of women's different socialization in Western culture.

(Hinz-Bode 2006a: 65)

Hinz-Bode does not fully accept either position and offers a reading that goes beyond the early essentialist approach. She suggests we should not dismiss the male characters as inferior or useless patriarchs but that we read Glaspell's message as embracing both men and women; for Hinz-Bode, *Trifles* "simultaneously enhances the notion of meaning as created in constitutive contact in a dramatic argument in which 'communication' becomes equivalent to 'life' itself for *all* characters" (*ibid.*: 56).

However, we should not dismiss as irrelevant the "bonding" of Mrs. Hale and Mrs. Peters and their piecing – or quilting – together for us a picture of the absent woman and her life. As the two women, who had previously barely interacted given their different social standing, gather the few pieces of clothing Minnie has asked for, we learn from their comments that Mr. Wright was "close" (Glaspell 1920c: 40) and that Minnie did not participate in the social life of the community:

> She didn't even belong to the Ladies Aid. I suppose she felt she couldn't do her part, and then you don't enjoy things when you feel shabby. She used to wear pretty clothes and be lively, when she was Minnie Foster, one of the town girls singing in the choir.
>
> (*ibid.*: 40)

Mrs. Peters, the Sheriff's wife, is new to the town and initially supportive of the work her husband does; feeling superior to her companion, a mere farmer's wife, she reprimands Mrs. Hale for her indignation at the men "coming out here and trying to get her own house to turn against her" with a curt "But Mrs. Hale, the law is the law" (*ibid.*). And yet it is Mrs. Peters, having been reminded by the Attorney that she is "married to the law" (*ibid.*: 45), who, somewhat ineffectually, attempts to hide the strangled canary. The Attorney's dogmatic comment on her status is less meaningful than the memories that poor Minnie has rekindled: memories of her homesteading days in Dakota after the death of her first child when she knew "what stillness is" (*ibid*.: 44). She also remembers the fury that dominated her when a boy killed her favorite kitten: "If they hadn't held me back I would have – (*catches herself, looks upstairs where steps are heard, falters weakly*) – hurt him" (*ibid*.: 43).

Mrs. Hale also comes to empathize with the absent Minnie, whom she had known as a young girl, and laments that she had not visited more often:

> I might have known she needed help! I know how things can be – for women. I tell you, it's queer, Mrs. Peters. We live close together and we live far apart. We all go through the same things – it's just a different kind of the same thing.
>
> (*ibid*.: 44)

Although it is too late for the two women to help Minnie, Glaspell does give them the power that comes from choice: they choose silence – that is, they choose not to disclose what they have found.[6] In their decision to hide the motive for murder that they have found, and in their coming together, bridging the class difference that separates them socially, they mitigate "the effect of isolation upon the human spirit and [affirm] the importance of the human community for the individual" (Noe 1981: 79), thus exemplifying the importance of women bonding and working together that the feminists of the 1970s advocated. For Karen F. Stein, "solving the murder is not a disinterested act [for Mrs. Hale and Mrs. Peters], but a cooperative endeavor which leads them to a knowledge essential for their survival as females in a hostile or indifferent world" (Stein 1987: 256). Their bonding, however, is not shown to be necessarily permanent, nor is Minnie's future settled, for although Glaspell makes a "gesture toward narrative closure" (Gainor 2001: 51), she has not resolved the crime to the satisfaction of any conceivable male jury and we can only wonder what Mrs. Hale and Mrs. Peters' relationship will be in the future: will a shared consciousness of guilt, of obstructing justice through their silence, be sufficient to overcome class barriers? Nor do we learn what fate awaits Minnie; the men's conviction of her guilt has been questioned or, at least, put into perspective for us by the women's discoveries and intuitions. However, we do know that Margaret Hossack was found guilty but then released from prison, and Patricia Bryan and Tom Wolfe, who have interviewed family members, seem to think the murder was committed by a third party (Bryan and Wolfe 2005). This virtually open ending and Glaspell's Brechtian distancing of the women from the audience and the other characters impose on us – as spectators/readers – the function of a jury, thus making us ponder the "very nature of criminality" and its relation to "an enforced alienation from society" (Alkalay-Gut 1984: 7).

Our picture of the absent Minnie is built on the comments of the two women in her kitchen that are reinforced through the tightly knit symbolism of the play. Minnie's name is "derived from the German word for *love*" (Alkalay-Gut 1995: 72), and, of course, her maiden name, Foster, is resonant of care and nurture. Her married name, Wright, is an ironical pun on her rights under the law, on that old dream of finding a "Mr. Right," and on the act of writing: Minnie, by her very absence, causes her story to be written for us. The quilt Minnie is making highlights her unfulfilled desire to give and receive love and warmth: significantly, the pattern and the method she has chosen show her love of color and her loneliness. As Alkalay-Gut has pointed out:

> Not only is quilting a simple communal task in which the trivial becomes integrated vitally into a larger framework, but it also makes use of hidden patterns and significances. . . . Minnie's patchwork would have been knotted and not quilted because knotting is easier and can be worked alone.
>
> (*ibid.*: 79–80)

The quilt becomes a complex metaphor for Minnie's solitude – but also for the process of detection, of interpretation and of writing, a piecing together of isolated fragments that form a whole.

Minnie's absence, however, is more than just a theatrical device that allows this piecing together of snippets of information. The fact that neither she nor her husband, the victim of her supposed crime, are present allows Glaspell to manipulate the information in such a way that we empathize with her and with the two women who are on stage observing the details in the kitchen for us. The men's conviction that Minnie is guilty rings hollow precisely because they are convinced even before they find any evidence; while the women, initially swayed by the men's certainty, slowly piece together a different truth.

The re-visioning and re-reading of women's texts in the 1970s allowed critics to realize the extent of the influence of the two spheres and to understand that although the "pressures and oppressions of gender may be as invisible as air, they are also as inescapable as air, and, like the weight of air, they imperceptibly shape the forms and motions of our lives" (Gilbert 1986: 33). *Trifles* (and "A Jury of Her Peers") exemplifies these pressures and oppressions in its language, its structure and its action. The language that Glaspell uses in *Trifles* looks forward to her more complex experiment of *The Verge*, which *The Outside* also prefigured. The hesitant mode of expression of Mrs. Hale and Mrs. Peters shows that they are grappling with new concepts, with as yet inchoate ways of seeing their lives, indicated by the dashes Glaspell inserts between words, as, for example, in Mrs. Hale's painful articulation of her sense of guilt at having abandoned Minnie: "I stayed away because it weren't cheerful – and that's why I ought to have come. I – I've never liked this place" (Glaspell 1920c: 42). The three men, whose relationships are determined by hierarchy and class, are even more importantly separated from the women by gender; they are not interested in what the women may have to say and scorn their preoccupation with "trifles." Glaspell carefully indicates in her stage directions the tone of voice that the men employ when they do deign to speak to the women: the County Attorney, for example, addresses them "*facetiously*" or "*as one turning from serious things to little pleasantries*" (*ibid.*: 43, 45). Annette Kolodny was the first to highlight the significance of the "necessary (but generally ignored) gender marking which *must* constitute any definition of 'peers' in the complex process of unraveling truth or meaning" in her ground-breaking analysis of "A Jury of Her Peers" (Kolodny 1986: 55). The men consider themselves superior and their task infinitely more important than any of the trifles that concern the women; they are "inadequate readers" (*ibid.*: 57), incapable of reading these trifles because to do so would destroy the male solidarity that empowers patriarchy. In one of the earliest readings of "A Jury of Her Peers," Judith Fetterley reminds us that "it is nothing less than the story of men's systematic, institutionalized, and culturally approved violence towards women" (Fetterley 1982: 153). The male cama-raderie that unites the men prevents them from recognizing that Mr. Wright may not have treated his wife correctly and that his behavior could be read as the missing "reason" for the crime. The women, on the other hand, through their process of uncovering the clues, learn that they form a class apart from the men, and that in order to save themselves they must acknowledge their bonds: the bonds that oppress them and, just as importantly, the bonds that unite them and, through union, confer empowerment.

Performances of *Trifles*

Although *Trifles* is undoubtedly Glaspell's most performed play, such performances have been mostly by amateur or university ensembles requiring a short play with few actors and a simple, realistic set. The Internet Broadway Database (http://www.ibdb.com/show.asp?ID=8881) lists two productions of *Trifles*: the Washington Square Players' production at the Comedy Theatre in August (*sic*) 1916, and one performance at the Frolic Theatre on 10 May 1928.

The thirty-minute, Oscar-nominated movie of "A Jury of Her Peers" made by Sally Heckel in 1980 has recently been released on DVD (www.wmm.com) and captures the desolation of Minnie's lonely life on the farm through the subdued colors and slowly paced action. The bonding of Mrs. Hale and Mrs. Peters is convincingly done by Diane de Lorian and Dorothy Lancaster. A more recent movie of *Trifles*, by Jonathan Donald Productions (www.jonathandonaldproductions.com), tellingly brings to life the hierarchical squabbles of the three men and tends to add more glamour to the story than Glaspell could have intended. Both make good use of the naturalistic qualities of the story/play and the symbolism to heighten the suspense and mystery. In 2003, in collaboration with Dora Galesso, an innovative film-maker, Lucia Sander, a freelance academic and actress working in Brazil, made a postmodern version of the play that she uses as a starting point for an intimate conversation with Glaspell and a discussion of her work and life (http://paginas. terra.com.br/arte/performarte/html/pag1_ing.htm).

Probably the first fully professional performance of *Trifles* took place in March 2007 at the American Century Theatre of Arlington, Virginia. The director, Steven Scott Mazzola, also included *Suppressed Desires* in *Drama under the Influence*, a collection of short plays by women written during the Prohibition Era. Although both *Trifles* and *Suppressed Desires* were staged with realist sets, lighting and costumes, the casting for *Trifles* was non-traditional in that Mrs. Peters was played by an African-American actress. The fact that such casting worked well is testimony to the universality of the play – historically it is unlikely that a Sheriff's wife in a small Midwestern town in 1900 would have been anything but of Anglo-Saxon origin. The universality of *Trifles* is also attested to by a student production in October 2006 at SuZhou University, China, directed by Alexander Moffet, as part of the Twelfth National Symposium on American Drama and Theater (www.susanglaspell.org).

5 Key plays II
The Verge

The Verge (1921) was the last play that Susan Glaspell would write for the Provincetown Players. She wrote it for an audience that she had come to know intimately, an audience that, for almost seven years, the Players had been training to appreciate their spirit of serious and yet playful innovation, and it marked the culmination of her theatrical development. With *The Verge*, Glaspell was finally able to break through the despised "patterns" of Broadway plays (Glaspell 1927: 248) she had been escaping from in her earlier work. With this full-length drama, she demanded more from her audience than she had ever dared before, provoking extreme reactions from spectators and reviewers. On the whole, women responded positively to this play, while male colleagues and reviewers were frequently baffled. One contemporary reviewer noted scathingly that "Nothing pleases the merry, merry Greenwich Villagers so much as a well misdirected idea which nobody quite understands" (Dickinson 1921). Others, however, recognized that Glaspell was stretching modernist, avant-garde and feminist concepts of theater to their very limits and were able to praise even if they did not quite understand the play. Ludwig Lewisohn, writing for the *Nation*, celebrated the "touch of that vision without which we perish" communicated by *The Verge*, and he praised both the "dramatic structure" of the play, which he considered to be "clear and clean and firm" and the "delicately and precisely wrought" dialogue (Lewisohn 1921). Kenneth Macgowan, an influential drama critic of the time who congratulated himself on his openness to

avant-garde developments in the theater, managed to fuse both
negative and positive reactions in his review for the *New York
Evening Globe* when he wrote:

> It is impossible to call the effort of the play a success, as other
> plays achieve their purpose. It is just as impossible to deny
> that, for the tiny audience of the keen, the sensitive, the
> genuinely philosophic, here is the most remarkable dramatic
> document that they have ever come across. However much
> of *The Verge* is unclear in the theatre, there must always be,
> for its special audience, extraordinary passages of meaning.
> (Macgowan 1921)

It is hardly surprising, then, that reactions to the play were
mixed. In the first place, audiences were disconcerted by the
subject matter: Claire Archer, an experimental botanist on the
point of unveiling a new plant called "Breath of Life," does not
want to deal with the demands of her uncomprehending family –
daughter Elizabeth, sister Adelaide and husband Harry. She seeks
reassurance from her lover Dick and her friend Tom, but the
conflict between her ambition to create new life and her need
of human relationships grows until, at the close of the play, she
strangles Tom, the one man who attempts to understand her
desire to go beyond convention. Second, the language of the play
confounded many, even among Glaspell's professed admirers,
who were unable to assimilate the movement from dialogue
bordering on comedy to free verse exploring the predicament of
humankind trapped in social stereotypes, as, for example, in
Claire's words: "Stabbed to awareness – no matter where it takes
you, isn't that more than a safe place to stay? . . . Anguish may
be a thread – making patterns that haven't been" (Glaspell 1922:
86). And then the innovative stage design which relied on
German expressionism, a trend as yet barely known in the United
States, perturbed the audience. Even the Provincetown audience,
prepared for innovation by six seasons of plays by Glaspell,
O'Neill, Edna St. Vincent Millay, Djuna Barnes and others who
had departed from the conventions of realism, found it difficult
to accept a play that, as C. W. E. Bigsby would write in 1987, is

"a radical revisioning of all aspects of theatre" (Bigsby 1987: 19). *The Verge* is an example of the fusion of varied theatrical genres – comedy, melodrama, social criticism, tragedy – and European "-isms" that American theater was making its own. The play bears the imprint of Strindberg, Ibsen, Shaw or Coward, while at the same time it is a profound feminist revisioning of the thinking of the late nineteenth and early twentieth centuries.

Curiously enough, a Nietzschean comment made by Eugene O'Neill regarding his own play *Diff'rent* comes to mind when attempting to summarize the plot of *The Verge*: "Only through the unattainable does man achieve a hope worth living and dying for – and so attain himself" (O'Neill 1921). But when Glaspell's protagonist attempts to "attain herself," the play must be read as a reflection on the norms of society that imprison women or as a symbolic breakthrough into another dimension. Throughout *The Verge*, Claire struggles to overcome the limitations of personal relationships, of family life, of science and nature and of all that holds human beings within bounds; she stands on the verge of society and therefore of sanity.

The Provincetown Players' production of *The Verge*

The Verge was performed, as were all of Glaspell's plays of this period, at the Playwrights' Theater on Macdougal Street in Greenwich Village by the Provincetown Players. It was the first bill of the 1921–22 season and opened on 14 November, directed by her husband, George Cram Cook. The normal five days of performances was extended to eighteen, and then, from 6 to 16 December, the play was taken by the Theater Guild to the Garrick Theatre for matinee performances, and returned to the Playwrights' Theater from 26 to 31 December.

As was usual with the Players, the actors were either members or friends, but the role of Claire requires a sensitive, strong actress, and Margaret Wycherly (1881–1956), a friend of Glaspell and a professional actress, gladly accepted the part.[1] Wycherly was a fellow-member of the Heterodoxy, a feminist club that gathered "unorthodox" women twice a month for discussion of taboos and forbidden topics (see Schwarz 1986), and, after seeing Glaspell's *Bernice*, she had begged her to create a strong woman protagonist for her – but one that would appear on stage (Anon. 1921a). As Cheryl Black points out, Wycherly had studied acting at the American Academy of Dramatic Art, where she had learned to reject the traditional, melodramatic acting methods (Black 2002: 85). Although Wycherly's acting in *The Verge* was generally praised as magnificent and moving, it took a woman reviewer, Maida Castellun, to appreciate just how well she understood Glaspell's Claire:

> Margaret Wycherly transcends herself . . . an actress who has always scorned the patterns of the stage, lends her intelligence, her sensitive intuitions, her poetic beauty and her artistic sincerity to make Claire live, and transcends anything she has done before . . . the signs of genius on the verge of madness relentless in its truth.
>
> (Castellun 1921)

Glaspell's *The Verge* is a challenge for even the best-trained director and designer; judging by contemporary reviews, both director George Cram Cook and designer Cleon Throckmorton were stimulated to do their best work. Cook was known to be eccentric in his directing, but he had acquired experience with the Players and – most importantly – in *The Verge*, he had a professional actress in the main role. The positive reviews imply that he was capable of directing her and of respecting Glaspell's explicit stage directions, the mood and import of which he presumably shared, as when, in Act I, Claire suddenly affirms: "The war. There was another gorgeous chance." Glaspell leaves no doubt as to how she wanted these words spoken: she indicates that they should be said with a tone of mockery that "*gives true expression to what lies somberly in her*" (Glaspell 1922: 70). On the other hand, *The Verge* also demands a measure of poetic diction that could, in the hands of an insensitive director or actress, lapse into needless sentimentality. Claire has a number of speeches that are poetic articulations of her dilemmas, such as her attempt to explain her experiments to her daughter Elizabeth (*ibid.*:

76–77), when she speaks of the son who died in infancy and was "movement – and wonder. . . . His little bed was by the window – he wasn't four years old. It was night, but him not asleep. He saw the morning star – you know – the morning star. Brighter – stranger – reminiscent – and a promise" (*ibid.*: 87), or when she uncovers the Breath of Life plant (*ibid.*: 96). The critic Alexander Woollcott objected to such moments as "helplessly loquacious" (Woollcott 1921), and yet, as we have already seen, Lewisohn praised Glaspell's use of language, indicating that a convincing measure of sensibility and rationality had been achieved.

Cook's other directorial challenge would have been to orchestrate the moods of the play, allowing the flippant tone of "satiric comedy" (Anon. 1921c) in the opening of Act I to come through and yet segue into Claire's urgent need to express her ideological position with regard to her experiments, her yearning for the "great leap" and her exasperation at anything that "scuttled right back to the trim little thing[s]" of convention (Glaspell 1922: 70). Margaret Wycherly would have known how to avoid melodrama, particularly in her interactions with Tom (played by Henry O'Neill (1891–1961) in his first role for the Players),[2] the friend and confidant whom she strangles at the end of the play because he finally offers her the conventional love that she had requested in a moment of weakness but is now convinced would stifle her:

> No, I will beat my life to pieces in the struggle to . . . Not to stop it by seeming to have it. (*with fury*) I will keep my life low – low – that I may never stop myself – or anyone – with the thought it's what *I* have. I'd rather be the steam rising from the manure than be a thing called beautiful! (*with sight too clear*) Now I know who you are. It is you puts out the breath of life. Image of beauty – *You fill the place – should be a gate. (in agony)* . . . No! You are *too much*! You are not *enough* . . . Breath of Life – my gift – to you!
>
> (*ibid.*: 99)

Glaspell's bold, unprecedented stage directions as to the settings were faithfully carried out by Cleon Throckmorton

(1897–1965), a young scenic designer who was "both an artist and an artisan" (Deutsch and Hanau 1931: 69) and who, after the success of his designs for Eugene O'Neill's *The Emperor Jones* and Glaspell's *The Verge*, went on to work for the Civic Repertory Theatre, the Group Theatre and the Federal Theatre Project. For *The Verge*, he designed two sets, both highly expressionistic in their depiction of Claire's yearnings: Acts I and III take place in the greenhouse which is her laboratory; and Act II in the tower, her private space. Both are womb-like habitats where she takes refuge from family and social duties in her urge to escape all patterning of life. As did Glaspell, Claire wants to break out from the restrictive patterns of nature and society and yet, in the stage directions at the beginning of the play, Glaspell emphasizes the hopelessness of such an endeavor since all manifestations of life are organized in forms that repeat themselves:

> *The frost has made patterns on the glass – as Plato would have it – the patterns inherent in abstract nature and behind all life had to come out, not only in the creative heat within, but in the creative cold on the other side of the glass. And the wind makes patterns of sound around the glass house.*
>
> (Glaspell 1922: 58)

Nonetheless, both the playwright – in her readiness to experiment with new theatrical forms – and her protagonist – who yearns to transcend what is known – dare to abandon the stultifying self-reflexivity of the "herd" that Nietzsche's Zarathustra shuns. The greenhouse, as Glaspell insists, is not a place where *"plants are displayed, nor the usual workshop for the growing of them, but a place for experiment with plants, a laboratory"* (*ibid.*). One of Claire's experiments creeps along the back wall; it is a *"strange vine"* that is *"arresting rather than beautiful"* and it grows in the shape of a cross *"if you happened to think it that way"* (*ibid.*). There is an entrance from below, through a trap-door in the floor, thus symbolically implying two levels of action or thought. Glaspell specifies that, as the curtain opens, the stage should be dark except for a shaft of light from below which, as it falls on one of Claire's *"strange plants,"* projects a shadow. This somewhat Gothic, surreal effect is heightened by the wind, and then by the appearance of a dark figure – Anthony, Claire's assistant – who blocks the light as he climbs up the stairway. Throckmorton was able to achieve the effect Glaspell wanted thanks to his successful experiments with shadows and silhouettes the previous year when working on O'Neill's *The Emperor Jones*. For that play, Cook, carried away by his need to transcend the possibilities of their small stage, had built a plaster cyclorama, "modeled on those in use in the art theaters of Europe" (Deutsch and Hanau 1931: 61) that reflected light, creating an illusion of infinite space.[3] This allowed Throckmorton literally to play with the lighting and give Claire's greenhouse a sense of mystery and of a bizarre world of undreamed possibilities which is dissipated when the lights come on to reveal the plants in the startling "*sunshine of a snowy morning*" (Glaspell 1922: 58). An unidentified cutting with a photograph of Act I in the Provincetown Scrapbook (reel 2) held by the New York Public Library for the Performing Arts gives a sense of the effect achieved: we see Tom knocking on the greenhouse door in his futile attempts to enter Claire's space and we register the luminous outside created by Cook's dome beyond the glass walls. One spectator's reaction to the whole play sums up the effect it had on him in the following words: "I sat breathless, drugged with its luminous color, the music of the lines, and with the irresistible acting of Miss Wycherly. Must one really bother about meanings in a play so beautiful!" (Anon. 1921b).

Throckmorton put the dome to even better use in Act II, where the action takes place in Claire's tower room which is "*thought to be round but does not complete the circle*" (Glaspell 1922: 78). This cave or womb-like space is separated from the public by a wall with a "*huge ominous window*" (*ibid.*) through which Glaspell wanted the spectator to observe the action. This daring innovation embodied the modernist challenge to theatrical illusionism: the spectator has no need to suspend disbelief; s/he is clearly on the outside and by shamelessly gazing in on the tormented woman is violating her inner sanctum. Access to Claire's space is again through an opening in the floor and all we see of the spiral staircase is the *"delicately distorted rail"* that echoes the distorted tower room:

> *The back is curved, then jagged lines break from that, and the front is a queer bulging window – in a curve that leans. The whole structure is as if given a twist by some terrific force – like something wrong. It is lighted by an old-fashioned watchman's lantern hanging from the ceiling; the innumerable pricks and slits in the metal throw a marvelous pattern on the curved wall – like some masonry that hasn't been.*
>
> *(ibid.)*

The whole is reminiscent of the broken lines and contrasting planes of the German expressionist film *The Cabinet of Dr.*

5.1 *The Verge*, Act II, Playwrights' Theater, 1921. Photograph reproduced by courtesy of the Billy Rose Theatre Division, the New York Library for the Performing Arts, Astor, Lenox and Tilden Foundations

Caligari (1919), which had been released in the United States in the spring of 1921. Expressionism had originated in Germany in the late nineteenth century as a form of artistic protest against social conventions, and is best exemplified by Edvard Munch's painting *The Scream* (1893). *The Verge* is indeed an expression of Claire's anguished "scream" at all that holds her back from fulfilling her personal and professional yearnings. Theatrically, her state of mind is expressed in the settings, the closed spaces of the laboratory and the tower room into which she retreats from her social and family obligations. As Mardi Valgemae points out, German experiments in expressionism were, by this time, known to New York avant-garde artists, but audiences shunned its excesses, described by an anonymous reviewer in 1926 as "hard to swallow" (quoted in Valgemae 1972: 1). According to Valgemae, Kenneth Macgowan, "In one of the first applications of the term to a New York production . . . called Throckmorton's scenic approach in *The Verge* 'expressionistic'" (*ibid.*: 26). This, coming from Macgowan, who would define expressionism as the "way of escape" from realism, which he defined as "a cramp upon art" (Macgowan and Jones 1923: 7), was praise indeed!

Although Macgowan applied the term "expressionistic" only to Act II of *The Verge*, Steven Frank, in a recent essay, argues specifically that the influence of *The Cabinet of Dr. Caligari*, the expressionist film *par excellence*, can be felt throughout Glaspell's play – not only in the distorted tower and the contrast of light and shadow of Act II, but in the emotional states and facial appearance of the characters and in the "bizarre plants" (Frank 2003: 124–26) of Acts I and III. Frank, comparing the photograph of the original Provincetown production with *Dr. Caligari*, argues that:

> The two settings are thus also alike in how they position the actors; in both, the human figures are dwarfed by the harsh lines that extend and converge high above them, creating a metaphor for how the individual is overshadowed by authoritarian forces in the modern industrialized world.
>
> (*ibid.*: 121)

He suggests convincingly that *The Verge* should not be read as the depiction of a woman's descent into insanity, but rather as an expression of the "collective angst" (*ibid*.: 125) that characterized expressionism:

> And just as the mad scientist, as represented by Caligari, works outside the realm of conventional scientific inquiry, and is therefore exiled, even hunted down, by the community at large, so too is the Woman Artist, in her attempt to subvert patriarchal artistic forms, ostracized and labeled "mad."
>
> (*ibid*.: 126)

Thus, in *The Verge*, Glaspell not only created the first American fully expressionistic play, but by placing a woman artist at its center, she extended to women the angst and anger at society that German expressionism had presented as characteristic of men.

Later productions of *The Verge*

Glaspell's work was popular in Britain, where she was viewed as on a par with Eugene O'Neill, or, by some, as even better. R. Ellis Roberts of the *Guardian* declared Glaspell "the greatest playwright we have had writing in English since Mr. Shaw began" (Roberts 1925); prestigious avant-garde institutions such as the Cambridge Festival Theatre, the Liverpool Repertory Company and the Gate Theatre performed Glaspell's plays, while her plays and novels were published in London by Ernest Benn and Victor Gollancz (see Papke 1993). On 29 March 1925, the Pioneer Players performed *The Verge* at the Regent Theatre with Sybil Thorndike (1882–1976) playing Claire and her husband, Lewis Casson (1875–1969), in the part of Tom; the play was produced by Edith Craig. Reviewers praised Thorndike's performance enthusiastically, and preferred to concentrate on Claire's horticultural activities and her sanity or on the symbolism of the play rather than give a sense of the production or setting. As the New York critics had in 1921, the London reviewers fall into two camps in their evaluation of *The Verge*, going overboard in their praise or their condemnation. James Agate, the renowned

London drama critic, stated categorically that "*The Verge* is a great play" (Agate 1926: 98). Others, such as Hubert Griffith in the *Observer*, concentrating on Claire, damned the play as an unconvincing portrayal of insanity – and yet the anonymous reviewer of the *Daily Telegraph* could declare: "Herein is Miss Glaspell's triumph, that she makes you accept Claire as that one person in a million whose vision is clear, and whose speech, howsoever transcendental, is sincere and true" (Anon. 1925e). The more cerebral critic of the London *Times* declared: "Claire's history is an intellectual adventure and a deeply moving piece for the theatre" (Anon. n.d.). Others, however, were clearly not up to the challenge, as evidenced by the review in the *Morning Post*: "But although one may feel dimly that Miss Glaspell's intention is to state some problem or problems which to-day are agitating our most thoughtful women, her action and dialogue is so choked by symbolism that it is impossible to discern precisely what she has at heart" (Anon. 1925c). A baffled reviewer for the *Yorkshire Post* simply came out "holding [his] head, totally unable to think" (Anon. 1925a). What was recognized as Glaspell's feminist stance, possibly enhanced by general opinion on the work of the Pioneer Players, provoked the paternalistic comments of J. Forbes Robertson, who considered Glaspell's "mind [to be] unfettered by masculine predilections" and so ends his review with: "The drama of Susan Glaspell more nearly touches greatness than any yet created by woman" (Robertson 1925).

But Sybil Thorndike's comments best illuminate the play, which she regarded as symbolic, and definitely not realistic. She assured G. D. Cummins of the *Yorkshire Post*, who interviewed her, that, "With uncanny skill, Susan Glaspell has tried to grasp at the unknown, the intangible." She believed that Claire was "as daring in her new and extended vision of life as Christ or Buddha" and that, although her murder of Tom may "represent negation" to many people, she considered it to be "affirmative-positive" – an attempt to reach the truth. She also gave Cummins Edith Craig's opinion of the play: Craig had suggested *The Verge* to Thorndike, indicating that it "contained much that was difficult to understand, [but that] it was a play of such uncommon power it might be considered a masterpiece" (quoted in Cummins 1925).

The next documented performance of *The Verge* was not until 16 March 1991; this was at Brigham Young University, produced by the English and Theatre/Film departments. The producer and director, graduate student Robert Paxton, did without the tower wall that Glaspell specified should separate Claire from her audience, and used a naturalistic approach. Two reviewers, Gerhard Bach and Claudia Harris, believed that the audience was "challenged in a very modern way to step outside the boundaries, to see beyond the conventional, to confront otherness" (Bach and Harris 1992: 95). The detailed description they give of the murder shows how Paxton's direction attempted to clarify Claire's frenzied repetition of the word "gift" during the last moments of the play:

> Under Paxton's direction, the choking scene at the end of the play becomes the "gift" Claire proclaims it to be. Tom's death becomes a passionate act of love: Claire first caresses him from behind, then tightens her grip, pulling him back to her down on the stage, lying with him between her legs, cradling him in her arms.
>
> (*ibid.*: 95)

The Studio Theatre of Glasgow University produced *The Verge* on 4 May 1996, directed by Stephen J. Bottoms, who, rejecting naturalistic, realistic or symbolic approaches to the play, conceived of a production "driven by a blatantly postmodern collaging technique, pushing each moment to its logical extreme in order to create a jarring, unstable experience. . . . I wanted simply to generate conditions in which Glaspell's script could really breathe" (Bottoms 1998: 132). He was convinced that "any attempt at production would stand or fall on the question of how it dealt with Claire's linguistic 'excesses'" (*ibid.*: 128). Agreeing with the critic Marcia Noe that Glaspell's use of language in this play is a "radical example" of the playwright's attempt to "break free of the prison of forms" (Noe 1995: 138), Bottoms was against cutting these "linguistic 'excesses'" – as the almost simultaneous Orange Tree Theatre revival in London did freely (Bottoms 1998: 129).

Bottoms's highly experimental production was inspired by Michael Vanden Heuvel's *Performing Drama/Dramatizing Performance* and by Diane Elam's *Feminism and Deconstruction* to generate a dialogic interpretation of Glaspell's *The Verge* as regards the setting and the characters. His production was limited both by scarce resources and by the theatrical space, a black box studio. However, Bottoms made the best possible use of the space by placing his audience on three sides of a central raised acting area, thus achieving the "warped perspective" (*ibid*.: 132) demanded by the play, particularly in Act II. In this way, although there was no physical separation between the audience and Claire, he was able to give the spectators what he called a "mouse's eye-view" of the stage: "spectators found that actors close up would tower overhead, with actors at the other end of the stage viewable in their entirety through the legs of those nearby" (*ibid*.: 132). Also, by raising the acting area, he could place a trap-door in its floor and so allow Glaspell's characters to emerge as if from a different world, as she had specified. Unable to give the effect of intimate space that Glaspell's stage directions indicate in her descriptions of the glass greenhouse and the twisted tower, Bottoms used the available space imaginatively to create a comparable "gulf of comprehension and communication" (*ibid*.: 133). He placed Tom, Dick and Harry outside the acting space on a raked set of rostra along the fourth wall of the studio. In order to reach Claire, the men bridged the gap between their rostra and her space by placing *hanamichi*-like planks and walking across.[4] Although in the Japanese *kabuki* theater these paths run through the audience and serve to create greater intimacy between spectator and player, Bottoms used them to trap the audience in an inner space with no exit. At the same time, the sense that the men were invading Claire's space was intensified.

What Bottoms understood as the "dialogic relationship between text and performance" was heightened by the use of video monitors which decentralized the spectators' attention, preventing a monologic or unitary experience. The projections of

5.2   Edge Vine (Alison Reeves), Claire (Judith Milligan), Dick (Jamie Small) and Harry (Alistair Rolls) in Act I of the University of Glasgow Studio Theatre's production of Susan Glaspell's *The Verge*, directed by Steve Bottoms. Photo: Leslie Black (Every attempt has been made to contact the photographer and request permission to use this photograph)

large, distorted shots of greenhouse plants in Acts I and III, and of "constantly shifting images of gothic roof vaulting and spiraling stairs" in Act II, reflected Claire's anguished mind (*ibid.*: 133). The screens were also used for Elizabeth, Claire's daughter: rather than give her a real stage presence, Bottoms made her into a virtual image, so solving one of the dilemmas of feminist criticism regarding *The Verge* – the need to account for Claire's cruel rejection of her daughter. By repeating the image of a huge, plastic, doll-like figure on three large screens he invested in Elizabeth the oppressive power of conformism, making Claire's rejection not only comprehensible but a psychological necessity.

The multiple perspectivism of Bottoms's interpretation of the play, and the restricted means of adequately reproducing the stage directions in the acting area at his disposal, suggested the device of having the stage directions read out by a female narrator in the role of stage-manager. Together with the projected images, this contributed to the creation of a visual and auditory experience for the audience that reproduced Claire's distraught imagination fulfilling Glaspell's desire to provoke audience participation (Glaspell 1927: 248). In another important innovation Bottoms transformed the Edge Vine into a "movement role for a female performer [. . . thus] suggesting women's desire for a different life form/pattern . . . a powerful image of a thwarted female desire for breaking out" (Aston 1997: 231).

The postmodern, probing approach Bottoms brought to Glaspell's play revealed the complexity of the secondary characters, particularly the three men, whom the actors were able to portray as the "slightly grotesque cartoons" their names – Tom, Dick and Harry – imply, but also as "living, breathing people" (Bottoms 1998: 137). In this way he gave credence to Claire's relationships with these men. Bottoms also supplies an answer as to why Claire kills Tom in the last scene of the play, a moment that has also bewildered feminist critics unwilling to accept violence from women (see Malpede 1995: 126 and Noe 1995: 131). In the Brigham Young production the murder was seen as an act of love on Claire's part; but here, Claire, astounded by Tom's sudden turn to conformism, kills him in order to "free him . . . from becoming Elizabeth" (Noe 1995: 144).

Bottoms cast a physical/visual performer as Claire rather than an actress used to working with words; he sensed that it was more important for the person playing the part to "interpolate *herself* actively into the undecidable blanks of the text" (*ibid.*: 138) than to attempt to interpret the text. Aston, in her review of the production, admitted that Judith Miller "offered a very convincing and commanding performance as Claire" (Aston 1997: 231). Miller's analysis of Claire helps understanding of this complex figure:

> It's that fear of failing. Not of failing other people or of not being famous or not being a success, but of failing yourself, of never satisfying yourself, of never being able

to achieve what you need, or even recognizing what you need to achieve it.

(quoted in Bottoms 1998: 146)

At almost exactly the same time, opening on 1 May 1996, London's Orange Tree Theatre also produced Glaspell's *The Verge*, directed by Auriol Smith. Judging from reviews, in spite of Glaspell's stage directions, this production, although played in-the-round, was more conventional than the Glasgow venture and drew "heavily on a realistic acting style" (Aston 1997: 229). Isla Blair as Claire was highly praised by the *Guardian*'s Michael Billington – "a stunning performance" (Billington 1996) – and by Elaine Aston, who noted that "So much of what Claire tries to speak, or rather unspeak, Blair spoke gesturally rather than verbally – especially through a patterning of arm, hand and finger movements" (Aston 1997: 229). Just as Margaret Wycherly had emphasized Claire's physical presence – one reviewer criticized her for "Forest of Arden[ing] around like a British Rosalind" (Young 1921) – so Blair's performance was highly corporeal. As Aston perceived, she

> played between outward explosion and inward constraint, enacting Claire's struggle as a dangerous and exhausting experiment with the "life" force. When, for example, she destroyed the Edge Vine because it had turned back on itself, Blair's body exploded with transgressive pleasure and energy, then subsided into quiet release.
>
> (Aston 1997: 230)

Juliet Nichols's set designs were "marvellous" (Billington 1996), efficiently adapting the relatively new Orange Tree Theatre venue (opened in 1991), built as a theater-in-the-round, to the needs of the play. Auriol Smith had the audience "seated around the edges of the set" so that spectators "claustrophobically bordered the inside, but were able to see outside, beyond the glass of the conservatory" (Aston 1997: 229). Nichols's set subverted the theatrical involvement just as powerfully as Glaspell's specification of a real fourth wall had done in the original 1921 production, although in a different way. According to Aston, the set

> successfully incorporated the spectatorial experience of being dis/placed on the margins [and] . . . further suggested the possibility of new forms in its "incompleteness": cut-away glass panel doors opening onto the conservatory and to Claire's most special plant, Breath of Life, along with a sloping desk and expressionistic doors leading to new possibilities in the twisted tower.
>
> (*ibid.*: 229)

However, the "*marvelous pattern*" of light that Glaspell had specified for the tower was disappointingly simplified by Joe White into a subdued amber flush that pervaded the acting space; all the same, it did lend a dream-like quality to Claire's desperate search for "radiance lighting forms undreamed" in her dialogue with Tom (Glaspell 1922: 86).

5.3   Orange Tree Theatre of Richmond production of *The Verge*, Act I. Photo: Paul Thompson. Reproduced with permission of Paul Thompson Photography

Reviews of the Orange Tree Theatre production of *The Verge* echoed the divided criticism that the 1921 production had received: Jeremy Kingston, writing for *The Times*, considered *The Verge* to be "demented in spirit," "turgid in dialogue" and "opaque nonsense"; so frustrated did he feel by the play that he barely managed to reach the end "without breaking the furniture" (Kingston 1996). On the other hand, for Billington, the play is an example of how Glaspell "cross-breeds American realism and European symbolism and, in the process, produces something both original and strange" (Billington 1996). He affirms that the play is "a pioneer work of feminist drama" (*ibid.*). However, to limit interpretations of *The Verge* to feminist considerations is to do a disservice to both the play and its author. The multiplicity of approaches that recent scholarly publications have applied (see Carpentier 2006 and Carpentier and Ozieblo 2006) leave no doubt that this is indeed a modernist play that combines a Jamesian interest in the workings of the inner mind with the need to make things new while yet recognizing the myths or beliefs of a previous era as highly significant. Thus Claire, intent on destroying the old, the Edge Vine that goes the way of a cross in its refusal to reach new life, still refers to God who, she feels, is "not far off" (Glaspell 1922: 78) as she joins the "hymn-singing ancestors" she despises to intone "Nearer, my God, to Thee" (*ibid.*: 78, 77). By the end of the play, Claire has achieved the transcendence Hegel accorded to men and become her own God, a creator and a destroyer of life. She has also become a free agent, resisting all interference from the patriarchal sphere, thus defying thinkers such as Nietzsche, who held that women were but the playthings of man. Glaspell does not explore the consequences of Claire's acts – and this refusal irritated reviewers and critics who, as we have seen, unable to understand Claire, reduce her to a mad-woman. Steven Rathbun was one of the few critics who understood Claire's insanity, presenting it in almost existential terms:

> [Claire] is the most anarchist of anarchists and knows no law
> or rule of human conduct except the gratification of the

needs of her real self. . . . Most of all, she seeks freedom from herself, and she is constantly endeavoring to break through her chrysalis and get a new personality that will make her different. And when she cannot move on to a world of her own creating, insanity, with its loss of memory, takes away the sting of defeat.

(Rathbun 1921)

The close relationship Susan Glaspell had always enjoyed with her audience gave her the confidence necessary to write a play such as *The Verge* and test the limits of the spectator's imagination. It is safe to say that she succeeded: her friend Hutchins Hapgood, who was horrified by what he considered to be an "expression of half-mad feminism" when he saw the Provincetown production of *The Verge*, was amazed at the extreme reactions of her Heterodoxy co-members who "seemed to be worshiping at some holy shrine; their voices and their eyes . . . full of religious excitement" (Hapgood 1939: 377). An appreciative reviewer of the first London production commented: "We are not used to being made to think in the theatre in these days; and *The Verge* keeps you thinking hard with barely a respite" (Anon. 1925a). Glaspell's ability to reach her audience and leave a lasting effect was recognized by another British reviewer who made a subtle distinction between the heart and the mind: "Susan Glaspell's appeal is first to the mind and, when she reaches the heart, she does so completely and in a way not to be lightly forgotten by those who have yielded to its power" (Royde-Smith 1926: 25).

It is, of course, useless to speculate what other plays Glaspell would have written if she had not put her devotion to her husband and her desire to participate in the Greek adventure before her love of the theater or if, on her return to New York after Cook's death, she had been welcomed by the Triumvirate that had taken over the Playwrights' Theater. If O'Neill had been as supportive of Glaspell as she had been of him in 1916 when he was searching for a theater to perform his plays, she may well have continued as a playwright, going beyond *The Verge*. Given not only a lack of such support but a clearly hostile attitude, she turned most of her energies back to the novel, the genre that she had initially chosen as her favored mode of expression.

Part II

Sophie Treadwell

Jerry Dickey

6   Life and ideas

Treadwell is one of those fascinating people whose life was
full of adventure but about whom little was ever recorded.
. . . Nobody knows what she was like, but she must have
been pretty tough and fiercely independent. She was the first
female American war correspondent, she sued the actor John
Barrymore over copyright and won, and was a veteran of
30 or so theatrical flops. Inexplicably, there is no biography
of her.

(Gore-Langton 1993)

The quotation above, written for UK newspaper the *Daily
Telegraph* fourteen years ago, encapsulates the still-prevalent
view of Sophie Treadwell: that a smattering of details about her
life and exploits suggests a woman of extraordinary determination, originality and influence. As the author of thirty-nine plays
– including seven that were produced on Broadway between
1922 and 1941 – numerous journalistic articles, and fictional
stories and novels, Treadwell amassed a prolific output as a
writer. Shortly before her death in 1970, she wrote to her friend
and fellow-writer Gerald Brenan that "from childhood on
[writing had been] my drive, my excitement, my pleasure,
my joy" (Treadwell 1969). Yet, with the one exception of her
1928 drama *Machinal*, Treadwell was often unable to relay that
joy to her audiences, and critical reception to her plays during
her lifetime was mixed, at best. Perhaps as a result, her overall accomplishments until recently have seldom received the

documentation they seem to deserve. Most standard texts of theater and journalism history, and indeed most autobiographical and cultural writings by her better-known contemporaries and associates, mention her only in passing, if at all. Why the discrepancy? Were her achievements underestimated in her own day, and can their significance be fully appreciated only with the advantage of time and distance? Was she ahead of her time, or was she an individual who absorbed the ideas of her time and occasionally translated them into sensational but temporal media events? The contemporary critical reception to Treadwell's work has not yet reached a decisive consensus.

Feminist theater scholars have rightfully championed her best-known play *Machinal* for its merger of an innovative theatrical style with an insightful indictment of patriarchal society in modern America. Then and now, the play has been favorably compared to the works of more critically acclaimed male authors such as Elmer Rice, Eugene O'Neill and Sinclair Lewis (see Dickey 1997a: 69). Yet many of Treadwell's other Broadway plays were often dismissed by critics for presenting unsympathetic central characters, simplistic or unpleasant themes, and poorly developed plots. It has always been *Machinal* that has kept Treadwell's reputation alive, including revivals of the play for television and off-Broadway in the 1950s and 1960s, decades in which Treadwell had turned primarily to fiction and virtually given up hope of securing production in the commercial theater for any of her later plays.

The overwhelming critical attention for *Machinal* has resulted in a somewhat inaccurate record of Treadwell the playwright. Most critics associate her with radical experimentation in form and content. But while some of her other plays share the feminist concerns and innovative style of *Machinal*, a great many of them are rather traditional, attempting to adhere to principles of the late nineteenth-century well-made play structure. Furthermore, feminist scholarship has yet to address fully the contradictions within Treadwell's plays. While a work like *Machinal* powerfully presents a woman's resistance to patriarchal controls, a number of Treadwell's female characters are unable to maintain such resistance, often choosing to return to a relationship in which power is deferred to a male partner. As Louise Heck-Rabi noted, "Like Glaspell, Treadwell strove to represent feminine vacillation and desperation in the search for selfhood in an altering and amorphous society." Treadwell, whom Heck-Rabi believes should be "[p]roperly considered a realist," is most noteworthy today for "her role of agent-for-change in the maturation of American drama in the first half of the twentieth century" (Heck-Rabi 1976: 217, 223–24). Finally, as will be discussed later in this chapter, critics have barely begun to address Treadwell's occasional expressions of social conservatism, especially beginning in the 1930s when aspects of her thought and writing kept her out of step with the majority of the New York theater community.

The resuscitation of Treadwell's career by feminist scholars accelerated after prominent revivals of *Machinal*, first by the New York Shakespeare Festival in 1990 and then by the Royal National Theatre in London in 1993. Originally published in 1949 in John Gassner's now long out-of-print *Twenty-Five Best Plays of the Modern American Theatre, Machinal* reappeared in 1981 in Judith Barlow's anthology, *Plays by American Women: 1900–1930*, flanked by the first doctoral dissertations on Treadwell's career in 1976 and 1982 (Heck-Rabi 1976; Wynn 1982). The latter dissertation offered the first detailed biographical overview of Treadwell based on her surviving manuscripts and papers, which are housed today in the University of Arizona Libraries Special Collections. A slow but steady and increasing stream of critical commentary has followed these dissertations, and additional biographical essays appeared from 1995 onwards (see Steed 1995; Dickey 1997a; Dickey and López-Rodríguez 2006). While *Machinal* still receives the lion's share of critical attention among Treadwell's works and is regularly produced on US college and university campuses, other plays are now attracting critical comment and production. Two plays have received their premieres recently: *Intimations for Saxophone* at the Arena Stage in Washington, DC, in 2004 and *The Eye of the Beholder* at The American Century Theater in Arlington, Virginia, in 2007. And, at long last, the first collection of Treadwell's selected writings in journalism, fiction and drama was published in 2006 (Dickey and López-Rodríguez 2006).

6.1 Sophie Treadwell. Photo: by Sherril Schell. Reprinted with permission from the Roman Catholic Diocese of Tucson and Special Collections, University of Arizona Library; Sophie Treadwell Papers, ms. 318, box 23

Early years

Treadwell's childhood was indelibly marked by her family relations, so much so that one might argue that nearly all of her work as a writer consisted of an attempt to reconcile conflicting impressions and emotional experiences of these early years.[1] As a young girl, Sophie was presented with two diametrically opposed female role models. Her grandmother, Anna Gray Fairchild, was a Scottish immigrant who, after the death of her husband, maintained a 150-acre ranch near Stockton, California. The young Sophie was deeply impressed by this fiercely independent woman, who, Treadwell's later husband stated, had "crossed the plains in a covered wagon in '49 and shot Indians when the routine chores were done" (McGeehan 1931: vii). For decades in her adult life, Treadwell would return to this ranch for solace and respite. Conversely, Treadwell's mother, Nettie Fairchild Treadwell, remained overly dependent to a neglectful husband, Alfred B. Treadwell, who first separated from his wife and child when Sophie was six. Sophie would later write that this period of abandonment seemed to "end my childhood of itself" (Treadwell 1908). The young Sophie was disgusted by her mother's intermittent reunions with Alfred over the next two years, as well as her inability to follow through on her later desire to divorce him. Nettie moved into increasingly meager accommodations and assumed menial jobs barely to make a living in the absence of financial support from her non-responsive husband, a life that as a young adult Sophie termed "too painful to be disturbed even in memory now" (*ibid.*). As Sophie matured, she clearly attempted to model her life after her independent grandmother, but deep down held suspicions that she had inherited her mother's weaknesses and co-dependency. The women who occupy the central positions in her plays often reflect this ambivalence: they seek lives on their own but frequently stop short of leaving their domineering husband or lover.

An unresolved attraction to her absent father additionally complicated Sophie's childhood. She would occasionally spend summers with Alfred in San Francisco, where he served in a variety of elected public offices, including City Prosecutor and

Police Court Judge. It was Alfred who exposed Sophie to the theater by taking her as a young girl to see Helena Modjeska perform in *The Merchant of Venice*, thus sparking her interest in the arts (Wynn 1982: 4, 28–29). Perhaps more importantly, Sophie identified herself with her father's mixed ethnicity. Both Alfred's father and grandfather were Englishmen who migrated to Mexico and married Mexican women of Spanish descent. Although born in Stockton, Alfred was taken to Mexico at the age of eight after the deaths of his parents and grandmother. There, he received a Catholic education steeped in foreign languages – Spanish, English, French, Italian and Latin – before returning to California aged twenty. Nettie often reminded Sophie that her olive skin and dark features were evidence of the "Mexican in you" as derived from Alfred (Dickey and López-Rodríguez 2006: 245). For Sophie's mother and extended family of aunts and cousins, this inherited Mexican-ness was associated with unreliability and wildness. But Sophie appeared to remain only half convinced that her ethnicity consisted of these undesirable traits, typically preferring to idealize the Mexican character as possessing an innate affinity for the natural world and as something fiercely proud and masculine. Her romanticizing of these ethnic qualities is sometimes plainly evident, as when she posed for photos in Mexican Indian dress (see *ibid.*: 68ff.), or as a journalist when writing sentimentally about an orphaned half-Indian girl from Mexico who answered the "call of her blood" by running away to sleep outdoors (Treadwell c. 1909).[2] Yet her ambivalence about her ethnicity remained, perhaps as a result of her father's vehement public denials of his Mexican heritage. In her work as a journalist, Treadwell often took up the subject of Mexico itself, alternately praising the Mexican character and at other times terming it "basically Indian, basically primitive, basically not creative – acceptive rather than creative" (Treadwell 1924b). The characters of Latino heritage or mixed ethnicity in her plays range from the sympathetic and heroic, as in *Gringo* (1922) and *Hope for a Harvest* (1941), to the stereotypically comic, lusty and menacingly violent, as in *The Right Man* (1908), *Gringo* and *The Last Border* (1944). Above all, her mixed heritage undoubtedly contributed to her sense that she never quite belonged in any one place, or to any one social group or organization. Her middle name, Anita, which she sometimes included on the title page of her manuscripts, reflects both the Anglo (her grandmother Anna) and Mexican (Spanish for "little Anna") aspects of her identity.

Although her adolescent school years had led her to conclude that she was "not 'smart' at all . . . a gawky uninteresting girl of sixteen" (Treadwell 1908), Treadwell flourished at the University of California at Berkeley, where exposure to new experiences provided a much-needed sense of self-confidence. At the time of her entrance to the university in 1902, student enrollment had swelled to over 2,600, and co-eds had for the past twenty years enjoyed many of the same privileges as male students. It was in part due to the ongoing promotion of women's rights on the Berkeley campus that the state of California granted women the right to vote in 1911, a full nine years before the Nineteenth Amendment to the Constitution offered the same rights to women throughout the nation (Pettitt 1973: 159). The year after Treadwell's arrival on campus, the now-famous Greek Theatre, a gift from William Randolph Hearst, was erected and significantly advanced theatrical activities and performances, giving the entire community of Berkeley "a cultural transfusion" (Writers' Program 1941: 66–71, 87–90). It was in this Greek Theatre that Treadwell saw Sarah Bernhardt perform the title role in Racine's *Phèdre* in 1906 (Treadwell n.d.a). While she worked toward completing a Bachelor of Letters in French, Treadwell served as one of the editors for the college humor magazine, participated on the ladies' crew team, acted frequently in the drama club, and, like her father, concentrated her study on foreign languages. To meet financial obligations and prepare herself for employment, she studied shorthand and typing at a commercial school, taught English as a second language at night, and worked in the circulation department of the *San Francisco Call*. But the rapid increase in activities coupled with working jobs to support herself proved physically difficult for Treadwell, and she began experiencing a variety of nervous ailments that were to plague her for the rest of her life. Of these years, she later wrote that "my brain got so active I could not sleep and this wore me out" (Treadwell 1908). By the end of her senior year, she suffered a complete "breakdown" and for two months was unable to walk. During these college years, Treadwell also began writing short fiction, songs and early sketches and plays.

Activism for women's rights

Treadwell's exposure to the growing women's rights movement while at Berkeley shaped many of the experiences of her early professional life, including her involvement with women's suffrage. Her marriage in 1910 to renowned sports columnist William O. McGeehan seemed almost immediately to exacerbate her concerns about a woman's loss of identity and autonomy in marriage, anxieties that had formed early in life from watching her mother's responses to an inattentive husband. Within six months of their marriage, McGeehan placed Treadwell in St. Helena Sanitarium in California to receive treatment and recuperation for what was diagnosed as "nervous prostration." From their correspondence at this time, it is clear that it would be McGeehan who would determine when Treadwell was well enough to return home, although he accepted this duty reluctantly: "I can't make your decisions for you," he wrote to Treadwell, "because I love you so. In that everything even to the buttoning of your little shoes is a momentous problem over which I pause and tremble. I am only the second" (McGeehan 1910). Very little of Treadwell and McGeehan's correspondence has survived, so the letters from this period, which include McGeehan's frequent uses of diminutives in reference to Treadwell, such as "my little girl" (*ibid.*), provide suggestive glimpses into the nature of their early relationship. Treadwell's sudden rise in popularity in San Francisco as a writer of sensational serials between 1914 and 1915 proved difficult for McGeehan to accept and seems to have been a primary motivating factor in his decision to leave California and accept a position with the *New York Evening Journal*. As a result of this, for a time, Treadwell made cross-country trips between San Francisco and New York.

Whatever dissatisfactions there may have been in their marriage, it is clear that Treadwell always retained tremendous respect for McGeehan, and her early involvement in organizations and causes advocating women's equality were inspired more by the condition of her parents' marriage than her own. In 1914, she joined a group of fellow-journalists and women's suffrage advocates in a 150-mile march from New York City to the State Legislature in Albany to deliver a petition demanding the right to vote. Ishbel Ross recalls that "No one took suffrage seriously at this stage, except the suffragists themselves," but an adventurous group of women journalists – including Treadwell, Dorothy Dix and Emma Bugbee, the latter the only woman reporter on the *New York Herald Tribune* – "marched side by side with the militants and shared in the brickbats and cheers" (Ross 1936: 123–24). The resulting human interest stories published by these journalists "helped the status of the women reporters in New York," and thereafter "the *Tribune* girls were brought downstairs to the city room" where women's news became a regular feature (*ibid.*: 125).

A few years later, Treadwell joined the women's rights organization, the Lucy Stone League, adopting its motto and principal platform: "My name is the symbol for my identity and must not be lost" (Kramer 1949: 9).[3] Only rarely did she identify herself publicly or professionally as Sophie Treadwell McGeehan, preferring to use only her given and maiden names even before the League successfully lobbied in 1926–27 for a woman to copyright under her own name and not her husband's. Some of her friends, such as New York theater critic Percy Hammond, could never understand why Treadwell and other Lucy Stoners took such offense to adopting the names of their oft-famous husbands: "'Miss Sophie Treadwell' is an expression of the particular individuality of one of its [the League's] most fervent protagonists. So why should Miss Treadwell suffer from so incompetent a description as is her married name, 'Mrs. William O. McGeehan?'" (Hammond 1925: 45). Upon their respective moves to New York City, McGeehan and Treadwell not only maintained separate surnames but separate residences at times, another practice promoted by leading members of the League, such as its president, Ruth Hale. Treadwell and McGeehan's relationship at this time appears to have evolved into the sort of marriage built on mutual friendship, independence and openness to outside relationships practiced by many progressive artists and literati of the time (see Black 2002: 9–31). McGeehan, whom Ishbel Ross called "the shyest and most silent of men" (Ross 1936: 470), seems to have grown content to let Treadwell assume the decision-making role in their marriage. In his humorous account of his automobile travels through Eastern Europe titled *Trouble in the Balkans*, McGeehan never identifies Treadwell by name as his traveling companion, referring to her consistently as "the lady who is driving me" (McGeehan 1931: v–viii). Since the couple had a German chauffeur for the trip, McGeehan's reference to Treadwell was ironically figurative – an inside joke for those who knew the couple – rather than literal.

In addition to her support of women's suffrage, Treadwell advocated increased sexual freedom for women. Between 1916 and 1919, she maintained a passionate affair with the noted painter Maynard Dixon, a relationship that most likely served as the backdrop to such works as "Letters from 'A' to 'B'" (c. 1915) and the one-act play *The Eye of the Beholder* (1919).[4] Sexual independence and birth-control rights for women are frequent subjects in Treadwell's plays. Yet her central female characters are not of uniform class, ideology or behavior. Plays such as *Constance Darrow* (c. 1908–09), *O Nightingale* (1925) and *Machinal* center on the experiences of a somewhat overly trusting woman embarking on a new career or just entering the still male-dominated workplace. These plays typically present an awakening experience that challenges or destroys the women's idealistic assumptions about the interplay between love/family and work/career. While these working women often make diverse decisions, they are typically unified on key issues such as birth-control rights. For example, the "Maternal" scene in *Machinal* presents a compelling portrait of a woman resisting childbirth and the impending maternal role insisted upon by her doctor and husband as natural for women. Conversely, Constance Darrow argues desperately for her right to bear a child despite her husband's insistence on aborting it. Treadwell's plays, taken together, are consistent only in their advocacy of women's right to choose for themselves.

Another type of female character developed in Treadwell's plays is that of the sophisticated modern woman, the so-called "New Woman" liberated from Victorian mores and patriarchal social custom. Plays such as *You Can't Have Everything* (1925), *Ladies Leave* (1929) and *Three* (1936) present women seeking to redefine their traditional roles in marriage, often through sexual awakening via an extramarital affair. Treadwell presents these women as socially elite, enormously articulate in their reasoning, and ultimately supremely comfortable in their unconventionality. Many other female characters fall between these polarities of the working "everywoman" and the literate "New Woman," but almost always they are forced to try to reconcile their needs for companionship, love and family with a desire for autonomy, self-fulfillment and individual expression.

That Treadwell's professional careers as a journalist and playwright came of age during the years of the First World War should not go unnoticed. Like many women of her day who had been among the first to attend university or enter new fields of employment previously restricted to men, Treadwell also sought to become actively engaged in the events of the new global war. Ishbel Ross cites Treadwell as one of the first women journalists to cover a foreign war (Ross 1936: 377). But like many other women with similar ambitions, such as Jane Grant and Rheta Childe Dorr, Treadwell found herself denied access to the front lines because of her sex. Determined not to return to the States empty-handed, she chose to remain in Europe to cover the effects of the war on returned, wounded soldiers and the civilian population. Her article for *Harper's Weekly*, "Women in Black," is an outstanding example of her ability to turn the tragic repercussions of the war into poetic metaphor: "Women in black. They are all over this land. It is late spring – spring in France! But the fall sowing was lead and powder; the winter rains, blood and tears; and the spring has its flowering in women in black" (Treadwell 1915c: 111).

From modernist salons to Broadway

When Treadwell moved from the West Coast to New York, she found herself at the epicenter of change in modern America. During the latter part of the nineteenth and the beginning of the twentieth centuries, the United States emerged as an industrial power and global empire while its urban centers swelled with eighteen million immigrants drawn to America's promise of freedom and opportunity. Yet the response to such changes by Treadwell's generation ultimately received definition by intellectuals, artists and social activists dissatisfied with the country's increased focus on consumerism and inequities in social justice. Fueled by internal dilemmas such as a widely uneven distribution of wealth, industrial exploitation of workers, and racial and gender injustices, this generation began to envision a sweeping transformation of a new, modern America, including a rejection of Victorian-era views of the prevailing social order and objective reality. Moral codes, such as the sexual double standard, were increasingly seen as hypocritical, and the nineteenth century's tendency toward binary oppositions, such as superior/inferior class, black/white, male/female, was viewed as a contributor to social fragmentation.

In New York, intellectuals and artists often formed relatively small, like-minded enclaves to share and debate ideas. These loosely formed groups received stimulus when joined by expatriated avant-garde artists from Europe, many of whom were fascinated by the technology and vibrant energy of the New York metropolis or who, after the outbreak of the First World War in 1914, sought refuge far away from the conflict. The salon of Mabel Dodge Luhan at 23 Fifth Avenue and the meetings of the Liberal Club on Macdougal Street in Greenwich Village, for example, have been widely recognized by cultural and art historians as fertile sites for radical discourse and progressive reform. Between 1915 and 1920, Treadwell became the habitué of another salon, one hosted by modern art collectors Walter and Louise Arensberg in their apartment on West 67th Street. According to Robert M. Crunden, "Of the three major New York salons, that of Walter and Louise Arensberg was the least known to the public and remains the least documented" (Crunden 1993: 409). At the Arensbergs', Treadwell formed close associations with the likes of Arthur Cravan, Henri-Pierre Roché, Robert Allerton Parker and Beatrice Wood.[5] Salons like the Arensbergs' encouraged a cross-fertilization of ideas across a wide spectrum of disciplines, and through their writings, discussions and relationships, these modernists sought to challenge social limits on the individual and the artist.

The impact of European ideas on modernist art in America found initial expression in the field of visual art. In 1913, the first major exhibition of modern art in America took place at the Armory on East 26th Street in New York. The now famous Armory Show, with its motto "The New Spirit," featured approximately 1,300 deliberately iconoclastic works of art by European avant-garde artists such as Pablo Picasso, Henri Matisse and Georges Braque. The artistic innovation seen in the Armory Show exhibition manifested itself in a variety of distinct forms and styles, many of which adopted or earned labels such as cubism, symbolism, expressionism and Dada, among others. Perhaps the visual artist who best synthesized the impulses among these various schools was Marcel Duchamp, whose *Nude Descending a Staircase* had proven the most shocking of works at the Armory Show. The Arensbergs were attracted to Duchamp's painting, purchased it, and displayed it in their apartment from 1915 to 1921 (Macleod 1999: 207). Treadwell befriended Duchamp at the Arensbergs' apartment, which by 1918 housed "one of the finest collections of modern art in America" (Naumann 1980: 3). Duchamp's use of new materials and redefinition of the spectator's role in relation to the art object clearly influenced Treadwell's developing artistic aesthetic. His "ready-mades" transformed everyday objects into works of art and reflected his dual obsessions with the machine and chance in shaping art for the modern world. Duchamp argued that the art work itself should no longer be seen to possess "meaning," but rather the spectator must interrogate the work and thus join in the act of creation. As he wrote, "the creative act is not performed by the artist alone; the spectator brings the work into contact with the external world by deciphering and interpreting its inner qualifications and thus adds his contribution to the creative act" (Duchamp 1989: 140).

One of Duchamp's assisted ready-mades, *With Hidden Noise* (1916), exemplifies the active role the spectator should now play in artistic creation. The ready-made consisted primarily of a ball of twine sandwiched between two brass plates, fastened together by four long bolts on each corner. Inside the ball of twine, another individual was to insert – without identifying for Duchamp or viewers – a small object that would produce a noise as it rattled around inside. *With Hidden Noise* redefines artistic collaboration as Duchamp, according to Caroline Cros, "shared authorship, entrusted someone else to 'finish' the piece, and since the contents were a secret, left the final results entirely up to chance" (Cros 2006: 60). Duchamp produced three versions of *With Hidden Noise*: one he kept; a second was given to Walter Arensberg, who added the hidden noisemaker; the third was given to Treadwell, who most likely similarly concealed a secret object (*ibid.*).[6] This art work, then, serves as a lasting symbol of Duchamp's artistic influence on Treadwell. Some of her most innovative plays are similarly designed to activate the audience into completing the art work. Some of her one-act plays of this period and later full-lengths such as *Machinal* (see Chapter 9) and *Intimations for Saxophone* (1934; see Chapter 10) employ fragmented, suggestive narratives and performance conventions designed to encourage theater spectators to fill in the gaps so that, as Treadwell stated, "*the audience discovers, – writes the play*" (Treadwell *c.* 1936a: n.p.).

For many playwrights similarly influenced by modernist art ideas, the emerging little theater movement provided an ideal haven for dramaturgical experimentation. Although Treadwell served on the initial producing committee and was "the first woman to assume individual control of a production" (Black 2002: 96) for the Provincetown Players, she never became an official member of the group and for the most part eschewed involvement with such little theaters. Rather, she kept her sights on the commercial Broadway theater, hoping, it seems, for a larger platform for her plays to receive widespread critical and popular attention. When her plays were produced in more intimate performing spaces, they were usually offered as self-produced showcases in rented, summer or community theaters. Treadwell used these non-commercial venues primarily as tryout houses, with the ultimate goal of refining the text to attract commercial production. In retrospect, this preference for Broadway often worked against her. She frequently found herself at odds with its practices. She detested its stagger system in which producers held productions indefinitely in an assembly line, its use of play doctors, and the increasing dominance of the director as the guiding visionary of theatrical production (see Dickey 2003). In a 1943 letter to a friend, the Russian critic and designer Alexander Koiransky, Treadwell summarized her frustrations after a meeting with producer John Golden and others who demanded revisions to her play *Highway*:

> There were there, besides Mr. Golden and I, the man he wanted to manage, the man he wanted to direct and an agent. Everyone talked except, of course – me (the eternal onlooker). . . . I am tired of plays standing on my shelves just because they are different – just because they are not like other people's plays.
>
> (Treadwell 1943)

When her dissatisfactions became too much for her to bear, Treadwell opted to produce her own plays on Broadway, as with *O Nightingale* (1925) and *Lone Valley* (1933).

Treadwell's self-fashioning: a tourist among the ruins

Treadwell's propensity for outspoken condemnation of the very venue to which she aspired ultimately may be the primary reason for her relative erasure from historical record. Although she could be charming and self-effacing in intimate settings, typically she was presented in the press – and often through her own writings – as an intimidating and difficult personality (see Dickey and López-Rodríguez 2006: 2–3 and Dickey 1995). Her closest friends often reprimanded her for her "definite perversity"

(Koiransky 1944) in deliberately marketing scripts she knew would be unappealing to Broadway producers. Treadwell's acknowledged "repugnance – detestation of *most* people" (Treadwell 1958) carried over into her general distrust of agents and producers. Thus, while she rewrote many of her plays tirelessly, rarely did the revisions bring them any closer to meeting producers' suggestions or demands. It may have been acceptable at the time for a male playwright like Eugene O'Neill to adopt an attitude of scorn toward the commercial theater and still receive Broadway productions, but it was an entirely different case for women playwrights, a bias Modjeska had warned Treadwell about years earlier in urging her to submit her plays under a male pseudonym (Modjeska 1908).[7] One of Treadwell's more noted women contemporaries, Rachel Crothers, found success largely because she was adept at tempering her feminist concerns within a form that was acceptable to Broadway producers and audiences.

At times, Treadwell seemed totally unable to assess the theatrical climate of the day. After her return from Russia in 1933, for example, she aggressively marketed her anti-socialist play *Promised Land* despite the fact that a strong leftist leaning, such as that seen in the Group Theatre, dominated Depression-era New York theater. Treadwell's last Broadway play, *Hope for a Harvest* (1941), received nearly universal dismissal for what most critics saw as a simplistic call for Americans to recapture their greatness by embracing their long-lost work ethic and agrarian roots, traits Treadwell believed were now found only in recent US immigrant populations. Her indignant response to the critics' rejection, an article in the *New York Herald Tribune* titled "I Remembered a Big White House," exemplifies her tendency toward defensiveness. Citing the success of the play's out-of-town tryouts, Treadwell believed the Broadway production failed only due to the provincialism and snobbery of New York's cultural elite: "Americans seem to recognize [the validity] of my play – even New York Americans. Not first-night New York Americans – they did not recognize it at all" (Treadwell 1941). After *Harvest*, Treadwell isolated herself from the same New York community of artists and intellectuals she had so fully embraced in the Arensbergs' salon in the 1910s. After this point, although she continued to write plays throughout her life, she turned her attention more toward fiction and even sought a new sense of community through living in various locales in Europe and Mexico before spending her final years in Tucson, Arizona.

The reaction to *Harvest* encapsulates Treadwell's difficulties in a nutshell: she was often uncompromising, brutally honest in her outspokenness, and more comfortable in a relatively isolated exploration of artistic and cultural ideals. McGeehan's introduction to his travel book begins with this description of his wife:

> The lady who is driving me was looking over the map of the world with me and we charted a course from New York to Istanbul, . . . zig-zagging here and there to look at a ruin – not that I care for ruins after thirty years of newspaper work but the lady who is driving me likes ruins.
>
> (McGeehan 1931: v)

A decade and a half later, Treadwell visited a very different set of ruins from those of the classical civilizations of the Mediterranean and the Balkans – those of post-Second World War Germany. In an editorial for the *New York Herald Tribune* in 1949 titled "A Tourist among the Ruins," she implied that the US shared culpability in the human destruction of the war: "I wish that every American would come to see these living ruins – see them, feel them, know them. For they are our ruins. We made them. For whatever reason and out of whatever desperate necessities, they are our accomplishment" (Treadwell 1949a). This article provoked angry responses in letters to the editor, signaling that Treadwell's isolation from her native populace was complete. Her grandmother's family ranch near Stockton, which had provided Treadwell with a place of respite and recovery but had also served as the locale for her poorly received novel and play versions of *Hope for a Harvest*, now only provided yet another reminder of the relative failure, excepting *Machinal*, of her work to garner popular or critical acclaim. She finally sold the ranch in 1954.

Many years later and in failing health, Treadwell took stock of her writing and concluded:

> I suddenly realized the devastating truth that I wasn't a good writer. I went back over everything I had done and saw that it was all no good. Corny. I tried to console myself by telling myself that I had been born and formed in a corny age. But I knew that others had been born in exactly the same age and had not been weakened or distorted by it.
>
> (Treadwell 1969)

This self-assessment was undoubtedly too harsh. Treadwell did not live long enough to enjoy the rediscovery of women dramatists of her generation by feminist scholars. Nor did she encounter the enthusiastic reception now given to ethnic studies, a field to which her early writings on Mexicans and Mexican-Americans form a significant contribution. As Miriam López-Rodríguez has noted, these writings occurred "years before the Chicano movement entered American literature" (Dickey and López-Rodríguez 2006: 7). Treadwell also did not live to see the acceptance of her finest play, *Machinal*, into the canon of great American dramas of the twentieth century. For these factors alone, much more critical enquiry is needed into Treadwell's writings. It is the intent of the chapters that follow to provide an overview of the current critical and artistic discourse surrounding her plays, and to encourage the broadening and deepening of this dialogue for the future.

7 Early plays

Sophie Treadwell's playwriting apprenticeship was a lengthy one. She began writing plays while still in college and continued to do so for the next sixteen years before gaining her first Broadway production. During this time, even while working as a full-time journalist, she completed an average of over a play a year, including nine full-length works. Although she often received encouragement from mentors like Helena Modjeska or agents or producers, Treadwell saw only two of her plays produced during this period. The first was a short sketch titled *Sympathy* (*An Unwritten Chapter*), which grew out of a popular serial for the *San Francisco Bulletin* and was produced during a one-week run in 1915 as part of a vaudeville bill in that city's Pantages Theatre. The other was a single performance of her play *Claws* (later retitled *The Love Lady*) in which she acted and produced herself on New Year's Eve 1918 at the Lenox Little Theatre in New York.

Although she studied and practiced drama at the University of California at Berkeley, she never had any formal training in playwriting. Treadwell's plays from this early period, 1905–21, display a wide range of subjects and styles, including short comedic sketches, psychological and historical character studies, nonrealistic one-acts, and full-length comedies and dramas. As it is not possible to discuss each of these plays in the space available in this text, this chapter will examine a few representative texts highlighting some of Treadwell's most significant forms and themes.

Women's rights: *A Man's Own* and *Rights*

The first and last plays of this period, *A Man's Own* (*c.* 1905) and *Rights* (1921), provide interesting bookends to Treadwell's early development as a playwright. They both reflect Treadwell's interest in using drama to explore issues related to women in modern society. Although vastly different in tone (comedy and historical melodrama) and length (short one-act and full-length), their central female characters reflect personal experiences and beliefs rooted in Treadwell's own life. Together, these two plays, along with others sandwiched between them, such as *Le Grand Prix* (*c.* 1906–07), *Constance Darrow*, *Guess Again* (*c.* 1915–18) and *The Eye of the Beholder*, pose the question as to where or to whom does a woman's supreme duty lie: to her family, to her husband, or to herself?

A Man's Own

Written while in college, *A Man's Own* is one of Treadwell's earliest surviving plays. It is a relatively simple sketch of a young woman, named only as Girl, who works for low wages in a department store. After being snubbed for a raise by the male store manager, Martin, the Girl sneaks into the store owner's office to steal what she feels is her due. Discovered by the owner, a "*quiet, self-centered*" man named Curtis (Treadwell *c.* 1905: 1), the Girl defiantly tells of her hardships, including a lack of education, a deceased mother, and a father who ran away when she was young. As the story unfolds, Curtis recognizes the Girl as his own daughter, and the play ends with the Girl sidling up to her father and asking that he tell the manager to raise her salary.

The play demonstrates that even at this early stage of her work in the theater, Treadwell possessed a facility with dramatic dialogue, situation, and overall theme. In the speech of the Girl in particular, the writer displays the sense of comic timing and verve that would reappear in her social comedies, such as *O Nightingale*, *You Can't Have Everything* and *Ladies Leave*. The play also reveals that, from the very outset of her playwriting,

Treadwell's primary concern would be with the changing role of women within the established patriarchal and economic structures of American society. As in her later drama *Machinal*, she focuses on the plight of a young working woman whose experiences may be viewed as so typical that she initially appears in the drama as an anonymous archetype, simply the "Girl" or the "Young Woman." Treadwell wrote *A Man's Own* at a time when young women's entry into the urban, corporate workplace initiated new discussions about women's independence and domestic obligations. Although focusing primarily on the office space in her study *Engendering Business*, Angel Kwolek-Folland's observations apply equally to the retail sales floor:

> Women's presence in the office work force challenged the Victorian ideal of separate public and private worlds for men and women, with the result that debates over definitions of manhood and womanhood were woven into corporate life from the beginning of the financial industries' modern development.
>
> (Kwolek-Folland 1994: 4)

Treadwell's awareness of this new merger of public and private domains for women became a recurring issue in many of her early plays and journalistic articles and serials.

Like Treadwell herself, the Girl comes from a home in which the father abandoned his familial responsibilities, leaving mother and daughter to fend for themselves. The Girl understands very well, as did most working women of her time, that a secretarial or retail sales job did not equate with financial independence. For many, it was a necessary way of adding much-needed income to her family, with whom she still lived. Curtis easily dismisses the Girl's complaint about the low hourly wages of his thousand-strong female workforce by saying, "Some of them have homes," and it "is not my business – just your bad luck" (Treadwell *c*. 1905: 12) when he learns that the Girl's mother has died and she has no family support. The store superintendent, Martin, also had previously dismissed her request for a raise from her unlivable salary of six dollars a week by asking, "Haven't you

got any friends . . . gentleman friends?" (*ibid*.: 10). By 1912,
conditions like the Girl's were so typical that the social activist
Jane Addams wrote of her fear that the male-managed corporate
workplace combined with women's relatively low wages would
tempt female workers into "a vicious life" of providing sexual
favors for money or developing misguided romantic attachments
(Addams 1913: 213). The Girl in *A Man's Own* remarks on
the easy prey the young saleswomen represent to their male
customers, not because of any solicitousness on their part but
only because they were so obviously "young and . . . poor"
(Treadwell c. 1905: 11).

The Girl displays a keen awareness of the economic situation
in which she finds herself, and her rebellion against gender
inequity in the corporate workplace serves as the focus of this
short play. She knows the numbers of women in the store's
employment, their salaries, her length of service without adequate compensation, as well as her low market value. There are
a "dozen girls," she acknowledges, "waiting to step into my job"
(*ibid*.: 12). Once she is discovered attempting to steal she displays
little hesitancy in voicing demands for what she feels is money she
has earned. That Treadwell chose to foreground this rebellion
should not be lost in the play's use of melodramatic contrivances,
most notably in the father–daughter reunion at the end. Yet even
when using well-worn dramatic devices such as this one, one can
gauge in this early play that Treadwell is not going to develop
into a dramatist who simply follows form. Despite the sentimental reunion of father and daughter, once Martin re-enters at
the end of the play it is clear that all will not end in familial bliss.
Curtis does not acknowledge to Martin the true identity of the
Girl; nor does she demand he do so. She quietly leverages her
new knowledge to get a pay raise in return for not causing a
scandal for her father. It is truly "a man's world," as Treadwell's
contemporary Rachel Crothers titled her 1910 play, and it is
"a man's own" interests that matter. While those interests are
financial more than familial, at least Treadwell's Girl better
understands the true nature of the social and economic world in
which she lives, and she can now begin to use this awareness to
her advantage.

Rights

The play at the opposite end of Treadwell's apprenticeship period took a celebrated historical figure for its subject. As Nancy Wynn has suggested, Treadwell perhaps composed *Rights* in 1921 to capitalize on the passage the year before of the constitutional amendment granting women the right to vote (Wynn 1982: 64). Based on Mary Wollstonecraft, the play uses the backdrop of the French Revolution to examine both Wollstonecraft's feminist arguments in her work *A Vindication of the Rights of Woman* (1792) and her relationship with her first husband, the American Gilbert Imlay. Thus, the discourse of the play alternates between the philosophically political and the intimately personal. Treadwell's three-act play dramatizes Wollstonecraft's philosophical debates with the likes of Thomas Paine and William Godwin (her second husband), her love for Imlay, and her subsequent rearing of their child alone after Imlay's frequent business trips and casual affair with another woman.

Wollstonecraft's philosophies and life experiences undoubtedly appealed to Treadwell on a variety of levels. Mary urges her sister Eliza to continue her education and leave her brutish husband back in England: "Independence is a powerful tonic," she asserts (Treadwell 1921c: I, 3). When a letter from her brother arrives announcing an offer of marriage to an English squire, Mary – much like Treadwell herself – voices her disgust over witnessing her mother endure her husband's abuses and decries the institution of marriage as an unequal partnership. Mary explains the premise of her book to Godwin and Imlay:

> I do not wish [women] to have power over men, but over themselves! . . . The helpless – the degraded position of women is the presumption of my mind – for that reason, I am opposed to marriage. . . . I will not submit to an institution I wish to see abolished. My doctrine is simply that marriage, as it has become, is wrong! But that an attachment, in some degree permanent, between persons of opposite sex – is right!
>
> (Treadwell 1921c: I, 30, 34)

Later, Mary – like so many of Treadwell's female characters – has difficulty reconciling her desire to be with Imlay with her own demands for independence. The pregnant Mary tells her sister Eliza that she feels married to Imlay even though no conventional ceremony has taken place. And late in the play, as Mary is despondent from the exhaustion of pursuing her writing and caring for her baby girl, she acknowledges that these dual obligations have provided the historical rationale for men relegating women to the domestic role. Thus, Treadwell's portrait of Mary Wollstonecraft is not without the same doubts and inconsistencies that Treadwell herself often expressed. It must be noted, however, that *Rights* ends with Mary's rejection of the unfaithful Imlay and his offer of financial support, as well as her momentary thoughts of suicide, in order to continue to care for her child. She does not allow Imlay to have any legal rights over her through marriage or child support, and the play's ending vindicates Mary's independence.

The subject of Mary Wollstonecraft would have had particular resonances for many in Treadwell's social circle and fellow-members of the Lucy Stone League. Many of these modernists were at the time actively debating the role of marriage and women's sexual freedom. Emma Goldman in *Marriage and Love* (1911) denounced marriage as a formal social mechanism for depriving women of their sexual freedom and ability to work outside the home. Goldman also posited that women should be free to have children without being married. Una Stannard notes that when Floyd Dell moved to Greenwich Village in 1913, "he immediately noticed the number of couples who were living together under two names" (Stannard 1977: 175) – some were married, some were not. Although Wollstonecraft referred to herself as Mrs. Imlay while living in Paris in 1793, modern feminists generally favored the retention of "Miss," along with their given surnames, thus making it impossible to tell by title alone whether a woman was married. These practices became the cornerstone of the Lucy Stone League, effectively putting Emma Goldman's foundational premise into effect: "Now that woman is coming into her own . . . the sacred institution of marriage is gradually being undermined, and no amount of sentimental lamentation can stay it" (Goldman 1916: n.p.).

Although Treadwell continued to revise *Rights* for the next two decades (see Dickey 1997a: 94–95), the play was never produced and has attracted almost no critical attention. Wynn believes its philosophical arguments and love story "both posture in predictable ways," and that its "complex, ironic portrait of a woman who speaks of freedom for women but who wants to belong to a man was unsatisfying and probably unpopular" (Wynn 1982: 72). The play is noteworthy, however, as an indicator that Treadwell viewed her own feminism within a long, sweeping historical context and that her own contradictions and inconsistencies were shared by one of the icons of the women's rights movement.

Experimental one-act plays: *To Him Who Waits* and *The Eye of the Beholder*

Upon her move to New York in 1915, Treadwell worked for a year as a journalist for the *New York American* before deciding to reject an offer for a long-term contract in order to pursue her playwriting career. Between 1915 and 1918, she composed half a dozen one-act plays, employing widely different styles and subjects. Two of these short plays, *To Him Who Waits* (c. 1915–18) and *The Eye of the Beholder*, are especially note-worthy for their use of nonrealistic conventions and, for that time, experimental dramatic constructs. These two plays best exemplify Treadwell's eagerness for artistic experimentation as a result of her interactions with the Arensbergs' circle, and they set the precedent for her later nonrealistic plays *Machinal* and *Intimations for Saxophone*.

To Him Who Waits

To Him Who Waits dramatizes a highly symbolic battle of wills between the sexes. Set outside "*a lonely cabin in the mountains at nightfall,*" the action of the play is underscored by "*the faint music of a violin, as though played far off, high up*" (Treadwell c. 1915–18: 1). A Man, "*huge, heavy insistent, powerful,*" brings clothing and food for the advancing winter to the cabin's lone inhabitant, a Woman, "*slim, passionate, eerie*" (*ibid.*: 1). The

Man's presence is repugnant to the Woman, who lives her days in spiritual communion with her dead lover, a slim youth with a violin who brought the Woman to the cabin. The Woman vows to die before giving in to the persistent sexual advances of the Man: "That is why I tell you it is useless that you come to me way out here – again and again – it is useless – you waste your time – I have too strong a will!" (*ibid.*: 4). The Man, however, claims he will simply stay and wait for the Woman's will to break: "Everything comes to him who waits" (*ibid.*: 2). When the Woman describes her lasting affection for her deceased lover, the Man grows violent and "*flings her aside as though she were a rag doll*" (*ibid.*: 6). The frantic Woman holds off the Man with a stick and bolts herself into the cabin, "*in terror – as one trapped*" (*ibid.*: 9). The Man calmly lies down and stretches himself across the door, settling in to wait for the Woman's moment of weakness. The play ends with the Woman's despair:

> *([She] turns and goes up to the little table by the lamps – sits there, her hands held tightly before her – outside the cabin all is blackness – the faint music dies down – increases – dies down – increases – is very faint – there is – far off – the call of a lonely animal. The girl gets slowly to her feet – the music grows louder – desperately – the girl stands in the light over the outstretched man – her arms are held out to him as though strained that way against her will – her fingers are working.)* Come – in. *(The music breaks – stops. [The Man] jumps to his feet and starts in – he is a great shadow in the doorway.)* Wait – I must put out the light. *(She turns in – the light goes out. The man follows her.)*
>
> (*ibid.*: 8–9)

In the play's use of music for communicating internal emotional states and in the Woman's ultimate inability to resist the compulsive sexual attraction of the brutishly physical Man, the play prefigures Treadwell's innovative drama *Intimations for Saxophone*. Despite the Woman's protestations about her strong will to resist, *To Him Who Waits* suggests that in a woman's internal struggle between a conscious preference for a spiritual communion with a lover and a physical attraction – even an intellectually repugnant one – the latter will ultimately win out. The Woman repeatedly refers to her deceased lover as "alive," and says, "Always I have my hand in his! . . . Sometimes it is his hand – sometimes it is God's" (*ibid.*: 5). In contrast, she tells the Man that through his coarse sexual advances "it is you who are dead – dead! That is why I cannot bear to have you come near me" (*ibid.*: 5). Treadwell's alternation of lyrical and prosaic language in the play further accentuates this contrast between the two men:

> WOMAN: And when the night comes like now, he plays to me his violin. I sit under this great tree like we used to – and the music quivers on the leaves like drops of dew – it comes down upon [my] eyes like wet drops of dew.
> MAN: Does it come down upon your mouth like wet kisses?
>
> (*ibid.*: 5)

The Man represents pure sexual desire, not love. Even he acknowledges that his attraction to the Woman is beyond his control.

> WOMAN: Why don't you leave me alone?
> MAN: I wish to God I could.
>
> (*ibid.*: 2)

Nancy Wynn believes that in this play, along with *Machinal* and *Intimations for Saxophone*, "Treadwell presented most forcefully the central question for her female characters and probably for herself: Can a woman live freely and securely without the help of a man?" (Wynn 1982: 50). Wynn concludes that even though Treadwell's writings reveal her repulsion for women's dependence on men, the "revulsion did not extend to the men, themselves," even when the man in *To Him Who Waits* is "brutish, insensitive, an almost-Neanderthal representation" (*ibid.*: 50). Michael Cotsell, in *The Theater of Trauma*, finds the Woman's "body-language" in the play's ending "contradicting everything she says," and that "Treadwell sites 'To Him Who

Waits' exactly at the question of the female hysteric: was she coerced or did she want it?" (Cotsell 2005: 277). Louise Heck-Rabi concludes that the play is the "most striking and short" of Treadwell's frequent "male–female oppositions" (Heck-Rabi 1976: 24). When viewed within the context of Treadwell's plays as a whole, *To Him Who Waits* presents a symbolic exploration of the relationship between women's spiritual and sexual selves.

The Eye of the Beholder

Treadwell returned more forcefully to the notion of women's various selves in *The Eye of the Beholder* (copyrighted 1919). In this play, the action centers on a young woman named Marcia Wayne.[1] Except for a brief exchange with a servant at the beginning and two sentences at the end, one might conclude that the play does not depict Marcia Wayne at all, focusing instead on presenting through four vignettes the social roles to which others have categorized her. Thus, the audience sees Marcia as those around her see her, with her costume and mannerisms changing accordingly. Her husband, Mr. Wayne, sees her in *"a slim flesh-colored negligee revealing her body . . . [her] every gesture is suggestive and enticing"* (Treadwell 2006b: 134). Her lover, Gregg, sees her in a *"simple frock of pink . . . giving her the sweet ingenuous look of a girl of eighteen"* (*ibid.*: 135). Her lover's mother, Mrs. Gregg, views Marcia in a dress of a *"brilliant rose color . . . a woman of the world of thirty"* (*ibid.*: 137). And her mother, Mrs. Middleton, sees her *"dressed as a little girl"* (*ibid.*: 139) in need of her mother's constant care. The play is Treadwell's first attempt to incorporate elements of expressionism into her dramatic writing, most notably by introducing subjectivity to the action through character mannerisms and costuming.[2] Only in the beginning and closing moments does the audience see Marcia as she is, in *"a formless wrap of white chiffon of long sleeves and high neck"* (*ibid.*: 134). At the play's end, Marcia, alone, utters simply: "Everybody understands a little. Nobody understands enough" (*ibid.*: 139).

This premise of the play clearly reflects Treadwell's early interest in the new psychology as advocated by Freud and Jung.

Noted psychiatrist Elmer Ernest Southard frequently attended the Arensbergs' gatherings, often asking guests to share their dreams for analysis (Naumann 1994: 28).[3] The new emphasis placed on the unconscious, coupled with the multiplicity of new freedoms offered to the individual by modern society, led many to question the very idea of a unified self. Instead, artists and intellectuals argued that the self was fragmented and that multiple, sometimes contradictory personalities could exist within one individual. The play's opening stage direction echoes this notion: *"The idea of the play is this: That each human being is, in fact, different personalities, depending on the eye of the person who sees him"* (Treadwell 2006b: 133).

Although this stage direction refers to "human being" rather than "woman," the structure and dialogue emphasize the play's specifically feminist focus. Miriam López-Rodríguez has aptly pointed up Treadwell's application of new psychological concepts to feminist concerns. In her introduction to the published version of the play, López-Rodríguez writes that the "fragmentary construction of identity is Treadwell's way of criticizing society's patriarchal stereotyping of women, its denial of the complexity of women's minds, and the resultant lack of identity in those females who perform the role imposed on them" (Dickey and López-Rodríguez 2006: 74–75). Treadwell was particularly attracted to the Jungian concept of individuation, a process of self-realization in which one discovers one's true inner self by integrating those aspects of the psyche that have the ability to become conscious.[4]

Typed notes in Treadwell's papers indicate that she was later drawn to Toni Wolff's "A Few Thoughts on the Process of Individuation in Woman" (1934), an adaptation of Jung's individuation process that included an identification of four types of women's personality: the mother, the hetaira or courtesan, the Amazon, and the mediumistic or psychically sensitive (quoted in Treadwell n.d.b).[5] Treadwell quotes Wolff's elaboration on the significance of these types:

> generally speaking feminine psychology must be understood as the relationship between woman and man, even in those

cases where it is not apparent on the surface, that is, in conscious life. . . . To sum up, we can say that the four feminine types of personality correspond to the four archetypal forms of human relationships between the sexes. . . . Thus formulated the mother type would correspond to the archetypal pattern of the wife, the hetaira to that of the lover, the Amazon to that of the sister, and the mediumistic type to that of the daughter.

(*ibid.*: 6)

Although written many years before Wolff's essay, Treadwell's *The Eye of the Beholder* offers a strikingly similar classification of women's personality types, most obviously in the mother/wife and mediumistic/daughter. Wolff's Amazon, which she defined as "That type of woman who does not have an instinctive relationship either to children or to a man, but is concentrated on herself and her own likes and talents" (*ibid.*: 2) is not present in Treadwell's play. Instead, for the vignettes with the lover Gregg and Mrs. Gregg, Treadwell employs what Wolff would later identify as positive and negative forms of the hetaira – respectively, "La Femme Inspiratrice; the muse" (*ibid.*) and "the seducer" (*ibid.*: 7). While Wolff believed that "women have somehow been more estranged from their real nature than men" (*ibid.*: 1), she argued that a woman "has to renounce the complete identification with one archetype" in order "really [to] find herself" (*ibid.*: 7).

The play's ending provides a hint of such a renunciation yet still invites audiences to construct their own meaning as to Marcia Wayne's identity, providing the sort of audience activation that Marcel Duchamp advocated for modern art. Wynn writes that the four differing views of Marcia "do not form a complete picture, leaving the central character of the play a mystery" (Wynn 1982: 51). López-Rodríguez, on the other hand, suggests that the play does offer a full portrait of Marcia's "individuation process" but the other four characters see only a portion of it. For the audience, López-Rodríguez writes, "It may not be a full picture, as we are never presented with her own concept of herself, but at least it is closer to truth than the image held by the other characters" (López-Rodríguez 2006: 135). She also compares the play to Susan Glaspell's *Trifles* (1917) and *Bernice* (1919), plays in which the largely absent central female subject is similarly constructed by those around her (*ibid.*: 128). When *The Eye of the Beholder* received its much-belated premiere in 2007 by The American Century Theater in Arlington, Virginia, this shared dramaturgical technique was plainly evident when it was produced back-to-back with *Trifles* as part of a bill of one-act plays by modern American women playwrights.[6]

In this production, director Steven Scott Mazzola tightly choreographed the actors' movements, a "stylized approach" that one critic felt was "Eastern influenced, almost Kabuki" (Jackson 2007). To underscore the theme of Marcia Wayne's obscured identity, Mazzola kept the face of the actress, Lauren Judith Krizner, hidden until the play's final moment. As Krizner progressed through the four vignettes, her face was alternately obstructed by her hair or hands or by turning her back to the audience. In the scene with her lover's mother, Marcia's entire body was seen only in silhouette through transparent screens, moving seductively as the temptress she was imagined to be. For the final moment, Krizner, curled on a chair down center, slowly unfolded her body and revealed her face for the first time. The speed of the production emphasized the play's brevity. One audience member commented, "I wanted to see it again, it went so fast" (*The Eye of the Beholder* 2007). Critics found the play "a fascinating vignette" (Krentzlin 2007) and an "incisive inquiry into roles and objectification" (Graham 2007).

Merging journalism and theater: *Sympathy* and *Madame Bluff*

Sympathy (An Unwritten Chapter)

Treadwell's background in journalism not only paved the way for her first produced play but repeatedly provided source material for some of her most successful stage experiences, especially *Gringo* and *Machinal*. Her earliest involvement in newsrooms came while still in college and at a time when the role of women reporters in America was changing drastically. From 1880 to 1900, the percentage of women journalists more than doubled (Lutes 2006: 8–9). Rival New York publishers Joseph Pulitzer and William Randolph Hearst had reconceived how women reporters might cover the news, especially emphasizing the *woman's reaction* to the story more than the news event itself (Ross 1936: 20). Nellie Bly, writing for Pulitzer's *New York World*, became the prototype of what became known as the stunt reporter, a journalist who concocted a daredevil activity or went undercover for an investigative exposé. Like Treadwell, Bly was "a gifted actress" (*ibid*.: 48), and she successfully posed as shop and factory workers, an insane woman, and a Salvation Army girl, among many others, while offering candid glimpses into lives about which most readers knew little (compare Treadwell's serial "An Outcast at the Christian Door" in Dickey and López-Rodríguez 2006: 28–43). Bly always wrote her stunt articles in the first person, and such personalization of the news ran counter to most editors' penchant for neutral objectivity in reporting. Through their stunt reporting, women such as Bly and Treadwell undermined the dominance of objective reason for the journalist – long associated as a particularly male trait – and instead insisted "on the significance of their own bodies as sources of knowledge" (Lutes 2006: 38).

Like Pulitzer, Hearst similarly favored women stunt reporters, first as publisher of the *New York Journal* and later in San Francisco. Ross notes: "It was not enough [for Hearst's stunt journalists] to report the acts of God. They had to make things happen – and the more startling the better" (Ross 1936: 576). Treadwell's editor at the *San Francisco Bulletin*, Fremont Older, "believed in manufacturing news too. He started a flock of girls doing unheard of things for newspaper copy, but all his ideas had the social services slant and he made crusaders of his reporters" (*ibid*.).

Editors like Older believed women possessed certain characteristics that made them especially suited to news and stunt reporting. According to Ross, Older felt women "had more facility of expression than men, were diligent workers, could get anything they wanted" (*ibid*.: 580). Older and others encouraged women to write in a particular style, one that emphasized emotional aspects of the story in short phrases or "word splashes" (Lutes 2006: 3), rather than the mid-Victorian "prosiness" customary at the time (Ross 1936: 62). A woman reporter in this vein soon garnered the moniker "sob sister," a derogatory phrase that in "three syllables . . . recast trailblazing professionals as gullible amateurs" (Lutes 2006: 66).[7] The function of the sob sister, according to Ross, "was to watch for the tear-filled eye, the widow's veil, the quivering lip, the lump in the throat, the trembling hand. They did it very well" (Ross 1936: 65). Treadwell's frequent use in her plays of "word splashes" offset by dashes reflects her earlier mastery of the sob sister style (see Dickey 1999: 71–72).

Most importantly, Treadwell learned from Older how to "manufacture" news. The editor preferred serials whenever possible to cover news events (Ross 1936: 580), and after the success of "An Outcast at the Christian Door" in 1914, Treadwell pitched and gained approval of an idea for another. "How I Got My Husband and How I Lost Him: the Story of Jean Traig" appeared in fifty-four installments beginning in November 1914. Treadwell's serial offered a first-person narrative of a young working girl and would-be actress in San Francisco. The serial was billed as a factual account: Traig had told her experiences to Treadwell, who turned them into a compelling story. Unbeknown to readers, however, the story was complete fiction, probably based on Treadwell's own experiences, and a model was hired to pose as Traig for the photographs accompanying the installments (Wynn 1982: 43). The serial became a tremendous sensation in San Francisco, and during its later installments advertisements began appearing for a stage play based on an unpublished episode in Traig's life written by Treadwell and starring Traig herself.

As produced at the Pantages Theater in February 1915, the short, twelve-page play titled *An Unwritten Chapter* (later renamed *Sympathy*) dramatizes a wealthy man's attempt to parlay a dinner invitation to an impoverished and hungry Traig into a sexual encounter in his apartment. When the man persists despite Traig's many objections, she shoots him with a revolver she had concealed in her coat and escapes. Although a very brief sketch, the play generated enormous public response. Edgar T. Gleeson in the *Bulletin* wrote that the "playlet" attracted "capacity houses, which in point of actual numbers and general enthusiasm shattered all Sunday records at the Pantages Theater" (Gleeson 1915). Earning the then-considerable sum of $190 royalty for the one-week run, Treadwell had found a way not only to manufacture news but to parlay this news into a stage success.

Madame Bluff

Treadwell had first shown an interest in merging journalism and drama in an earlier unpublished and unproduced play, *The Settlement* (1911). Although that play featured a brassy, young female reporter, the play's theme of the power of media to build up or destroy reputations was largely subsumed within a melodramatic plot. After her return from the First World War, Treadwell again took up this theme in one of her best early comedies, *Madame Bluff* (1918). In this three-act play, a young French girl, Simone de Byng, arrives in New York posing as the widow of a poet–soldier and looking to sell her sentimental story for profit. When her invented story is smelled out by Camille Jones, a former sob sister journalist, Simone explains: "(*Lip trembling*) I just want to geef the lecture and have a little success – American girl came to Nancy last year for the war – she explain me what it is the success in America – she say it is the beeg stories in the paper and notheeng what is true" (Treadwell 1918: I, 14). Rather than exposing Simone, however, Camille sees the opportunity to embellish the story and pave the way for their ultimate collaboration as writer and actress in the burgeoning motion-picture industry. Camille "springs into action with her ex-news room finesse":

> (*To Simone*) Now for the publicity end! We got to work quick! These boys [reporters] out here hungry for stuff! . . . Well that stuff you pulled wasn't so bad at that – got to put some zazz into it though. (*Looking at her*) You're a Countess

– Countess de Byng – widow of the young poetic Count René de Byng. Your father isn't a little professor! He's a big one! Biggest in France! Biggest in Europe! . . . All right – that'll do for a starter – till I think up something new – now don't let 'em know you're going into [motion] pictures! That'll crab everything! What you pulled isn't so bad at that when we do spring the picture end – we'll do it right – patriotic purposes – something like that.

(*ibid.*: I, 17)

The "Madame Bluff" of the title refers to the French Simone, but it might apply just as easily to Camille and her fellow-journalists for their ability to bluff, to pose or present a false image of the truth.

Madame Bluff is a clever, comedic work, but Treadwell was well aware that the journalistic bluff often had serious consequences, even though she herself may have practiced such deception. Her papers contain a single undated typed page that reveals her concern for journalistic responsibility. In part it reads:

The machinery for deceiving people, or at least for preventing them from getting an accurate view of the real struggle going on in the world, has never, it would seem, reached the perfection of the present day.

Nowadays, the vast majority of human beings in all countries are at the mercy of the newspapers for information about the world. And the newspapers mislead them atrociously.

(Treadwell n.d.c)

Treadwell repeats this same basic idea in her plays of the late twenties. In *Machinal*, she depicts two reporters reaching exactly opposite conclusions to courtroom proceedings. And in *Ladies Leave* (1928), a recurring theme is the media's reliance on advertising in shaping publication content and in selling consumers false images of beauty and necessities. Yet, it was another of Treadwell's sensational news stories that would provide her with her first foray into Broadway play production, *Gringo*.

8 Broadway and later plays

For two decades, from 1922 to 1941, Treadwell successfully obtained productions of seven of her plays on Broadway. During this period, she wrote five other full-length plays that remained unproduced, as well as two others – *The Love Lady* (1925) and *The Island* (copyrighted 1930) – that she self-produced in private performances at New York's Heckscher Theatre and the Edmond Town Hall in Newtown, Connecticut, respectively. During these decades, Treadwell also continued her development as an actor and director, tried twice to work in Hollywood doing film adaptations and script revisions, and advanced her reputation as a professional journalist with several series of articles on Mexican culture and politics.[1] She composed another seven full-length dramas – some re-workings of earlier plays, and at least one intended primarily for television – from 1942 to the mid-1950s. Thus, as with the preceding chapter, space does not allow for a discussion of each of these dramatic works. Instead, the focus here will be on Treadwell's plays presented for Broadway audiences, as these were the works that largely shaped her critical and public reputation in her own time. This chapter will also briefly discuss two of Treadwell's later works that received stage and television productions, while her most noteworthy stage success, *Machinal*, will be discussed exclusively in Chapter 9.

Gringo

During 1920–21, Treadwell wrote several feature articles on the aftermath of the Mexican Revolution for the *New York Tribune*, a newspaper where McGeehan had advanced from a sports writer to managing editor in 1921. Treadwell's articles included extensive, front-page features on the assassination of Mexican President Don Venustiano Carranza, the first interview with President Alvaro Obregón after he took office, and growing tensions resulting from Americans' "ill concealed racial disdain" for Mexicans and "air of moral superiority" regarding US corporate interests in Mexico (Treadwell 1921b). Her journalistic coup, however, was an exclusive interview with the revolutionary leader Pancho Villa at his remote hacienda in Canutillo, Durango, a 25,000-acre ranch across the border from Parral, Chihuahua. Treadwell was the only American journalist to gain access to Villa after his retreat to this secluded location, which he purchased from the new Mexican government in exchange for forgoing armed resistance (Willeford n.d.). These articles – especially the Villa profile – provided the raw material for Treadwell's first play on Mexico, *Gringo*, and America's growing interest in that post-revolutionary nation created the momentum needed for its Broadway production. The articles and play proved so successful that when Treadwell began another series on Mexico for the *Herald Tribune* in 1924, she was identified as "one of America's best informed authorities on Mexican affairs" (Treadwell 1924b).

When Treadwell visited Villa over four days in the late summer of 1921, she sought to find the truth behind the myth about the man. Villa had been a prominent figure in the American press and consciousness since 1913, when his battlefield bravado first garnered widespread publicity. Some daily papers offered admiring, sympathetic portraits of Villa as the heroic general and deferring friend to the US, most notably the *New York Times* and Hearst's *San Francisco Examiner* (Anderson 2000: 178–83). But not all the American press trusted Villa. The *Chicago Tribune* and *Los Angeles Times* were chief among newspapers that emphasized Villa's military defeats and cruel, sometimes vicious leadership. At times, these attacks echoed prevalent stereotypes of the era about the Mexican character as backward and morally deficient. The *Times*, for example, referred to him as a "savage" who fought not for his country but for a love of "plunder"; he was, the paper wrote, "as unscrupulous a ruffian as ever murdered a friend" (quoted in *ibid.*: 168). The *Saturday Evening Post* even dismissed Villa in unmistakably racially prejudicial terms: "Probably a majority of Mexicans are of pure, or mixed, Indian blood. . . . They are animals, señor; they are not people. That is the real problem in Mexico" (quoted in *ibid.*). Such attacks on Villa in the press increased after his raid on Columbus, New Mexico, left eight American soldiers and ten civilians dead and resulted in General "Black Jack" Pershing's vain, ten-month cavalry pursuit through northern Mexico. The media's use of Villa to perpetuate Mexican stereotypes undoubtedly fueled Treadwell's desire to talk with the man herself and set the record straight.

In her subsequent profile, titled "A Visit to Villa: A 'Bad Man' Not So Bad," Treadwell focuses on him as a family man and a pensive, caring leader of the Mexican poor. Her article affords Villa ample opportunity to revise the historical record of his raid on Columbus, the kidnapping of the American Joe Askew, and many battlefield exploits. Her unbridled enthusiasm for her subject gushes forth at the end of the article:

> Yes, I believe in Francisco Villa . . . in the sincerity of his feeling for his country and for his people. . . . I, for one, know of no man to whose integrity to protect and to whose power to defend I would more confidently intrust either "my money or my life." Viva Villa!
>
> (Treadwell 1921a: 66–67)

It is nearly impossible to read Treadwell's article today and not surmise that she was in many respects either naïve or politically motivated, as she allows Villa's personal charisma and unsubstantiated claims to dictate the tenor of the piece and shape her interpretations. Treadwell also omits unsavory aspects of Villa's character, such as his mistreatment of former wives. But this fact does not deny the significance of her accomplishments. Not only was she, as a woman journalist, able to arrange and navigate the potentially dangerous journey to Canutillo, but she offered in the words of the *New York Tribune*'s editor "a Villa hitherto a stranger to the American press" (*ibid*.: 44). Regardless of one's point of view about Villa's revolutionary actions, Treadwell's article humanized for Americans a complex, quasi-mythical figure too often dismissed within racial stereotypes.

Treadwell's fascination with Villa is clearly reflected in *Gringo*, which features an unpredictable, one-eyed bandit named Tito who disrupts greedy American mining interests in Guerrero, Mexico. The mine owner's half-Mexican daughter, Bessie (Besita), shocks the sensibilities of the American characters by professing her love for Tito and riding off with him at the play's end. In addition to numerous Mexican characters, *Gringo* features several expatriated Americans. One, the titular character Chivers, hypocritically treats his native mine workers "like children" (Treadwell 1922: I, 9) despite fathering a half-Mexican daughter and maintaining a Mexican lover. Another, Leonard Light, a blacklisted socialist, loathes his native country and despises "those Americans who spend all their lives out of America and bragging about it all the time. Mexico's full of 'em" (*ibid*.: I, 6).

Despite its title, Treadwell attempted to focus the play on Tito and his charismatic, persuasive power. In Act I, Tito recruits revolutionaries with Villa-esque ease by denouncing American economic interests in Mexico and Mexicans. He rallies the mine workers, saying:

> Why don't you stay on top of the earth – you fellows – where the sun is? . . . Moles can't enjoy the sun! You are moles – not men! . . . If you were men you would live like men! You would stay on top of the ground where, if there is no sun, there are stars! . . . You dig in the dark for gold! And you give the gold away! . . . The Gringoes have the gold you dig – you don't! . . . We should live like men! Not like beasts of burden! Burros! . . . (*Sudden ringing voice*) Who comes with

> me? A horse and a gun and the sun with Tito! Or a pack and
> a pick and the dark with this poor [Gringo]?
>
> (*ibid*.: I, 33–36)

Unlike the Villa portrayed in her news profile, however,
Tito is presented as someone who cannot completely be trusted.
He acts against his written word; and his treatment of women,
including the young Besita, is violent and fickle. After literally
stealing her away from her father, Tito dismisses Besita's
new-found affection for her captor, saying, "You've got too
much energy for me! You wear me out! (*ibid*.: III, 3). Yet, despite
Tito's disinterest and her earlier denouncement of him as "only
an Indian" (*ibid*.: I, 31), Besita ultimately rejects her Anglo
identity by choosing a life with her bandit lover. "I've never been
happy in my life before," she tells her father. "And here I am!
I love to live out under the sky! And I love Tito and I!" (*ibid*.:
III, 16).

Produced and directed by Guthrie McClintic at New York's
Comedy Theatre in December 1922, *Gringo* ran for thirty-five
performances. Several critics applauded the play's extensive use
of local color and its seemingly authentic portrayal of Mexican
banditry, many citing Treadwell's journalistic experience in
support of their conclusions. Treadwell herself wrote of the
similarities between Pancho Villa and José Ruben as Tito, noting
especially an "amazing" likeness to their voices (Treadwell
1923). Some, though, felt Treadwell tried to adhere too strictly
to historical accuracy, resulting in a diffuse plot or a missed
chance at creating a play of nationalist sentiment. James Craig in
the *New York Mail* wrote: "Here was a superlative chance to
'get' a Mexican bandit and thereby make amends for that con-
spicuous failure in 'getting' Villa" (Craig 1922). And Alexander
Woollcott in the *New York Herald* believed Treadwell not only
offended the Babbits of America who think their country the
"best under the sun," but the "editors of *The Nation* and other
of the more audible radicals" by portraying a conscientious
objector as a "whining, ungenerous poltroon" (Woollcott 1922).
For the most part, critics misread or did not respond to the play's
open criticism of American racist attitudes toward Mexicans.

For example, in his two reviews for the *New York Times*, John Corbin was deeply drawn to the "finely imagined and remorselessly psychological" character Besita (Corbin 1922a), ultimately concluding that as part Mexican and part American she stands as "a document on the evils of mongrelization" (Corbin 1922b), even though Treadwell clearly intended her as a heroic and sympathetic figure. Treadwell's social commentary remained hidden within multiple plot lines full of adventurous, melodramatic complications and secondary characters. Heywood Broun's review for the *New York World* sums up the overall critical response to *Gringo*, stating that the play showed "great promise and some extraordinarily interesting achievement" (Broun 1922).

The profile of Villa and the play it inspired served as a springboard for Treadwell's return to Mexico in 1924 and 1943 to write two series of articles for *New York Herald Tribune*. An outline for this first set of articles survives in her manuscripts. Titled "The Mirage of Mexico," Treadwell formulates the general theme of the series: "Nothing in Mexico is ever quite as it seems. Form and reality are widely separated. Between them, a no man's land of rumor, intrigue, pretense, indirection" (Treadwell 1924c). The causes for this mirage, according to Treadwell, are both psychological and historical. Psychological because of general confusion over "the character and temperament of the people"; historical because of the "constant imposition of alien forces upon a subject and abject people." As a result, Treadwell notes the "difficulty of arriving at anything approximating the truth" (*ibid.*). Taken collectively, Treadwell's writings attempt to present Mexican life, politics and culture from within while urging her fellow-Americans to view Mexico in terms other than those defined by US notions of race or nationalistic interests.

O Nightingale

Just as Treadwell was entering the world of commercial theater in New York, she was also beginning to experience dissatisfactions and new techniques that would lead her to seek reforms to Broadway practices. In January 1923, she sat in on a series of lectures in New York by Richard Boleslavsky, an expatriated member of Konstantin Stanislavski's Moscow Art Theatre. Treadwell soon joined a small collective of theater artists who studied all aspects of play production with Boleslavsky in a summer retreat in Pleasantville, New York. Her involvement with this group stemmed from her desire for more autonomy as a playwright in the play production process. In a series of lectures she gave for Boleslavsky's American Laboratory Theatre in the winter of 1925, she enumerated her objections to Broadway practices, including the relegation of the playwright to the role of a voiceless observer during the rehearsal period. Treadwell informed the students of her belief that the playwright, not the director, was *the* true creative force in theater, and that conflicting visions between playwright and director often precluded the realization of true works of art onstage (see Dickey 2003).

An important consequence of Treadwell's summer study with Boleslavsky was her new-found confidence to begin producing and directing her own plays, thus asserting her overarching vision as playwright on the production process. In January 1925, she produced, directed and acted in her play *The Love Lady*. And in April of that year, she became what critic Percy N. Stone called Broadway's only "playwright–producer–director–actress" (Stone 1925) when she acted in and co-produced her comedy *O Nightingale*. This is a simple comedy about a young Midwestern girl, Appolonia (Loney) Lee, and her attempts to break into the theater industry in New York. Loney takes dance lessons from a former Russian star (the role played by Treadwell under the pseudonym Constance Eliot) and receives advice from a chorus-girl neighbor about needing a male sponsor for her show-business ambitions. Initially, Loney rebuffs the latter advice, idealistically proclaiming, "And what of talent? What of character? It's character that wins! AND talent! And faith? Faith is what does it! Why, it moves mountains! Sometimes something sweeps over me and I feel I could do anything. Conquer – the world!" (Treadwell 1925: I, 23). Finally, after being wooed by an unscrupulous marquis with promises of introducing her to theater producers, a disillusioned Loney finds comfort in the tender love of a young visual artist.

In performance, the play hinges on the ability of an actress to capture the innocence of Loney, a quality that critics largely applauded in Helen Hayes's tryout performances and in Martha-Bryan Allen's rendition on Broadway. Nevertheless, the character's incredible naïveté proved the biggest hurdle to the play's critical success. The critic for the *New York Daily News* wrote: "In these days of the jazz age, we never surmised there was so much innocence in the world" (L. 1925). Another reviewer felt that Loncy's "excessive lack of sophistication . . . leads you to suspect that she is not very bright" (Anon. 1925). Some critics simply found Loney's resilient idealism to be unrealistic. The reviewer for the *New York World* offered a particularly intriguing comparison of Loney to Treadwell's previous Broadway ingénue, Besita, in *Gringo*:

> *Gringo* . . . was not a conspicuous success, probably because a public which loves to sentimentalize over young girlhood, hates to watch it chase one-eyed [Mexican] Bad Men. . . . It is probable that the heroine of *O Nightingale* will capture the imagination of her audience where her rowdy young predecessor failed. But in the midst of her prettiest speeches and most earnest evidence of charm, your mind turns back wistfully to the dogged, dirty-faced little baggage who trotted contentedly after her Mexican and was thoroughly deplorable and utterly alive.
>
> (S. 1925)

Robert Benchley offered a pithy response that serves as a summary of the critical reaction to *O Nightingale*, calling it a "quite nice" play "performed by nice people" (Benchley 1925). It ran for twenty-nine performances on Broadway and sparked brief interest from Fox as a film vehicle for Janet Gaynor (Heck-Rabi 1976: 60).

The play has attracted little scholarly attention. Louise Heck-Rabi wrote that in *O Nightingale* Treadwell found the formula for a funny play that she never used again:

The action moves from one reliably sentimental situation to another, to a final love-conquers-all curtain: loss of innocence; a mistaken identity; a meeting of aged lovers long estranged; a chance of a lifetime squashed; rapport between a titled foreigner and poor American artist, and the experienced chorus girl learning from a newcomer.

(*ibid*.: 54)

Nancy Wynn and Michael Cotsell, though, see a disturbing aspect to the play's love finale, both implying that Treadwell's unresolved attraction to her father provided the source for Loney's ultimate desire for a protector rather than a lover. "Through much of the play she appears in her child-like nightdress" (Cotsell 2005: 277), and in the character of the artist "Loney gets her wish – a surrogate father" (Wynn 1982: 95).

Ladies Leave

In the spring of 1927, Treadwell called upon her background as a court reporter in gathering material for her finest success in the theater, *Machinal*. Although not functioning in an official capacity for a newspaper, she attended the sensational murder trial of Ruth Snyder and Judd Gray. Snyder, a Long Island housewife, and her lover Gray were subsequently convicted and executed for the murder of her husband. *Machinal*, copyrighted a mere four months after the execution, utilized a style combining expressionist and realist dramatic conventions to explore the circumstances that might have led to the woman's journey to murder. As will be discussed in the following chapter, *Machinal* garnered widespread critical praise and established Treadwell's reputation as a daringly innovative playwright.

If the style and subject of *Machinal* caught Broadway audiences by surprise, then so did Treadwell's next play, *Ladies Leave*, produced and directed by Charles Hopkins at his self-named intimate theater in October 1929. At this time, however, audiences and critics were still fresh from Treadwell's non-traditional *Machinal*, and thus were disappointed with her new, rather polite comedy of manners (Waldorf 1929). Set in the New

York apartment of J. Burnham Powers, editor of the popular magazine *Ladies Home Companion*, the play dramatizes the changing moral sensibility of Zizi, Powers's young wife. Under the influence of a visiting psychoanalytic author from Vienna, Zizi seeks self-realization first by taking a lover, then by rejecting both husband and lover in favor of leaving for Vienna.

Treadwell's subtitle, "A Modern Comedy of Morals," provides a springboard for discussing the play's main features. The dramatic conflict of the work centers on a debate between traditional and "modern" life, with the progression of Zizi's character moving from one realm to the other. At the outset of the play, Powers, the bastion of traditionalism in the play, tells Jeffer, the visiting author, "I want security in my life! I realized my safety – my salvation lay in the one hope of finding somewhere an old-fashioned girl – untouched by modernity – and marrying her" (Treadwell 2006a: 143). Powers found such a girl, Zizi, after returning to his home town, and in the years since their marriage he has blindly believed in his "security" without noticing Zizi's growing dissatisfaction as a result of her exposure to "New York ideas" (*ibid.*: 189). When a young author, Phil, attempts to persuade Zizi to have an affair with him, he calls upon the stagnating effects of her traditionalism:

> Your sensibility's dulled! Oh, the immorality of withholding yourself from love – of immolating yourself behind a vain, stubborn, small will – all because of cowardice and a small-town mind – you are small-town, you know! When you're middle-aged, you'll be a female edition of Powers himself!
>
> (*ibid.*: 152)

Phil's use of the term "immorality" reflects Zizi's central obsession and the key to her transformation, referenced in the "morals" of the play's subtitle. While Zizi has resisted Phil's advances for months, she gives in to them only after hearing a lecture by Jeffer in which he claims that self-fulfillment in the modern world can be obtained only by opposing the stifling effects of Victorian morality. Zizi explains to Phil that their affair began because Jeffer "came, and just by a word, a casual word, he changed everything! . . . Moral! – the word 'moral.' . . . 'Immorality is moral'" (*ibid*.: 173). Throughout the play, Treadwell associates the term "immoral" with any action that suppresses the authentic self, while "moral" is associated with actions that unlock this authenticity. Late in the play, Zizi explains that she has "lost some taboos" (*ibid*.: 184) and that her sexual affair with Phil was "an end in itself, unimportant"; yet, "as a means" to "coming out," it was "powerful" (*ibid*.: 184–85). Jeffer notes that prior to this affair, Zizi appeared "covered over . . . smothered – buried" (*ibid*.: 183). Through this inversion of traditional morality, the extramarital affair allows Zizi to cease thinking of herself as someone's possession, which in turn allows her to experience a new sense of love for her husband. "Not wonderfully," she tells Powers, "not magnificently, not anything like that – still, it was love – then – for the first time" (*ibid*.: 191).

Just as Treadwell inverts customary definitions of morals, so does she attempt to alter traditional associations with the generic term "comedy" found in the subtitle. The ending of *Ladies Leave* resists the traditional comedic resolution involving reconciliation and pairing off of the sexes, such as that found in her previous Broadway comedy, *O Nightingale*. When both her husband and lover refuse Zizi as something other than a possession, she calmly orders her servant to pack her trunks as she departs for Vienna. While Vienna is Jeffer's home and the center of psychoanalytic practice, Treadwell implies that Zizi selected the destination almost on a whim, not as an attempt to pursue a love interest or seek counseling: "The world's full of trains and boats," as she tells Powers and Phil (*ibid*.: 194). The only substantive explanation she offers the astounded men for her departure is that she, like most modern women, has learned "Not to kid ourselves" (*ibid*.: 195) with the illusions and misplaced moralities of her mother's generation.

The relatively easy demeanor conveyed through Zizi's final departure may have contributed to most critics' lukewarm response to the play's subject and themes. Bide Dudley in the *New York Evening World* wrote: "I feel sure it must be about something. . . . But just where it attempts to go – in fact, just why it starts – I can't make out" (Dudley 1929). The critic for the *New York American* felt that "The curtain was dropped with the play – or at least its problem – still going on" (Anon. 1929). Some, though, praised *Ladies Leave* as "a slick comedy" (Cushman 1929) and "the most sophisticated play of the season" (Longacre 1929). Numerous critics praised the set design of Robert Edmond Jones while faulting the general overacting of most of the cast (Riley 1929; see also Dickey and López-Rodríguez 2006: 77). Louise Heck-Rabi later stated that Treadwell's play failed because it "negates the image of the American husband" (Heck-Rabi 1976: 109). Michael Cotsell sees in it a combination of "anxiety and narcissism," connecting the departure of Zizi to Treadwell's own "flight from trauma" to Vienna after a nervous breakdown following the closure of the play (Cotsell 2005: 281).

Lone Valley

For her 1914 stunt serial "An Outcast at the Christian Door," Treadwell's editor Fremont Older asked her to disguise herself as a destitute "girl of the underworld" and report on what life was like on the streets.[2] In her drama *Lone Valley*, which opened at the Plymouth Theatre on Broadway in March 1933, Treadwell once again returned sympathetically to the subject of the prostitute. Three earlier versions of the play under various titles had been circulating in tryout cities as far back as 1927. When no commercial New York producer would option the play, Treadwell decided to produce and direct it herself (Mantle 1933). Set in an isolated ranching community, *Lone Valley* is the first produced play of several that Treadwell placed in Western, rural settings. The play depicts the efforts of a former prostitute, Mary, to reform her life and recuperate from a recent illness. She tentatively returns the affections of a homely but good-hearted nineteen-year-old ranch hand, Joe, but their planned marriage is stopped by a self-righteously moral sheriff. Mary willingly leaves the town and Joe, but the young man soon forsakes his good reputation in the community and follows after her. Thematically, the play concerns itself with the sexual double standard found in small towns of rural America, and a redefinition of sexual morality is promoted through Mary and Joe's relationship.

Although the play had received some encouraging responses in tryout cities, New York critics almost unanimously felt its situation and themes too shop-worn. Brooks Atkinson felt the play was "out of the theatre's old clothes closet" (Atkinson 1933), and Bernard Sobel believed it to be a re-hash of Eugene O'Neill's *Anna Christie* and thought that it "seemed to belong to the vague dramatic past" (Sobel 1933). Only Treadwell's friend and fellow *Herald Tribune* writer Percy Hammond offered encouraging words. Calling Treadwell "one of the loveliest ladies this side of heaven," Hammond defended her choice to produce the play due to what he felt was its origin in factual circumstances (Hammond 1933). Another critic subsequently derided Hammond for being "an old softie" in defending a play that turned out to be "a boo-boo and a bore" (Anon. 1933a). *Lone Valley* closed after only three performances. Treadwell's next Broadway production, *Plumes in the Dust* (1936), similarly ended abruptly; this time after only eleven performances.

Plumes in the Dust

Although produced at the Forty-sixth Street Theatre in 1936, Treadwell's play about Edgar Allan Poe, *Plumes in the Dust*, most appropriately belongs to her early apprenticeship period. Under the title *Poe*, the play was copyrighted in January 1920, a full year and a half before Treadwell's other historical drama, *Rights*. This early version of the play served as the centerpiece of the much-publicized lawsuit Treadwell filed in October 1924 against John Barrymore and his wife Michael Strange.[3] The suit argued that Barrymore planned to appear in a Poe play written by Strange that was plagiarized from Treadwell's play, which Barrymore had been promising to produce for several years. The suit was dropped when Barrymore returned the manuscript of Treadwell's play and cancelled the production of Strange's version.[4] The press largely rallied to Barrymore's defense, branding Treadwell a publicity-seeking opportunist. This event undoubtedly marked Treadwell as a potential business hazard, and her subsequent difficulties securing commitments from producers seemed only to solidify her stance as a playwright's advocate.[5]

Even though the play underwent several revisions and titles before receiving production, the basic premise and structure remained the same. Having researched the subject for over two years, including gaining access to unpublished Poe materials from scholar J. H. Whitty and medical advice on delirium tremens from her friend Elmer Ernest Southard, Treadwell's versions remain consistently focused on four incidents in Poe's life. As she wrote to Walter Hampden in 1924: "I have not, as is usual in so-called historical plays, taken one more or less true incident and woven fancy around it. . . . Every fact, every situation, every character, and practically every line said by Poe, himself, is absolutely authentic" (Treadwell 1924a). A stage direction in one of the manuscripts of the play reveals that Treadwell deliberately omitted inserting her own interpretation of the events:

> *For [the play] tries to recreate this life as moving in the scenes and to the moods of its own time, without comment or slant from the author's time and moods. (It is hoped the audience will contribute this slant, and find its own pleasure in doing so.)*
>
> (Treadwell 1936: n.p.)

Treadwell's attempt at historical accuracy resulted in an episodic play spanning twenty-three years and more than two dozen characters.

Ironically, it was Barrymore's producer–director at the time of the suit, Arthur Hopkins, who brought *Plumes in the Dust* to Broadway in 1936.[6] Despite a celebrated performance by Henry Hull as Poe, most critics decried the genre of biographical drama as uninteresting (Gabriel 1936) and faulted the episodic plot structure for lacking the clear point of view Treadwell had carefully avoided (Coleman 1936). Richard Watts, Jr., however, praised Treadwell's "usual sympathetic understanding" in creating her artist–hero: "She persuades you that her central figure actually is a great literary artist, with a burning, inexhaustible passion for artistic creation" (Watts, Jr. 1936). Believing the play would prove a "regrettable but, I feel, an inevitable failure," Burns Mantle nevertheless stated, "But add the Barrymore appeal of twelve years ago and the Barrymore flair for misunderstood genius to such fading memories as Poe inspires and you have a strongly appealing combination" (Mantle 1936).

Hope for a Harvest

The critical and box-office failures of *Lone Valley* and *Plumes in the Dust* contributed to Depression-era years of professional and personal difficulty for Treadwell. After the deaths of McGeehan of heart failure in 1933 and her mother the following year, a disillusioned and exhausted Treadwell embarked on a lengthy steamer trip to the Middle and Far East. When she returned in July 1937, she moved to the family ranch she now inherited in Stockton. As I have noted elsewhere, the pattern of Treadwell's life and career to this point bore a strong similarity to that of Susan Glaspell: "Both women began in rural settings writing works of local color, moved to urban centers for intellectual and artistic stimulation, and returned after the death of their husbands to the type of rural environment that shaped their early lives" (Gainor and Dickey 2005: 49).

Treadwell's time on the ranch was one of reassessment and new directions. "I went there to live and to be a farmer," she later wrote, "led there by the memories of my childhood and seeking to find again the feeling of security, of plenty, of peace, that had always seemed to me to be there" (Treadwell 1941). Upon inheriting the ranch, Treadwell was surprised at its dilapidated condition and vowed to restore it to its former state of productivity. Her efforts eventually failed, and she cited her inability to find or create "the work, the good will, the co-operation of other people" necessary to make a farm community (*ibid.*). Treadwell hoped Americans would revive their belief in their country as a land of opportunity by learning from hard-working, recent immigrants. To further this desire, she wrote a novel and a play, both titled *Hope for a Harvest*.[7] While the novel contains many autobiographical elements, the play alters characters and situations more freely for dramatic effect.

The play centers on Lotta Thatcher, a middle-aged widow recently returned to the family ranch in California from war-ravaged Paris. Her efforts to revitalize the ranch and the attitudes of her pessimistic cousin Elliott are stymied until the son of a neighboring Italian immigrant agrees to marry Elliott's half-Anglo, half-Indian daughter even though she is pregnant by another man. The play ends with the promise of a business and perhaps romantic partnership between Lotta and Elliott, and their cooperative use of the ranch land with their Italian neighbors.

The play was produced on Broadway by the Theatre Guild in 1941 as a starring vehicle for the husband and wife team of Fredric March and Florence Eldridge. It had received exceptionally strong notices during out-of-town tryouts – a Boston critic calling it "one of the major theatrical events of this season" (Norton 1941) – so the Guild and Treadwell were dismayed by New York critics' rejection of the play's simple solution to a complex and important problem. Wolcott Gibbs in the *New Yorker* found the play "fairly dull and unlikely," offering a remedy that was little more than "pretty rudimentary economics." While he professed "highest admiration" for Treadwell, he could not help believing that "the soil is not exactly her theme" (Gibbs 1941). Guild co-producer Lawrence Langner, angered by the critics' dismissal, placed a large advertisement in the New York dailies "printing enthusiastic notices from over thirty out-of-town critics who liked the play. The results were instantaneous. Even those New Yorkers who had bought tickets seemed to want their money back!" (Langner 1951: 335). The play was aired on the Guild's radio show, *Millions for Defense*, before the play completed its disappointing run of only thirty-eight performances. In 1953, *Harvest* received a televised broadcast by the Theatre Guild in an adaptation by Norman Lessing.

Despite being one of only two Treadwell plays published in her lifetime, contemporary scholarship on *Hope for a Harvest* has been slow in forthcoming, perhaps due to the very traditional structure of the work. As Yvonne Shafer has noted, "It comes as something of a surprise to read *Hope for a Harvest* after considering earlier Treadwell's non-realistic works" (Shafer 1995: 267). Shafer nevertheless cites the continuing relevance of the play's themes – rampant consumerism, ethnic discrimination and ecological mismanagement – and concludes that "Treadwell used the metaphor of a decaying ranch as a symbol for an America in decline" (*ibid.*: 268). Richard Wattenberg more specifically views the play as subverting the traditional American frontier myth, as perpetuated in literature, theater and film:

> Treadwell reverses the hierarchy of the traditional frontier myth. Rather than focus on a dynamic male representative of Western savagery, a hero who protects the weaker female representative of Eastern civilization, she focuses on a self-assured female representative of civilization, a heroine who returns to her family homestead to find that her cousin and prospective lover, a "Westerner, a rancher – a characteristic, fine American type" has "gone to seed." . . . More importantly, he has lost the open-hearted optimism that was so characteristic of the Western male heroes.
>
> (Wattenberg 1995: 345)

Late in the play, Lotta's determination to "Work! – work hard and enjoy it! And enjoy what it gives me" (Treadwell 1942a: 89) effectively resuscitates Elliott's desire to cultivate his land. Wattenberg credits Treadwell with developing "what might be called a feminist frontier myth," one no longer marred by "male violence and aggression . . . in pursuit of easy gain," but instead dominated by those who "seek to live in harmony with the Western environment" (Wattenberg 1995: 348).

Later plays

After the New York failure of *Harvest*, an "awfully bitter" Treadwell saw only two more of her plays produced, and neither of them in New York theaters (quoted in Calta 1960). Her character study *Highway*, which chronicles the emerging love of a young woman who runs a highway diner in Texas, was first produced at the Playbox Theatre in Pasadena in 1944.

Reminiscent in tone and structure of William Saroyan's *The Time of Your Life*, the play was telecast a decade later by the Theatre Guild. Her last drama, *Now He Doesn't Want to Play*, was produced in 1967 by the University of Arizona Department of Drama in Tucson, where Treadwell spent her final years. The play had been reworked by Treadwell off and on for twenty-five years, and its stereotypical characters' romantic misadventures in Mexico City were appropriately dismissed by local critics as "quaintly dated" (Keating 1967).

Mostly, Treadwell spent the years after *Harvest* traveling between residences in Europe, Newtown, Stockton, Mexico and eventually Tucson. Beginning in 1949, she was accompanied on many of these trips by her son, a young boy whom she adopted as a baby in Germany (see Dickey and López-Rodríguez 2006: 200–01). Treadwell paid respect to McGeehan, with whom she had no children, by naming the boy William. She also turned more to the writing of novels, such as *One Fierce Hour and Sweet*, which was published in 1959. However, she continued marketing her plays, both old and new, while maintaining a rigorous daily writing schedule. Shortly before her death in 1970, she assigned the rights to her works to the Roman Catholic Diocese of Tucson, where proceeds would be used to support the education of Native American children.

9 Key plays I
Machinal

Treadwell called upon her background as a court reporter for the basis of her most successful play, *Machinal*. Produced on Broadway in 1928 starring Zita Johann and featuring a young Clark Gable, *Machinal* was based loosely on one of the most written-about murder trials of the twentieth century: the Snyder–Gray case. The New York papers assigned 180 reporters to cover the story, which fed the public's appetite for details about this seemingly normal housewife turned cold-blooded murderer. Although both Snyder and Gray were found guilty and executed, the media continued to focus mainly on Snyder, typically portraying her as an embodiment of evil or an inhuman monster (see Jones 1980: 251–66). When she became the first woman executed by electric chair in New York State, a reporter for the *New York Daily News* smuggled a camera into the execution chamber strapped to his leg. His photo appeared in print the next morning in an edition that sold out in fifteen minutes (Pelizzon and West 2005: 211). The curiosity about Snyder's motives later inspired James M. Cain's novels *The Postman Always Rings Twice* and *Double Indemnity*, both of which were turned into successful films in the 1940s.

Machinal undoubtedly owed some of its initial success to being one of the first fictionalized treatments of this case, but it has since been recognized as a seminal feminist play that, unlike Cain's novels, avoids delving into the sensational aspects of the story in favor of exploring the social conditions and gender inequities that might have led to this woman's act of violence.

The play

The play's title is taken directly from a French word meaning mechanical, automatic or fragmentary. Told in episodic, piecemeal fashion, *Machinal* chronicles the journey of a young female clerical worker, named at the outset only as the Young Woman, who reluctantly marries a wealthy executive of her company. The action of the play revolves around the reluctance of the Young Woman to accept traditional expectations for gendered behavior. Her central difficulty arises when, in the play's nine episodes, she is surrounded by examples of women who do fulfill these expectations without questioning them. In Episode One, her co-workers in the office fully expect that the boss's attraction to the Young Woman will lead to marriage. At their tenement home in the next scene, the Mother calls the Young Woman crazy when she shows the slightest hesitancy to marrying her boss, a man whose position as vice-president of the company ensures his decency and appropriateness as a husband. As the action dissolves into a honeymoon suite, her new husband (her ex-boss George H. Jones) dismisses her sexual anxieties as "nothing to cry about" (Treadwell 1949b: 26). In Episode Four, a nurse in a hospital's maternity ward cannot comprehend the Young Woman's refusal to take her own child to breast.

At this point in the play, the Young Woman begins to take a more active role in establishing a life for herself outside of her marriage, but again the voices around her help shape her actions. At a table in a speakeasy, a Woman ultimately relents to her male partner's urgings to follow through on an abortion: "Most women just . . . don't think nothing of it" (*ibid*.: 38). Meanwhile, at another table in the same scene, the Young Woman (identified for the first time by name, Helen Jones) meets a young adventurer recently returned from Mexico and leaves with him for a sexual encounter. Her sexual liberation in the scene in his apartment is immediately contrasted by a scene at her home, where her husband equates marriage with property acquisition in business. The play ends with the Young Woman on trial for murdering her husband and then in the prison cell moments before her execution.

The action is punctuated by a range of expressionistic devices, most notably lengthy interior monologues revealing the Young Woman's evolving psychological state, as well as a cacophony of city sounds and snatches of overheard dialogue on the periphery of the Young Woman's life. As I have noted elsewhere, *Machinal*, unlike other expressionistic plays of the 1920s, avoids dramatizing climactic scenes, choosing instead to focus on the conditions that lead up to and immediately follow such moments of conflict (Dickey 1999: 74). The opening stage directions for the earliest surviving manuscript of *Machinal* reveal that Treadwell conceived of the play's unique form in an effort to activate the audience's response. Since these extensive stage directions are significantly different from those accompanying the previously published version of the play, and since they offer insights into Treadwell's aims and desired aesthetic, excerpts from them are worth reprinting here at length:

> THE PLAN *is to tell this story by showing the different flat surfaces and hard edges of life that the woman comes up against; and disclosing her inner reactions to these flat surfaces and hard edges. This is done by eight acted scenes connected by monologues – spoken thoughts. These monologues are all the voice of the woman coming from out a dark stage (to an audience now trained to radio, and so accustomed to the drama of the lonely unaided voice).*
>
> *. . . Does their place in the plan of the play – connecting links, or better – connecting channels of action – demand that the thought move through them in an approximately straight line, or can one be permitted a nearer approach to the scatteredness, unexpectedness of the relaxed meditating mind?*
>
> *. . .* THE HOPE *is (by accentuation, by distortion, etc.) to create a stage production that will have "style," and at the same time, by the story's own innate drama, by the tremendous interest and curiosity already aroused in it by the actual and similar story of Ruth Snyder, by the directness of its telling, by the variety and quickchangingness of its scenes, and the excitement of its sounds – (and perhaps by*

the quickening of still secret places, in the consciousness of
the audience, especially of women) – to create a genuine box
office attraction.

(Treadwell *c.* 1928: n.p.)

Although Treadwell references Snyder directly, she is quick to
note later in these stage directions that the Young Woman is *"any*
ordinary young woman." Later manuscript versions omit all
references to Snyder, most likely in an effort to convey that the
experiences of the Young Woman in the play are not those of one
individual such as Snyder, whose demonization in the media
could lead to easy dismissal as being idiosyncratic. Rather, they
are those of the common, ordinary, young working woman, and
as such represent a potentially more widespread rejection of
traditional gender norms.

Also noteworthy in these stage directions are the comments
pertaining to the nonlinear, reflexive nature of the monologues
and the overall aim of consciousness-raising, especially for
women. The stage directions demonstrate that Treadwell hoped
to adapt various expressionistic devices that had been in vogue
on the American stage earlier in the 1920s. The techniques
typically included some combination of the following: an
episodic structure of short scenes chronicling a central character's
(usually a young man's) quasi-messianic quest; the depiction
of inner, subjective emotional states; distortion, exaggeration
or symbolism to evoke a dream-like quality, as though the action
is filtered through the mind of the central character; the use
of compressed syntax and staccato dialogue; and the use of
character types, especially for secondary characters. Treadwell's
familiarity with expressionism prior to writing *Machinal* can be
found in a guest review of new Broadway openings she wrote
in 1926. Although the epic nature of Franz Werfel's *The Goat*
Song impressed her, Treadwell voiced displeasure for some of
its heavy-handed use of expressionistic techniques, calling the
play "a Big Bertha, heavy, booming, devastating" (quoted in
Hammond 1926). She expressed appreciation for the "depth and
truth" of Eugene O'Neill's expressionist drama *The Great God*
Brown, but disliked his tendency to be overly confessional of

his own psychological makeup (*ibid.*). In *Machinal*, Treadwell sought to modify such approaches to stage expressionism for the expressed aim of creating a new aesthetic, one that might have a particular appeal for the female spectator (see Dickey 1995 and Walker 2005; and Chapter 10).

The Broadway production at the Plymouth Theatre, 1928

Modern psychology and Unconscious Projection

Elsewhere I have discussed Treadwell's experiments with expressionism within the context of theatrical practice of the late 1910s and 1920s, especially as influenced by the emerging awareness of Freudian and Jungian psychology (Dickey 1999: 75–76). For the original Broadway production of *Machinal*, Treadwell teamed up with two theater artists – producer and director Arthur Hopkins and designer Robert Edmond Jones – who shared strikingly similar thoughts to her own about the power of the theatrical event to stimulate the unconscious minds of those in the audience. One might well argue that it was the unique style of *Machinal*, more so than its feminist critique, that accounted for its critical success in 1928. While Treadwell's original stage directions clearly reveal that she had formulated this stylistic approach to the play's staging (see Wynn 1991), its realization came as a result of an especially harmonious collaboration.

Hopkins, for example, had earlier staged expressionist productions on Broadway, including several famous Shakespearean productions with Jones in the early 1920s. In his 1918 publication *How's Your Second Act?*, Hopkins articulates his staging theory of "Unconscious Projection." Briefly summarized, this theory espouses an attempt to create a stage illusion of such hypnotic power that it will stimulate a response directly in an audience's unconscious. Hopkins stressed this unconscious appeal due to his belief that one could never reach a consensus of reaction, and therefore a complete illusion, in the theater through *conscious* appeal. As he wrote: "I want the unconscious of the

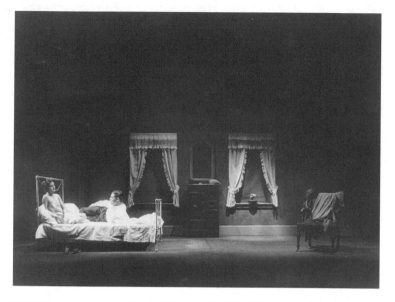

9.1 Zita Johann and Clark Gable in *Machinal*, Plymouth Theatre, New York, 1928. Photograph reproduced by courtesy of the Billy Rose Theatre Division, the New York Library for the Performing Arts, Astor, Lenox and Tilden Foundations

actors talking to the unconscious of the audience, and I strive to eliminate every obstacle to that" (Hopkins 1918: 16). The first step for Hopkins in achieving this goal involved stilling the conscious mind, a technique he says he learned from "The hypnotist" (*ibid.*: 8). Hopkins sought to render the conscious mind inoperative by eliminating from the stage all non-essential features, such as unnecessary scenery, props or acting tricks that might arouse the curiosity or focus of the conscious mind. Realism, for Hopkins, should be avoided at all costs due to its appeal to the audience's consciousness:

> An attempt at exact reproduction challenges the conscious mind to comparison . . . the result of the whole mental comparing process is to impress upon the auditor that he is

in a theatre witnessing a very accurate reproduction, only remarkable because it is not real.

(ibid.: 26–28)

Ultimately, Hopkins hoped that his approach to Unconscious Projection created an environment in which "All the repressed desires burst forth into flames in the theatre, and for a few hours they have full sway, to be silenced again until dreams have their way" (*ibid.*: 24). As with psychoanalytic technique, however, success depends on the ability of the conscious mind to integrate the expressions of the unconscious. Hopkins wrote that, in the end, his approach must "abide by the conscious verdict . . . all the unconscious reaction is wasted if the conscious ultimately rejects us" (*ibid.*: 9).

Similarly, Jones opposed realism in the theater, seeking instead to create a form of theater that suggests "images of a larger life . . . a visionary world all about us" (Jones 1941: 83). The year before *Machinal* went into production, he had been receiving psychoanalytic treatment from Carl Jung and Toni Wolff in Zurich, where he said he had "been working at intervals on a new set of trances, associating them just as one does with dreams" (quoted in McDermott 1984: 213–16). According to Dana Sue McDermott, Jones's subsequent writings on the theatrical artist's creative imagination reflect Jungian theories about the artist's intuitive ability to tap into the collective unconscious. McDermott writes: "According to Jung, something within the universal unconscious is striving for expression and the original manifestation of this striving is an intuition. The artist is compelled to reach for a means to express this intuition" (*ibid.*: 218). The same month that *Machinal* opened, Jones published an article in *Theatre Arts Monthly*, titled "The Artist's Approach to the Theatre." In this essay, he articulated the theatrical artist's "means" as a compelling, guiding "image," one that is not static but "in action" (Jones 1928: 629, 631). These images, when realized, possess the "hypnotic power" to draw the audience "into the mimic life that goes on up there on the stage. We become a part of it. We slip outside of ourselves into a larger existence" (*ibid.*: 630).

Critical reception

For the Broadway production of *Machinal*, Jones designed a lighting effect for the play's conclusion which may serve to illustrate his theories on the power of an image to elicit a Hopkins-like projection by the audience. This effect is described in one of Treadwell's post-production manuscripts of the play. After the Young Woman's final plea for a stay of execution is cut off and the Priest murmurs his prayer for mercy, the stage direction reads: *"Pause – overhead lights come up on Cyclorama, first faint blue, then red, then pink, then amber – they are thrown on FULL . . . PAUSE – . . . CURTAIN"* (Treadwell c. 1928–29: X, 2). Critics' responses to this lighting tableau must serve as some gauge of audience engagement. For some, like Morris Markey, the effect represented a hint of transcendence for the Young Woman, offering "a final, inarticulate assurance that wretchedness, murder, defeat are but passing things in a mysterious world" (Markey 1928). Stark Young wrote of the effect – executed on a bare stage devoid of actors – as "light growing brighter, flame colors at the bottom rising into blue, the moment of death for the tormented being in the electric chair" (Young 1928: 299). Other critics described the effect as "the migration of a woman's soul" (de Rohan 1928) and "one of the most impressive things the theatre has offered" (Pollack 1928). Jones's lighting and set designs combined with Hopkins's "economy and force" (Anon. 1928) in staging to create what Burns Mantle called "a production the mechanistic perfection of which leaves an old theatregoer gasping" (Mantle 1928).[1]

When Treadwell writes in her stage directions about the monologues in the play appealing to the *"relaxed meditating mind"* and to the narrative structure and use of voices and sound stimulating *"still secret places, in the consciousness of the audience,"* she is articulating an original dramaturgical equivalent of Hopkins's directorial and Jones's design theories. It is unfortunate, however, that Treadwell did not, like Hopkins or Jones, develop these ideas into a more detailed published statement. Many critics of the original production of *Machinal* acknowledged her unique achievements in playwriting, especially in adapting techniques seen in previous expressionist plays. Pierre de Rohan, in the *New York American*, noted Treadwell's abandonment of expressionist distortion in favor of a selective, simplified realism for scenes requiring a sense of intimacy: "She has created a complete picture of life's bitterness and essential meanness, painted with the oft-repeated strokes of the realist, yet achieving in perspective the sweep and swing of expressionism" (de Rohan 1928). In his introduction to the published version of *Machinal*, John Gassner noted that Treadwell's "unique" use of expressionism "was subdued and was given a muted musical function, being used as a sort of obligato to the heroine's failure. . . . If the author had poured the same story into the mold of an ordinary three-act realistic play, it would have been quite unremarkable" (Gassner 1949: 494). Robert Littell further commented on how Treadwell's original style elicited the type of Unconscious Projection sought by Hopkins and Jones:

> All sorts of things that do not strictly belong to the play, things that would be excluded by other playwrights, stray into *Machinal* and sink out of sight again, giving us overtones and glimpses and other dimensions which the ordinary self-contained play is too "well-made" ever to tolerate.
>
> (Littell 1928a)

Only a few critics focused on the feminist implications in Treadwell's play, with most obsessing on the Young Woman's resemblance or lack thereof to Ruth Snyder. Some suggested that the motives of Snyder and the Young Woman "may, further, exist in thousands of women not moved by them to violence" (Lockridge 1928), while the woman's execution "shows the vengeance of society for an act it did not understand well enough to forgive" (Littell 1928b).

Alexander Tairov's production at the Kamerny Theatre, Moscow, 1933

Despite a West End production of the play in London in 1931 (retitled *The Life Machine*) and aborted productions in Paris and

Germany (see Dickey 1997a: 70), the first European production of *Machinal* to receive critical acclaim was at Moscow's Kamerny Theatre in 1933.[2] As founding director of the Kamerny (Chamber) Theatre from 1914 to 1949, Alexander Tairov earned a reputation for sophisticated, formalist productions based on the theater's slogan, "the theatralisation of the theatre" (Markov 1935: 99). His early productions of classic plays by the likes of Shakespeare and Calderon typically featured constructivist settings, vibrant colors, choreographed movement and intoned dialogue. By the mid-1920s, however, this approach met with disfavor from Soviet authorities who now dictated a style of realism celebrating a proletariat hero. Between 1926 and 1929, Tairov redefined his approach to repertoire and style, most notably in productions of three plays by Eugene O'Neill, each of which he interpreted to underscore the corrupting effects of Western capitalism on the individual. When a translated version of *Machinal* made its rounds to various Moscow theater producers, Tairov selected it as a continuation of his anti-capitalist critique and invited Treadwell to attend rehearsals.[3]

In staging *Machinal*, Tairov sought to contrast the fragility of the Young Woman, Helen Jones, with the looming, impervious presence of the mechanized city. He suggested that the play contained only two characters, "Helen and the Town. . . . The chief theme is the Town – the machine – personified by a series of personages who have their own urban-mechanized rhythm, broken by the counterpoint of Helen's strivings, rises and downfalls" (quoted in Rubinstein 1933). Tairov perceived an inherent contradiction in Western culture: while it professed to champion the individual, its capitalist thrust served to depersonalize and standardize human life. He spoke of his aim in realizing this theme:

> I have tried to bring forth the internal emptiness of this civilization, to show the hypocrisy of its sacred institutions, to represent the deathly grip of its blindly moving wheels, which grind and destroy all human movements of the solitary beings who try to resist them.
>
> (*ibid.*)

Tairov's observations on Western culture had been recently stimulated by his company's five-month tour to Europe and South America in 1930, and his visual approach to *Machinal*'s production was inspired by his standing amid rushing traffic and neon lights on a busy street in Buenos Aires (Worrall 1989: 57). To emphasize the constant presence of the city, designer Vadim Ryndin constructed a series of ribbed, monochromatic screens extending the entire vertical space of the stage. When lit, these screens conveyed the illusion of skyscrapers, "like a looming mirage" in the background (*ibid.*: 58). Small wagons brought scenic pieces onto the forestage for the individual episodes, while transitions between scenes featured neon advertisements projected against the screens. Ryndin described the setting in detail:

> These advertisement signs moved by to music, creating a mood quite consonant with the form of the play. Also interesting was the fact that the skyscrapers hung not in one, but in many planes, and each skyscraper had its own relief. . . . [W]hen the projected neon signs moved across the ribbed surfaces of the skyscrapers, arranged in various planes, these depictions were "fractured," creating a very original scenic effect.
>
> (quoted in Torda 1977: 602)

Tairov coordinated the movement of the scene changes and the actors' characterizations with precise rhythmic detail, utilizing original music by L. Polovinkin as the unifying element. Each episode was given its own rhythmic quality. Tairov spoke of the first scene as an example:

> The telephone girl, the typist, the file clerk, and the bookkeeper play in turn. Everything is constructed on the interrelationship among them. As a result, this connection rhythmically and musically takes the form of a quartet, where each part, each 32nd note, each pause, each accented note is taken into consideration, resulting in a primarily syncopated design for this scene. The quartet turns into a

9.2 Alice Koonen (left) as the Young Woman in Alexander Tairov's production of *Machinal*, Kamerny Theatre, Moscow, 1933. Reprinted from M. A. Zelikson, comp. (1934) *Kamernyi teatr i ego khudozhniki: 1914 – xx – 1934*, Moscow: Izd. Vserossiiskoe teatral'noe obshchestvo (Every effort has been made to contact this publisher for permission to reprint)

quintet, when [George H.] Jones comes in, and even a sextet
when Ellen [the Young Woman] enters.

(quoted in *ibid*.: 603)

Throughout the play, Tairov established a rhythm for Alice
Koonen as the Young Woman that ran in counterpoint to that of
the other characters, most notably in the "terrifying" (Worrall
1989: 57) execution scene in the prison.

While Soviet critics applauded the technical prowess of
the production team, many decried Tairov's return to his early
formalist style which here de-emphasized all characters except
the Young Woman (Torda 1977: 603–04). As one critic wrote:
"But the people who are mutilated by the capitalist city are
non-existent apart from Koonen, and in their name alone was
it worthwhile staging Treadwell's play at all" (quoted in Worrall
1989: 58). Richard Watts, Jr., who had accompanied Treadwell
to Moscow, compared Tairov's production to that of Hopkins
on Broadway, concluding that "while the Kamerny production
is more effective visually, it probably lacks something of the
sympathy that Mr. Hopkins put into his version" (Watts, Jr.
1933). While in Moscow, Treadwell herself expressed deep
appreciation for Tairov's treatment:

Not only did I see touches of my play new to me . . . here in
the Kamerny Theater I . . . [also] sharply felt the horrifying
bulk and endless depth of the big city. While in America they
have reduced *Machinal* to a naturalistic illustration of the
personal drama of one small American woman, here they
have broadened this play to the limits of social tragedy.

(quoted in Torda 1977: 604).

Many years later, in 1947, Treadwell shared her views on
Tairov's production with Marie Darrach, comparing it with
other productions of the play and offering a slightly different
assessment of Hopkins's version: "Tairov accented the background – the machinal – etc. – made a huge production – with
special music – sounds – back drops etc. . . . Mr Hopkins gave it
a beautifully *balanced* production" (Treadwell 1947).

The New York Shakespeare Festival production, 1990

After Tairov's production, the fate of *Machinal* on stage mirrored that of Treadwell's career itself, receiving sporadic and occasionally well-publicized appearances. There were two televised broadcasts, one in 1954 on NBC and one in 1960 on ABC; Zita Johann reprised her role as the Young Woman in a 1944 radio broadcast and a late 1950s community theater production in Nyack, New York; and, most notably, it received a seventy-nine-performance revival off-Broadway at New York's Gate Theatre in 1960. For the next two decades the play fell into relative obscurity, with only a handful of productions at small professional theaters in New York, Chicago and San Francisco (see Dickey 1997a: 244–52). *Machinal*, as critic Linda Winer later wrote, had "been relegated to the ghetto known as women's-studies anthologies" (Winer 1990). It was one such anthology, Judith Barlow's *Plays by American Women, 1900–1930*, that caught the eye of New York actress Jodie Markell, igniting her passion for *Machinal*. Markell said, "Here was writing that was clear, precise, focused – and contemporary. I thought, 'Why haven't people been doing this play for the past 60 years?'" (quoted in Scott 1991: 36). Markell then set out to produce the play off-off-Broadway, persuading colleague Michael Greif to direct in a two-week run in 1989. New York Shakespeare Festival director Joseph Papp attended one of the performances and subsequently asked Greif to become one of three new directors-in-residence at the Festival (*ibid.*). For his first production there, Greif restaged *Machinal* with Markell as the Young Woman, opening at the Public Theatre/LuEsther Hall in October 1990. This production, more than any other single event, cast the spotlight back on Treadwell's work. And, unlike every previous major production of the play, this one came at the instigation of a woman, Markell.

Despite Markell's driving force, however, it was Greif's ensemble and transformational approach to staging that led primarily to its critical acclaim. One critic noted, "The cast of 15 seems twice that size – some actors play three or four roles" (Kirkpatrick 1990), appearing in speaking parts, as well as on- and offstage voices, singers, dancers, and a radio announcer introducing each episode. To emphasize the mechanistic environment of the play, Greif placed "the entire action within a skeletal factory that is constantly and subtly reconfigured to serve such settings as a speakeasy, a furnished room, a resort hotel, a maternity ward and a courtroom" (Rich 1990). In keeping with the ensemble approach, Greif frequently relied on actors to bring set or furniture pieces on and off the stage. He also established a strong visual concept in portraying the late 1920s era, relying heavily on a black-and-white motif in design and a chiaroscuro effect of concentrated light and shadowy silhouette, techniques which one critic felt evoked "Edward Hopper's urban America" (Tilles 1993: 20). But Greif did not treat the action simply as an excuse for picturization or period reproduction; instead, he often conceived of scenes in a manner to draw the audience into the realm of the stage action. The courtroom scene, for example, was staged with Markell as the Young Woman placed downstage center, facing the audience. The Judge was placed behind and high above her, leaving wide expanses of the stage for the two attorneys to roam, addressing in turn characters onstage in the courtroom and the theater audience as jury in the auditorium. When the audience laughed at the Young Woman's line about not wanting to hurt her husband by divorcing him, the Judge and Bailiff's call for silence was directed outward, toward the auditorium (*Machinal* 1990). Such scenes, according to Winer, contributed to Greif's "punchy, staccato black-and-white savvy that hooks right into Treadwell's pulp, unsentimental documentary style" (Winer 1990). The "painful volume" (Kirkpatrick 1990) of mechanical sounds between scenes further contributed to Greif's aggressive style of staging.

The critical response to the production focused evenly on the production values and the rediscovery of Treadwell's script. In addition to praising Greif's direction, several critics singled out Markell's "birdlike" performance as a "female Woyzeck" (Winer 1990). Frank Rich noted that "her anguished cries for peace and freedom are so affecting that they never fail to overwhelm the churning mechanical sounds of the hellish city engulfing her"

(Rich 1990). Kirkpatrick observed that Markell "half screams" her monologues (Kirkpatrick 1990), a trait especially noticeable in the maternity-ward monologue after the Young Woman's experience with childbirth (_Machinal_ 1990). Clive Barnes used a memorable simile that describes both Markell's performance and the production as a whole: "Jodie Markell is tremulously appealing, as sentimental and as right as a paper-flower drifting along a dirty, rain-swept gutter" (Barnes 1990). Some critics dismissed the play itself as a "theatrical curio" that post-feminist audiences would regard as "slight" (Beaufort 1990) or as "claptrap [that] does not improve with age" (Kissel 1990). A significant number of critics, though, hailed the text, calling it "an archeological treasure . . . an authentic artifact of a distant civilization and a piece of living art that seems timeless" (Rich 1990) and "a find, a virtually lost, or at best mislaid, American classic" (Barnes 1990). In concluding his remarks on Markell's emotional cries, Frank Rich wrote: "What the audience hears, of course, is not just the passion of a young actress, but the piercing voice of a forgotten writer who, in an act of justice unknown to her tragic heroine, has been miraculously reborn" (Rich 1990).

The Royal National Theatre production, London, 1993

For his second directorial project at the National Theatre, Stephen Daldry selected _Machinal_, which opened in October 1993. Daldry's previous production at the National, the year before, J. B. Priestley's 1946 drama _An Inspector Calls_, had received international acclaim, in part for its stunningly theatrical use of a complex scenic design.[4] For both productions, Daldry, the former artistic director of the small Gate Theatre in Notting Hill, assembled a team of designers and frequent collaborators seemingly eager to exploit the vast technical resources of the National: scenic designer Ian MacNeil, composer Stephen Warbeck and lighting designer Rick Fisher. The expressionist style of _Machinal_ provided more obvious opportunities for design extravagance, and Fisher later confessed that the collaborative team determined to outdo their previous hit: "The company line on it . . . is that *Inspector* was a hit single and *Machinal* was the concept album" (quoted in Lesser 1997: 56).

The resulting production of *Machinal* stunned even some of the most experienced theater critics. For the cacophony of sounds inherent in Treadwell's text, Warbeck enlisted a live, four-piece band that utilized violin, clarinet and electric bass, along with a variety of percussive objects such as filing cabinets and metallic pieces. Live sound underscored about a third of the play (*ibid*.: 216) and was augmented with manipulated sampling of sounds of steam-driven machines and buses' air brakes (Stickland 1994: 42–43). Masking along the sides of the National's Lyttelton Theatre stage was removed, exposing Fisher's lighting instruments and the painted, distressed-looking stage walls. Within this vast open space, MacNeil designed a massive, eight-ton steel grid that could be raised and lowered, effectively dividing the stage into front and rear sections, with the latter also potentially raked at an angle. As portions of the set moved during the playing of scenes, the crew and electricians were costumed in clothing of the 1920s and remained visible onstage while executing transitions. Not since Tairov's production in 1933 had *Machinal* been staged with such an overwhelming technical design.

Daldry excelled at making use of the sophisticated setting. Critic Graham Hassell described the first scene:

> The opening offers pure technical bravura: horizontal screens part like jaws to reveal a gaping space, the whole Lyttelton stage toothless and bare. Upstage, beams of light from left and right pinpoint a lone figure. As she walks gingerly forward a massive grid-iron factory floor descends from the flies accompanied by a cacophony of metallic strainings. Beneath it, a sectioned revolve shunts forward spinning a tableaux [*sic*] of 1920s New York office activity where our heroine arrives late for work. It's a mightily impressive, almost vorticist scene.
>
> (Hassell 1993)

Ruby Cohn noted that the large cast of twenty-seven actors "behave like automatons at work and at play, but these figures

9.3   Ciaran Hinds and Fiona Shaw in *Machinal*, Royal National Theatre, London, 1993. Photo. Ivan Kyncl. Reprinted by permission of Alena Melichar

are bounded by or lost in the intricate machinery of the Lyttelton Theatre – grid, traps, lifts, flies, slides, bridges, revolve" (Cohn 1993). At times, Daldry overtly converted the play's themes into striking visual images, perhaps most notably in the scene just prior to the murder as the Young Woman and the Husband sit on separate ends of a two-piece sofa:

> The husband sits on the left-hand two thirds, which is on top of a truck/meat rack, pushed on by crew, who recline nonchalantly underneath, while the Young Woman perches on the right-hand third, on top of a fork-lift truck that goes up and down, operated by the crew. The semantic emphasis on this allows him to not only have the lion's share of the sofa, but also control and communicate with the outside, whilst she is isolated and marginalised in her own hell.
>
> (Stickland 1994: 43)

The ever-changing nature of the massive scenic unit left critics to wonder if Treadwell's play maybe had "the life crushed out of it by the sheer weight and extravagance of the design" (Billington 1993). "At times," Roy Shaw wrote, "it was like being in a Sheffield steel works, complete with bangs and sparks flying" (Shaw 1993). Nevertheless, Peter Hepple expressed the view of many critics when he called Daldry's production "one of the most spectacular pieces of staging ever seen at the National" (Hepple 1993).

Despite having to perform on a set that one reviewer called "the least actor-friendly half acre of stage in the world" (O'Mahoney 1993), the production retained its human element in large measure due to the performance of Fiona Shaw as the Young Woman. Expressing deep admiration for the working methods of Daldry, Shaw not only overcame her initial trepidation about the setting but contributed to its original usage (*ibid.*). As John O'Mahoney wrote in regard to the staging of "one of the most striking moments in the play," the scene between the Young Woman and the lover, played by Ciaran Hinds:

> Originally the two were to be revealed lying in bed but on Shaw's suggestion they decided to experiment with a tableau on the grid. Now in that scene we see them standing almost in the air above us, both looking out on the city skyline as if perched on a fire escape.
>
> (*ibid.*)

Critics were nearly unanimous in their praise of Shaw, who played the Young Woman "with an intensity that tightens the throat" (Hagerty 1993). Several wrote of scenes with Shaw that were so emotionally unnerving that they were "almost too painful to watch" (Nightingale 1993). The final execution scene, especially, disturbed several reviewers. Barbara Nordern wrote: "The graphic quaking of her body as it is seared by the electric current, while a rainbow spectrum colours the smoke that rises from it, is extremely harrowing" (Nordern 1993). After this "terrifyingly logical climax," Louise Doughty wrote, "I was too stunned to applaud" (Doughty 1993). This treatment of the last scene perhaps reveals the ability of Treadwell's script to absorb a wide range of directorial approaches. There was no hint of the Hopkins and Jones transcendence in Daldry's version, only a suggestion of seared flesh. For Fiona Shaw, it was the play's "excessive relentlessness" that she found so appealing. "It really is on the wrong side of good taste," Shaw said, "which is the way a lot of life actually is" (quoted in O'Mahoney 1993).

Contemporary theoretical approaches

In 1998, Cary M. Mazer, a professor at the University of Pennsylvania, posted an online essay that posed the question: "Why's everybody suddenly doing an obscure 1928 play?" Citing that *Machinal* "used to be one of those plays that was only known to, and only read by, Ph.D. students in academic Theater Studies programs," Mazer marveled at the flurry of recent productions of the play on college and university campuses. He concluded that the highly visible productions by the New York Shakespeare Festival and the National Theatre helped demonstrate that the play affords exceptional staging opportunities for directors and designers. Additionally, Mazer felt, "It also helps that Treadwell's depiction of the Young Woman is so incontrovertibly feminist" (Mazer 1998). The two professional productions cited by Mazer coincided with the onset of a new wave of largely feminist critical assessments of the play and Treadwell's career. Kornelia Tancheva, for example, suggests that until recently Treadwell's subversively feminist themes in *Machinal* remained buried under the critical legacy of the original Broadway production. She posits that the women's rights movement had relaxed in the late 1920s after gaining the right to vote, and that the critics' responses to the play in performance focused instead on topics such as mechanization in the modern age, the play's unique theatrical style, and the story's basis in the Ruth Snyder case (Tancheva 2003).

Recent theorists have also re-evaluated the play's relationship to this case. Ginger Strand contrasted the language of *Machinal* with that of the media's accounts of the trial, concluding that the media "reconfigured, retold, and absorbed" the woman's story "into an ideology not her own" (Strand 1992: 167). Jennifer Jones examined the many similarities and differences between the play and the murder case, concluding that "*Machinal* is the testimony, disallowed by the court of law, that Treadwell wished to introduce into the court of public opinion" (Jones 1994: 486). Elsewhere, I have suggested that Treadwell's preoccupation with gender inequities in the judicial system originated in murder trials involving women defendants preceding the Snyder case (Dickey 1999: 71–72).

Several essays and papers appeared in 2005 that examined Treadwell's depiction of technology and the body in advancing her feminist statement. In a paper titled "Sophie Treadwell's *Machinal*: Electrifying the Female Body," Katherine Weiss focuses on the electric aspects of the play's mechanized era, specifically the historical use of electrotherapy in treating women diagnosed with symptoms of hysteria, symptoms similar to those Treadwell herself suffered. Weiss notes that electrotherapy was used either to stimulate the patient and dissipate over-excitement or to kill harmful, pathological aspects of the body or psyche. She also notes that electrotherapy's use coincided with the invention of the electric chair, which became US society's tool for removing what it felt were harmful individuals (Weiss 2005).[5] Thus, the Young Woman's anxiety stemmed from a fear over medical or social retribution for her behavior. Similarly, in an essay co-authored with J. Ellen Gainor, I have applied to Treadwell's plays Marianne DeKoven's theory that the ambivalence in many female characters of modernist women fiction writers may reflect a general fear of punishment for demanding female empowerment (Gainor and Dickey 2005: 46). Merrill Schleier, in a sweeping study calling upon "material culture, architectural history, gender theory, and historiography of nervous disorders" (Schleier 2005: 235) examines neurasthenic over-stimulation as a result of modernity. She concludes that "Treadwell combined her own knowledge of working conditions in the recently mechanized office with research on the origins and treatment of nervous disorders to create a dystopian environment where the female body and its internal processes are severely compromised" (*ibid.*). Julia A. Walker, in her study *Expressionism and Modernism in the American Theatre*, examines not only the typewriter and the electric chair as technological means of subordinating and suppressing women, but the patriarchal nature of the language of modernity. Walker asserts that Treadwell's belief in the inadequacy of language led her to co-opt expressionistic techniques:

> Treadwell seeks to resist the masculinization of language and meaning in the expressionistic form of her play. Through her use of bodies, voices, and words, she not only exposes the limitations of verbal signification alone, but affirms the meaningfulness of voice and gesture – those embodied forms of communication that do not deny the specificity of a gendered experience in the world.
>
> (Walker 2005: 238)

10 Key plays II

Intimations for Saxophone

Intimations for Saxophone (also titled simply *For Saxophone* in its later versions) occupies a critical position in Treadwell's career as a dramatist. Copyrighted in 1934 and revised over a period of seven years, *Saxophone* proved to be Treadwell's last foray into the expressionist style that she had used to such moving effect in *Machinal*. Her subsequent plays remained largely within the style of realism. In *Saxophone*, however, Treadwell sought to recapture what she had done best in *Machinal* – seamlessly marrying a novel theatrical style with timely feminist themes. The resulting play was perhaps her most ambitious theatrical experiment, as she sought to advance her explorations into creating a feminist aesthetic in the theater.

From the days of its earliest circulation in the mid-1930s and early 1940s, the novelty of the play's form proved its most compelling attraction. Treadwell's friend and trusted play reader, Alexander Koiransky, referred to *Saxophone* in a letter as: "a new kind of grotesque opera. . . . From the very start one is fascinated by a throbbing beat . . . It is like watching the graphic of a fever running along a chart and presently becoming a humming pulsation, a rhythm inside of oneself" (Koiransky 1935). Designer Robert Edmond Jones realized the rich potential the play offered for unique and theatrical staging and was reportedly "almost frothy at the mouth" at the prospect of producing the piece (Madden 1937). In a 1937 letter, he told Treadwell, "There are passages in *Saxophone* that are so original and brilliant I simply have no words for them" (Jones 1937). In another letter to the playwright, Jones elaborated: "You have a great idea here, the germ of a new theatrical idiom. It interests me enormously. . . . Here is a bold step into a new dimension, full of power" (Jones n.d.).

Jones's former protégé and renowned scenic designer Donald Oenslager held an early option on the play. But the poor economic climate of the Depression-era 1930s made it difficult to find financial backers for a play with large technical demands and what Jones terms a "depressed"-quality anathema to box-office success. Jones also believed that "as yet there is no adequate experimental theatre where such things could be put on" (Jones 1940). The play's episodic structure employing cross fades and dissolves convinced Treadwell that it was suitable for film. Yet, while Samuel Goldwyn script reader William James Fadiman praised the work for its "novelty . . . freshness . . . and most unusual" nature, he could not imagine a star actress "subordinating herself" to the play's technological effects (Fadiman 1935). The play also briefly attracted the interest in 1942 of Erwin Piscator, whose legendary epic and multimedia stage successes seemed an ideal match for the play's expressionistic and filmic devices. Yet, even prior to meeting with Piscator, Treadwell expressed doubts that he would "actually do the play" (Treadwell 1942b), perhaps because it lacked the overt political statements for which his productions were often known. It was to Treadwell's deep dismay that none of these production opportunities materialized. The play would have to wait nearly fifty years for its premiere at the Arena Stage in Washington, DC in 2005.[1]

The play

Like *Machinal, Intimations for Saxophone* features an episodic narrative that traces a young girl's progression from marriage and honeymoon through years of marital dissatisfaction with a wealthy husband. A prolonged sexual relationship with a lover helps prompt the young woman's rejection of her marriage in favor of an independent search for self-realization. The narrative structure in *Saxophone*, however, proves even more fragmented than that in *Machinal*, relying heavily on film techniques adapted for the stage to create what Treadwell called a sort of *"kaleido-scope of a very young girl"* (Treadwell *c.* 1936a: n.p.). Chief among these staging techniques is the use of *"an almost unbroken musical accompaniment."* Sensing that motion pictures and radio had altered audience's expectations for dramatic entertainment, Treadwell envisioned the play as *"really words for music"* (*ibid.*). While not literally scored, Treadwell suggests a wide variety of musical accompaniment, including a Brahms symphony, Hungarian gypsy improvisations, and especially a jazz saxophone. She also conceived of almost half of the play's scenes as being written for voices, with *"only one moment seen – the focal moment (something like a close-up in pictures)"* (*ibid.*). These offstage or disembodied voices frequently join with the musical underscoring to form a unique dramatic soundscape. Individual scenes are envisioned as being played in *"pools of light on a dark stage"* with very little scenery or props (*ibid.*). According to Treadwell's opening stage directions:

> *All the scenes of each act go one into the other through lights, voices, and music, so that the effect is of something seen, moving-by, and something overheard, – from all of which, a bit here and a bit there inconsequential and seemingly unrelated, the audience discovers, – writes the play.*
>
> (*ibid.*)

Treadwell's narrative merely suggests phases in the development of the inner life of the central character, with the ultimate aim, as in *Machinal*, of sufficiently stimulating the spectators' subconscious minds to the point where they would imaginatively fill in for themselves the narrative gaps between these phases.

Intimations for Saxophone survives in eight manuscript variants. For the Arena Stage production, dramaturg Michael Kinghorn created a faithful adaptation from these variants, following most closely three early manuscripts dated between 1934 and 1936: a copyrighted version at the Library of Congress (Treadwell 1934); a version at the University of Arizona Library Special Collections that Treadwell sent to Arthur Hopkins and subsequently marketed to other theater producers and play readers (Treadwell *c.* 1936a); and a similar version with heavily marked edits at the New York Public Library for the Performing Arts (Treadwell *c.* 1936b). The following plot summary is derived from these manuscripts and thus follows rather closely Kinghorn's as yet unpublished adaptation.[2]

The plot and themes

The main action of the play involves a young woman named Lily and her search for fulfillment, especially in regard to overcoming her repressed sexuality. The structure resembles an expressionist drama in the sense that the central character passes through various stations as part of a life-altering quest, and Treadwell often utilizes several short scenes to dramatize a single phase or station in Lily's journey. For example, the play's fifteen scenes – which Treadwell labels descriptively with captions like "At a dance" or "In a hotel room" (Treadwell *c.* 1936a: n.p.) – may be more easily discussed in terms of six primary phases of Lily's development.

The first two of these phases involve her movement from sexual innocence as an overly protected daughter of a wealthy entrepreneur to an idealized and worshipped wife of a timid man ten years her elder. At the play's opening, Lily, still under twenty years of age, has recently returned to her father's Park Avenue home after completing her education in a French convent. Amid a chorus of guests' gossiping voices, Lily and her arranged fiancé, Gilbert Lethe (called Gilly), haltingly become acquainted while dancing. The scene dissolves into a slow, low wedding march punctuated by the sound of doorbells, typewriters, sewing machines, and the voices of delivery men and servants making final preparations for the wedding. In isolated lighting, Lily's sexual chastity is symbolically represented as a suffocatingly heavy wedding dress and veil, into which she is fitted by a French maid. As the wedding music grows louder, spot lighting follows Lily's march in the gown across the stage to an awaiting Gilly. As they exit to a darkened stage, voices come from offstage:

MINISTER'S VOICE: Wilt thou have this man?
LILY'S VOICE: I take thee, Gilbert, to be my wedded husband.
GILLY'S VOICE: With this ring I thee wed.
LILY'S VOICE: With this body I thee worship.

(*ibid*.: I, iii, 13)

Lily's physical commitment to Gilly, however, is immediately tempered in scenes depicting their honeymoon getaway and their return six years later to their honeymoon hotel. Gilly is unable to profess his sexual ardor for Lily, whom he prefers to place on a pedestal and idealize. Psychologically dependent on his overbearing mother and affected by her sexual repulsion for his father, Gilly initially hopes Lily won't similarly despise him after the consummation of the marriage. Their ensuing comfortable but sexually unfulfilling marriage sends Lily into a deep state of ennui, characterized by the music of a saxophone in the distance, its "[s]o hungry – so lonely – and so empty" sound providing for Lily an apt metaphor for their "vulgar and stupid" years of marriage (*ibid*.: II, 4).

The third phase of Lily's development involves her impulsive search for sexual excitement. Over dinner at a hotel with her husband and their only slightly less wealthy friends, Billie and Millie (the rhyming name scheme underscoring the boredom of their lives), Lily is emotionally swept up in the onstage dance of a knife-throwing Russian dancer, Stanislos. That night, Lily and the dancer begin a lengthy affair, one that turns violently abusive toward Lily. From its outset, Lily is aware of the emptiness of this new relationship which is based solely on mutual self-satisfaction, yet she is tormented that Stanislos represents "some secret, dark destiny . . . from which she couldn't escape" (*ibid*.: IV, i, 8). Lily desperately seeks the advice of a noted Viennese author of psychological novels, Dr. Joseph Kartner. She misreads Kartner's compassion as a sign of love, however, and abandons her husband to follow the author when he returns to Vienna. This phase, in which Lily now seeks a romantic love of mutual affection, proves short-lived, however, when she learns that Kartner already loves another.

The remaining action takes Lily through two more stages: resignation and defiance. When she seeks rest at a European spa, she encounters a variety of lonely women similarly recuperating. One reads a book called *Enduring Passion*, a treatise that reduces sexual impulses and practices to pseudo-scientific, rational explanations:

> WOMAN WITH BOOK: This book enrages me! . . . It's called *Enduring Passion*.
>
> LILY: A novel.
>
> WOMAN: No – a treatise. How to make it last a lifetime. Can you think of anything more boring? Who wants it to last a lifetime? I don't, for one, do you? . . . Imagine writing a book about it – a scientific book about it. There is a chapter called "Some Aspects of the Kiss" with diagrams and definitions. Can you define a kiss?
>
> LILY: Not exactly.
>
> WOMAN: A kiss is a intermittent neuro-pneumatic massage. Do you believe that?
>
> LILY: If I did, I would never want to be kissed again.[3]
>
> (*ibid.*: IV, v, 44–45)

The woman rebuffs Lily's dismissal, claiming that women today suffer nervous conditions because they place too much emphasis on sex and should learn to use their "good manners and sense of humor" to endure an unhappy marriage (ibid: IV, v, 45). Despite the fact that the women in this spa are haggard, sick and lonely, Lily resigns herself to their apparent words of truth. When she subsequently tells Kartner in the play's final scene of her resolve to return to her marriage with Gilly, the music in the café changes quickly and Stanislos, visible only to Lily, begins his knife dance. Kartner becomes more concerned over Lily's faint appearance before the dancer's final knife strikes her (in one version of the play, Lily jumps in front of the knife).[4] In the end, Lily chooses to defy the social expectation that she should endure a loveless, sexless marriage, and her death represents her tragic inability to find fulfillment in either physical or romantic love.

In an alternate ending found in the earlier, Library of Congress manuscript, the final scene occurs on a café terrace. Lily, in traveling clothes, is amused by a fellow-American's difficulties with the German language. She confides to the American, a young man from Texas, that she is returning to the States, presumably to her husband. After the two share a brief exchange about the fierce nature of loneliness, the Texan offers Lily a ride in his car to Venice. "You are alone, ain't you," he asks. To Lily's "yes," he responds, "I thought so. You sure look it" (Treadwell 1934: n.p.). This more subdued ending of the play was used in the Arena Stage production. The tragic dimension that Treadwell pursued in later versions is replaced here with the faint hope of Lily obtaining the emotional and sexual relationship she so desires.

Aspects of the play reflect Treadwell's ongoing interest in Freudian and Jungian psychology. Nowhere is this connection more evident than in the figure of Joseph Kartner, a character based on the German author Jakob Wassermann. Now relatively forgotten, prior to the Second World War Wassermann proved one of the most prominent novelists of works exploring the human psyche. His influence on the character of Kartner may be traced to the 1934 manuscript. In that version, Kartner refers to the doctor in his new novel as Dr. Kerkhoven, a character who appears in Wassermann's most famous trilogy of novels.[5] The devotion with which Lily hangs on Kartner's advice parallels Treadwell's personal interest in the mind–body connection that is stressed so heavily in the writings of nontraditional analysts of psychology like Wassermann. Furthermore, *Saxophone* shares with Wassermann's novels an exploration of character transformation and change of identity. Although Wassermann remained skeptical over individuals' ability to change their nature, he believed strongly that new encounters with others held the potential to awaken dormant traits within each person. The concept of destiny or fate, for Wassermann, appears as a force of nature that arranges such new contacts for individuals. As he writes in *Doctor Kerkhoven*: "One of the fundamental laws to which our lives are subject is that which decides the kind of people we meet. This is an exact expression of the inscrutable will of the higher powers, which we call fate" (Wassermann 1932: 251). In Wassermann's novels, such new contacts hold a strange attraction for individuals seeking a change of identity. Similarly, in *Saxophone*, the characters of Stanislos and Kartner act as irresistible attractions that unleash Lily's dormant desire for love and sexual fulfillment, deeply ingrained impulses long smothered in her unadventurous marriage. Lily even uses the term "destiny" at several points throughout the play in reference to these men. John C. Blankenagel's conclusion regarding Wassermann's intent might apply just as well to Treadwell's in *Saxophone*: "he was endeavoring to delve into the hidden recesses of man's involved, irrational nature, and to probe more deeply into the mysteries of human conduct and relationships" (Blankenagel 1946: 20).

The Arena Stage production, 2005

The premiere of *Intimations for Saxophone* at the Arena Stage in Washington, DC, in January 2005 marked the first major production in over fifty years of a Treadwell play other than *Machinal*. Staged by the noted American director Anne Bogart in association with her SITI Company (the Saratoga International Theater Institute), this production reflects a growing interest in rediscovering neglected plays by Treadwell. *Intimations for Saxophone* poses tremendous challenges for a production team in terms of its variant manuscripts, suggestive rather than discursive narrative, and near-continuous reliance on film devices like voice-overs, close-ups, and extended musical underscoring. The Arena's choice of Bogart and the SITI Company seemed particularly apt for several reasons.

Co-founded by Bogart and Japanese director Tadashi Suzuki, the SITI Company is unique in its approach to actor training and collaboration. The company bases its work on two highly physical, yet very distinct, acting methodologies. The Suzuki Method consists of rigorous and disciplined exercises focused on the actor's center in the lower abdomen, a center viewed as the source of energy, balance, breath and vocal production. Bogart's method of the Viewpoints, derived from postmodern

dance, examines principles of time and space as a key to impro-
visational movement and acting. In his recent study of the SITI
Company, Scott T. Cummings summarizes the goal of using the
two methodologies:

> While other acting techniques focus on how to act . . . the
> SITI training centers on how to get ready to act. Emphasis is
> on achieving and maintaining a frame of mind, a physical
> and vocal condition, and a focus that prepares the actor to
> respond to an outside stimulus or event at any moment,
> to send and receive kinetic energy, and to execute a task or
> an action with clarity and precision.
>
> (Cummings 2006: 110)

In rehearsal, Bogart calls upon this preparation by the actor
as the basis for collective enquiry, improvisation and mutual
decision-making in staging a text. "The result," says Cummings,
"is work that is both highly calibrated and seemingly sponta-
neous" (*ibid.*). Such an approach seemed a perfect match for a
text that requires a host of characters and voices to create the
kaleidoscopic effect Treadwell desired.

The SITI Company possesses another quality that matched
Treadwell's script well, especially in regard to its heavy sound
demands. During previous SITI productions, Bogart has developed a unique collaboration with the company's sound designer,
Darron West. Like all the actors in the company, West attends
every rehearsal. He develops his sound design in response to
the company's improvisations, and as scenes rehearse he tests
various sound possibilities. Brian Scott offers a description of his
working methodology: "Darron hears the music that happens
when people say words on stage and then he lifts that musical
quality up by weaving things into it and around it, laying things
underneath and on top of it" (quoted in *ibid.*: 224–25). West is
also given free license to provide coaching to the actors. "He is,"
Cummings claims, Bogart's "alter ego in rehearsal" (*ibid.*: 225).

It should be pointed out that Michael Kinghorn was the initial
driving force behind this premiere of *Saxophone*. It was he who
suggested the play to Arena's artistic director, Molly Smith,

and faithfully collated the different versions of the script in his adaptation. In defining his role as adaptor, Kinghorn spoke of "standing in as playwright and dramaturg for the play's final phase of development" since "Sophie didn't have the chance to shape the play through rehearsal and production" (quoted in Minwalla 2005). Kinghorn chose to set the play in the 1920s, believing that its sensibilities were more in line with that decade than the Depression-era thirties in which it was written. This choice undoubtedly made the play more appealing to Bogart, who said, "It's one of the greatest discoveries in American theatre in the last 30 years. . . . I was born to direct this play. It connects jazz and expressionism with dance-theatre and oral traditions that feel both contemporary and conventional" (quoted in *ibid.*). Bogart believed that in *Saxophone* Treadwell "dealt with the sexual liberation of women, feminism and the push in the '20s to market and advertise directly to women. . . . It moves at break-neck speed, just like the era itself" (quoted in Blanchard 2005a). Smith similarly believed the play's Jazz Age feminism transcended its historical roots: "Women continue – even in this moment in time – to need to fight for their own freedom as thinking beings. And I think that's very much what Lily goes through in this play" (quoted in Chaney 2005).

To establish the atmosphere of the era, Bogart began her production with a lengthy, seven-minute prologue before any words were spoken. In this introductory sequence, men and women arrive separately in a nightclub and eye each other from tables scattered around a central dance floor. Eventually, a couple begins dancing the Charleston to the jazz rhythms of a club band, culminating in an energetically choreographed dance sequence for all the actors. As the dance opening transitioned into the first scene of the play, standing radio microphones around the edge of the stage allowed actors to adopt various characters and provide voice-over sequences or sound effects while still remaining visible to the audience (*Intimations* 2005). The opening effectively provided a nonverbal exposition of the era and established the voice-over convention that would carry on through the production. It also established the changeable quality of Neil Patel's simple but elegant setting, which consisted of an inlaid

10.1 Karron Graves hears a voice of hope on the radio in the Arena
Stage production of *Intimations for Saxophone*, Washington, DC,
2005. Photo: Scott Suchman. Reprinted by permission of Arena
Stage

wood platform with concentric squares that could be raised
or lowered to suggest different locales, such as Lily's sunken
bedroom later in the play.

In order to navigate the many scene transitions in the play,
Bogart relied on a transformational approach to acting and
movement. With Karron Graves (as Lily, appearing for the first
time with SITI) and Barney O'Hanlon (Gilly) as the exceptions,
the other eight actors in the company performed a variety of roles
and inanimate objects. For example:

> When Graves' Lily bravely sets off on an ocean liner for
> Europe, the ship is portrayed by a clump of actors moving
> briskly across the stage and representing both passengers and
> crew. . . . In a scene in which O'Hanlon's Gilly dresses for
> dinner, another actor serves as the sink, holding the basin

Gilly uses to shave; the same actor then becomes Gilly's closet, handing him a jacket.

(Rousuck 2005)

Additional dance and movement sequences were also injected between scenes, including one slow-motion movement collage late in the play in which the actors rewind memorable images from the preceding action. This scene's combination of "movement, stark lighting and off-kilter music" resembled for one critic "a 78 recording played backward to a crescendo" (Harris 2005). Such a scene represented both the best and worst in Bogart's staging. Its emphasis on technical precision and spectacle contributed to what many critics agreed was "a fusion of light, sound, music and movement that lavishes sophistication on this jazz era tale . . . a true feast for the senses" (*ibid.*). Yet, as some critics pointed out, the primary emphasis on visual elements overshadowed the emotional requirements of the text: "The atmospherics here are, in fact, all. . . . [S]tyle was everything" (Marks 2005). It appeared at times that Bogart did not trust the deliberate gaps that Treadwell had left in her narrative. The slow-motion scene mentioned above, for example, was intended to represent Lily's breakdown prior to going to the spa, even though Treadwell had not included such a scene in her text. Jayne Blanchard of the *Washington Times* noted the insertion of such a scene "in place of a satisfying resolution" was one of the "misfires" of Bogart's movement sequences (Blanchard 2005b).

As compellingly interesting as Bogart's staging proved from a visual point of view, the performances as a whole did not convey an emotional intensity. Karron Graves elicited praise for being "bright, clear and . . . flapper-like" (Anon. 2005), although her portrayal of Lily often appeared too self-assured, "coldly adrift" (Blanchard 2005b), and lacking the sense of urgency demanded by Treadwell's script. Consequently, her affair with Stanislos and subsequent departure from her marriage appeared more as casual diversions than as a desperate desire for mutually reciprocated love. Kartner's advice to Lily appeared too obvious, then, since a woman of her composure and wherewithal would most certainly have reached similar conclusions on her own. Jaclyn Levy believed that had Graves presented her character "as an individual, multilayered woman, Lily might have been able to cultivate an infinitely stronger rapport with the audience. Instead, her plight is viewed from a distance, detracting from the play's message about individualism and change" (Levy 2005).

Although secondary characters are written as broad types in Treadwell's script, it is nevertheless essential that they provide compelling foils prompting Lily's progression. In this regard, Graves was not helped by Barney O'Hanlon's portrayal of Gilly as a completely ineffectual and clownish companion. As Levy noted, "you lose any sympathy that might have been gained for Lily, when it is so obvious that the man she's married is a dolt" (*ibid.*). Bogart's priority clearly rested on the coordination of the extensive movement in the play rather than the emotional inner lives of the characters. Michael Kinghorn referred to this emphasis on movement in rehearsals as "hitting the pad," a radio term referring to timing an action to coincide with the exact duration of a musical introduction or sound effect (Dickey 2005). Although Bogart and West's collaboration has yielded many positive results in the past, in *Saxophone* it seemed clear that the "frenetic, even rhapsodic movement" timed to sound sequences did "little to illuminate the scattered remains of Treadwell's storyline" (Munch 2005).

In one respect, adapter Kinghorn viewed the play as Treadwell's female inversion of the traditional, male hero's quest for self-fulfillment found so often in romantic novels and expressionist plays. In another, he saw *Saxophone* in social terms, in which Treadwell attempted to indict American cultural and gender factors that created a double standard for women (Dickey 2005). Ultimately, he believes Treadwell "over-reached" in this play: "She wrote so much into the play – big themes, big ideas, thrilling spectacle – as if, in theatrical terms, she intended to paint the essence of her protagonist's soul against a vision of America itself" (Kinghorn 2005: 13). Several critics of the Arena Stage production felt the play's subject matter was too dated for a post-feminist age (see Marks 2005 and Harris 2005).

J. Wynn Rousuck's comments are typical: "*Intimations* might have seemed daring in the 1930s. But nowadays few eyebrows would be raised in this coming-of-age story about a woman forging her own identity separate from her husband, who is baffled and heartbroken by her departure" (Rousuck 2005). A few, however, believed the play still resonated well today (see Chaney 2005 and Thielman 2005). According to Dorothy Chansky, the play is an "invitation to rethink the terms of love and modernity for women brought up to think that marriage is (at least a big part of) their destiny" (Chansky 2005).

Kinghorn deserves much praise for resurrecting *Intimations for Saxophone* and shepherding its premiere. It is unfortunate that Treadwell never had the opportunity herself to witness such a realization onstage; one may only speculate on how such a production may have shaped her subsequent dramaturgy.

Contemporary theoretical approaches

While very little discussion of feminist themes surfaced when Treadwell first circulated *Saxophone*, a few recent scholarly examinations have addressed this aspect of the play. Wynn notes that *Saxophone* avoids the openly didactic approach found in many social dramas of the 1930s while addressing themes of "the place of women in marriage or on their own in society; surface living, easy morality, extra-marital relationships and personal freedom . . . for women" (Wynn 1982: 175). Elsewhere, I have discussed how the play, while focusing on a single woman's experiences, utilizes a montage of scenes to demonstrate how modern society's hegemonic notions of female gendered behavior impede Lily's progress toward self-realization: "Lily . . . learns indirectly . . . society's traditional imperatives concerning feminine desire: endure marriage, no matter how stultifying; avoid open expression or pursuit of sexual fulfillment; defer self-interest and egoism to the concerns of male partners" (Dickey 1999: 80). Ann M. Fox focuses on Treadwell's use of character types as representative of the fixed roles prescribed by modern society. She views the choices presented to Lily as exemplifying equally fixed and repressive life options:

But freedom to choose from a limited selection of typified experiences is not true liberty at all, as Lily finds. It keeps her trapped from the beginning to the end of the play, denies her complexity of character as a person, and keeps her within her set gender role, despite the illusion of autonomy. . . . The tragedy for Lily is not that she possesses inclinations toward each type of [romantic or sexual] "dream," but that she feels compelled to continually trade one type of one-sided existence for another.

(Fox 1993: 44)

Fox sees Lily's role in accepting her own stabbing at the play's end as an active form of resistance. "Only then," Fox writes, "has she made as free a choice as the world Treadwell depicts can offer" (*ibid.*: 45). Similarly, Michael Cotsell suggests that "It was never sex that Lily Lethe was seeking, but her life, and then (under the conditions in which she could not live) its end" (Cotsell 2005: 284–85). In this analysis, then, *Saxophone* echoes the ending of *Machinal*, in which a final, tragic image is presented of female resistance to restrictive gender roles in a patriarchal society.

The unusual early title of the play, *Intimations for Saxophone*, also encourages feminist interpretations. Treadwell's choice of the word "intimations" neatly encapsulates the play's form and intent – to intimate: to make known subtly, indirectly; to hint. It is a seldom-used word that, outside of occasional jazz musical references, most often resonates with Wordsworth's famous ode, "Intimations of Immortality from Recollections of Early Childhood." Curiously, though, the word also occupied a prominent place in Susan Glaspell's novel *Brook Evans*, published in 1928, just a handful of years before the composition of *Saxophone*. In that novel, "Intimations" is the name of a book of American poetry that Brook's son Evans buys for himself in Paris. "He liked the word intimations," Glaspell writes, "rather like a detective story, but on the trail of things you thought by yourself" (Glaspell 1928: 183). And in the novel's final pages, Evans is in America and resting besides the running brook from which his mother received her name. He ruminates on the nature and source of intimations he feels about his family's history: "Were they – the intimations – out of that place from which we do not speak? Were they from what we know, and never say we know, or only half know – dimly – and was it from there we sometimes – almost reached one another?" (*ibid*.: 311). While there is no way of knowing if Treadwell was influenced by Glaspell's prominent use of the word, it is worth noting that the idea of intimating informed the themes and narrative form of several plays by both women. Glaspell's early, one-act *Trifles* suggests that women are more likely than men to decipher intimations of female behavior. Her later *The Verge*, along with Treadwell's *Machinal* and *Intimations for Saxophone*, employs narrative and language constructs designed to suggest rather than delineate concrete or uncontested meanings.

Such a textual approach falls closely in line with the French theorists' concept of "*écriture féminine*," a connection that I have previously discussed with Treadwell's *Machinal* and *Saxophone* (Dickey 1997c: 178–79). As postulated by theorists such as Hélène Cixous, Luce Irigaray and Julia Kristeva, this concept seeks to identify a particularly female form of writing, one that is in opposition to language and narrative constructs associated with males, such as an emphasis on linear progression and reasoned, discursive expostulation of a thesis. As Marcia Noe has stated in applying this theory to Glaspell's *The Verge*, "*L'écriture féminine* is fluid, nonlinear prose, characterized by broken syntax, repetition, multiple voices, long, cumulative sentences, embedded clauses, parenthetical assertions and other disruptions of traditional prose style" (Noe 1995: 133). It is this form of writing, found in both *Intimations for Saxophone* and *Machinal*, that Treadwell hoped might have a special appeal in the audience's consciousness, as she stated, "especially of women" (Treadwell c. 1928: n.p.). As I have suggested elsewhere, Glaspell and Treadwell are now poised to receive their long-overdue recognition for the same type of narrative innovations in drama that are often attributed to American women writers of modernist fiction (Gainor and Dickey 2005: 46–47, 49).

Chronologies

Susan Glaspell

1 July 1876	Susan Glaspell born in Davenport, Iowa, to Elmer and Alice Keating Glaspell. Brother Charles (Ray) born in 1875; Frank in 1879.
1894–96	Writes for *Davenport Morning Republican*.
July 1896–July 1897	Contributes weekly column "Social Life" to *Davenport Weekly Outlook*.
September 1897	Leaves Davenport for Des Moines, Iowa, where attends Drake University, studying for degree in philosophy.
1899	Publishes stories in school magazine the *Delphic*. Graduates from Drake University.
1899–1901	Works as reporter for *Des Moines Daily News*; assigned to legislature and murder cases. Writes weekly column signed "The NEWS Girl."
3 December 1900	Publishes first report on the Hossack murder case that she would, in 1915, transform into *Trifles*.
1901	Returns to Davenport, to parents' home, to write.

Summer 1902	Registers for two courses at the University of Chicago Graduate School.
1904	Wins *Black Cat* Prize ($500) for short story. Her stories start appearing in popular journals and magazines, such as *Author's Magazine*, the *American*, *Booklovers Magazine*, *Harper's*, *Ladies' Home Journal*, *Leslie's*, *Munsey's*, the *Speaker* and *Youth's Companion*.
1907	Joins Monist Society in Davenport, founded by George Cram Cook and Floyd Dell. She and Cook fall in love but he is waiting for a divorce from his first wife in order to marry Mollie Price, by whom he will have two children before divorcing her.
1909	Travels with friend Lucy Huffaker in Europe and spends some months in Paris. *The Glory of the Conquered*, first novel, published.
1911	Novel *The Visioning* published.
1912	*Lifted Masks*, a collection of Glaspell's early short stories, published.
14 April 1913	Marries George Cram Cook. They live in New York and spend summers in Provincetown, Cape Cod.
1915	Novel *Fidelity* published. In July *Suppressed Desires* performed in Provincetown, inaugurating first Provincetown summer season.
Summer 1916	Second Provincetown summer season.
8 August 1916	*Trifles* performed on third bill of the season.
4 September 1916	Participants in this season of plays name themselves the Provincetown Players and decide to found a theater in New York that would be called the Playwrights' Theater.

	Cook leaves for New York to search out a suitable venue.
3 November 1916	Playwrights' Theater at 139 Macdougal Street opens.
15 November 1916	*Trifles* performed by Washington Square Players at the Comedy Theatre. During that same winter, it is also produced by the Neighborhood Playhouse.
9–14 March 1917	*The People* performed on eighth bill and repeated, together with *Suppressed Desires*, on ninth, a review bill.
2–6 November 1917	*Close the Book* performed on first bill of second New York season.
28 December 1917–3 January 1918	*The Outside* performed on third bill.
26 April–2 May 1918	*Woman's Honor* performed on seventh bill.
20–26 December 1918	*Tickless Time* by Glaspell and George Cram Cook performed on first bill of third season.
21–27 March 1919	*Bernice* performed on fifth bill.
1919–20	Leaving the Provincetown Players under the direction of James Light and Ida Rauh, Glaspell and Cook spend most of this year in Provincetown, where Glaspell writes *Chains of Dew* and *Inheritors*.
21 February 1920	Glaspell registers *Chains of Dew* with the Library of Congress.
21 March–10 April 1921	*Inheritors* performed as fifth bill of fifth season.
14 November–1 December 1921	*The Verge* performed as first bill of sixth season.
1 March 1922	Glaspell and Cook sail for Greece.

27 April–15 May 1922	*Chains of Dew* performed as sixth and last bill. The Provincetown Players announce an interim in their activities.
1922–24	Glaspell and Cook travel in Greece, spending most of their time in the village of Delphos.
14 January 1924	George Cram Cook dies. Glaspell returns to Provincetown, where she meets Norman Matson, with whom she will live until 1932.
1927	*The Road to the Temple*, Glaspell's biography of Cook, published.
1928	Writes play *The Comic Artist* with Matson. Novel *Brook Evans* published.
1929	Novel *Fugitive's Return* published.
1 December 1930	*Alison's House* opens at Eva Le Gallienne's Civic Repertory Theatre.
1931	*Alison's House* awarded the Pulitzer Prize. Novel *Ambrose Holt and Family* published.
1931–32	Glaspell and Matson live in England and travel in Europe.
1936–38	Glaspell appointed director of Midwest Play Bureau for Federal Theater in Chicago.
1939	Novel *The Morning Is Near Us* published.
1940	Children's novel *Cherished and Shared of Old* published.
1942	Novel *Norma Ashe* published.
1945	Novel *Judd Rankin's Daughter* published.
27 July 1948	Susan Glaspell dies of viral pneumonia and an embolism.

Sophie Treadwell

3 October 1885	Sophie Anita Treadwell born in Stockton, California, to Alfred B. and Nettie Fairchild Treadwell.
1890–91	Alfred moves to San Francisco, leaving wife and daughter.
1902	Moves with her mother to San Francisco. Briefly enters The Madames convent. Enrolls in the University of California at Berkeley.
1904	Works during the summer in her father's law office.
c. 1905	Writes her first play, the one-act *A Man's Own*.
1906	Graduates with a Bachelor of Letters in French. Suffers a nervous collapse, briefly rendering her unable to walk.
1907	In Los Angeles, appears as a character change artist in vaudeville under the name Willia Williams. Writes freelance articles for the *San Francisco Examiner*.
1908	Hired to type Helena Modjeska's memoirs.
1909	Hired by the *San Francisco Bulletin*, first in a secretarial capacity and then as a reporter.
27 January 1910	Marries well-known sports columnist William O. McGeehan. That summer, makes first stay in a sanitarium, suffering from weight loss and nervous exhaustion.
1914	Writes popular serial, "An Outcast at the Christian Door." Marches with suffragists on the New York legislature to petition the right to vote. Her father dies. McGeehan moves to New York City to write for the *New York Evening Journal*.

1915	Her first produced play, *Sympathy (An Unwritten Chapter)*, runs for one week at the Pantages Theatre in San Francisco. Writes articles from France during First World War. In fall, moves to New York City and works as reporter for the *New York American*.
1916	Begins frequenting the salon of Walter and Louise Arensberg. Begins affair with Maynard Dixon. Writes numerous one-act plays over the next three years.
1919	Copyrights *The Eye of the Beholder*.
1920	Covers the aftermath of the Mexican Revolution for the *New York Tribune*.
1921	Conducts exclusive interview with Pancho Villa in Mexico.
1922	*Gringo* opens on Broadway, 12 December.
1923	Studies acting with Richard Boleslavsky. *Loney Lee* (later *O Nightingale*) in tryout performances with Helen Hayes.
1924	Sues John Barrymore, citing plagiarism of her play on Edgar Allan Poe.
1925	Acts in private performances of her play *The Love Lady* in New York in January. Acts in and co-produces *O Nightingale* on Broadway, opening 15 April.
1927	Attends the Snyder–Gray trial.
1928	*Machinal* opens at the Plymouth Theatre on Broadway on 7 September for a ninety-one-performance run.
1929	*Ladies Leave* opens at the Charles Hopkins Theatre on Broadway on 1 October. Works briefly adapting scripts for United Artists.

1931	*Machinal*, re-titled *The Life Machine*, produced in London's West End. Novel on Mexico, *Lusita*, published. Travels with McGeehan through Eastern Europe.
1933	Produces and directs her play *Lone Valley* at Broadway's Plymouth Theatre, opening 8 March. Runs for only three performances. *Machinal* staged by Alexander Tairov at his Kamerny Theatre in Moscow in May. McGeehan dies on 29 November.
1934	Her mother dies in Los Angeles. *Intimations for Saxophone* copyrighted.
1936	*Plumes in the Dust* opens on Broadway, 6 November.
1938	Writes novel, *Hope for a Harvest*.
1941	Stage version of *Hope for a Harvest*, produced by the Theatre Guild, opens 26 November.
1942	Travels to Mexico as correspondent for *New York Herald Tribune*. Travels to Guatemala, Peru and Argentina.
1944	Works on screenplays in Hollywood during summer and fall.
1948	Travels to El Salvador and Panama.
1949	Spends two months in a sanitarium in Vienna. Adopts a German baby boy, naming him William. Begins lengthy travels between various parts of Europe.
1953	*Hope for a Harvest* aired on television, produced by the Theatre Guild.
1954	Sells the family ranch in Stockton.
1956–64	Lives in Torremolinos, Spain. Health begins to deteriorate after blackout spell in 1956 and mild stroke in 1962.

1959   Novel, *One Fierce Hour and Sweet*, published.

1960   *Machinal* revived off-Broadway at the Gate Theatre.

1963–65   Moves to Vienna and then to Tucson. Sells home in Newtown, Connecticut.

1967   *Now He Doesn't Want to Play*, her last play, produced by the University of Arizona Drama Department.

1970   Dies 20 February in Tucson after a massive stroke.

Notes

Introduction

1　John Reed, communist, journalist, and poet, died in Russia in 1920 and is buried in the Kremlin. He is best known for *Ten Days that Shook the World*, his account of the October 1917 Russian Revolution, published in 1919.

1　Life and ideas

1　The little theater movement was recognized as "the most interesting development of the past decade in our theatre" by the reviewer John Corbin (Corbin 1917).
2　Feminist interpretations of *Trifles* will be discussed in Chapter 4.
3　Originally published by Avon Books, this volume was reprinted by Applause Theatre Book Publishers in 1985.
4　Glaspell scholars Linda Ben-Zvi and J. Ellen Gainor are preparing *The Complete Plays of Susan Glaspell*, to be published by McFarland.
5　There are now available two full-length biographies of Susan Glaspell (Ozieblo 2000 and Ben-Zvi 2005) and a number of studies of her plays and novels. The earliest were those by Arthur Waterman (1966) and Marcia Noe (1983), and Noe's book remains a good starting point for the main facts of Glaspell's life.
6　Floyd Dell would later move to Chicago and then to New York; he was one of the founding members of the Provincetown Players. The intense admiration Dell felt for Cook ended abruptly as a result of, among other matters, the inept staging of his plays (see Ozieblo 2000: 108–09).
7　Cook was diagnosed as suffering from glanders, a disease normally contracted by horses and sometimes dogs, rarely by humans. For further discussion of his illness see Ozieblo 2000: 223–25 and Ben-Zvi 2005: 286–89.

8 The Federal Theatre, 1935–38, was one of the arts projects of the Works Progress Administration (WPA) created by F. D. Roosevelt's New Deal to give jobs to the unemployed (Flanagan 1969).

2 The short plays

1 The programs do not always indicate the director and designer. Given the by-laws of the Provincetown Players, we can assume that authors directed their own plays until early 1917, when Nina Moise joined them. The set design would also have been the responsibility of the authors/directors unless otherwise stated.

2 In the play *Chains of Dew* and the novel *Ambrose Holt and Family*, the protagonists Seymor and Lincoln make out that their self-sacrifice is for others, but it is clear that they need the burden of their chains, as the Mother in each work realizes.

3 At the time Glaspell was writing this play, Eugene O'Neill was living in a life-saving station that Mabel Dodge had done up as her summer home.

4 Glaspell would repeat virtually the same lines in *Chains of Dew* (performed in 1922), enabling us to read *Woman's Honor* as the germ of the later play.

5 See, for example, the anonymous review, "'Woman's Honor' Acted," *New York Times*, 21 May 1918.

6 Although this play is not overtly a feminist piece, note Glaspell's covert criticism of the role of both women, mere addenda to the active, thinking men.

3 The full-length plays

1 The manuscript of *Chains of Dew* is in the Library of Congress, deposited 21 February 1920.

2 There have been readings of *Chains of Dew* by members of the Susan Glaspell Society at conferences in Chicago and Philadelphia. See www.susanglaspell.org.

3 The first birth-control clinic giving information and fitting working-class women with contraceptive devices was opened by Margaret Sanger in 1916; the clinic was promptly closed and Sanger was put in jail. For Glaspell, who wanted children but was unable to bring a pregnancy to full term, the issue was theoretical rather than personal, but even so, she made it a central theme in *Chains of Dew*. A number of the women in her circle worked for the legalization of birth control in one way or another: Emma Goldman, Ida Rauh, and Mary Ware Dennett. See Gainor 2001: 170–98 for a detailed analysis of the struggle for birth control and its relationship to Glaspell's play.

4 At the Susan Glaspell Society reading of *Chains of Dew* at the SSAWW conference in Philadelphia, 2006, audiences responded to the comedy in the play but, in discussions following the readings, expressed concern at the ending. Pioneer feminist critic Judith Fetterley, recognizing the psychological depths the play probes, commented on its "dark" aspect.

5 Cheryl Black, when directing the reading of *Chains of Dew*, instructed the actor playing Seymore to try for a Cary Grant charm.

6 Glaspell requested Deeter not to perform *Inheritors* during the Second World War for fear that her words should be misinterpreted (see Ben-Zvi 2005: 380). For other performances of *Inheritors*, see Papke 1993: 43.

7 See photographs of the Metropolitan production of *Inheritors* at www.metropolitanplayhouse.org and on the Susan Glaspell Society website, www.susanglaspell.org.

8 The possibility that humankind descended from apes was, in the late nineteenth century, just beginning to work its way into public knowledge. As the young Felix Fejevary assures his father and Silas Morton: "The whole intellectual world is at war about it. The best scientists accept it. Teachers are losing their positions for believing it. Of course, ministers can't believe it" (Glaspell 1921: 116).

9 See Makowsky (1993) for an examination of Glaspell's early stories and novels as domestic fiction.

10 During the twenties, she wrote her two most complex modernist novels, *Brook Evans* (1928) and *Fugitive's Return* (1929), and the biography of her husband, *The Road to the Temple* (1927).

11 *Alison's House* was performed in London in 1932 at the Little Theatre (see Papke 1993: 85 for other performances) and has been revived recently by the Mint Theater (New York, 1999) and the MeX Theatre (Louisville, KY, 2004) but without critical success.

12 The typescript is in the Berg Collection at the New York Public Library.

4 Key plays I: *Trifles*

1 The New York Public Library does not identify the production or date this photograph. However, it is identified and dated in its reproduction in *Theatre*, January 1917.

2 Linda Ben-Zvi has studied Glaspell's reports of the Hossack murder in depth (Ben-Zvi 1995).

3 Hinz-Bode (2006a) questions the feminist perspective of *Trifles* criticism. For a brief survey of the debate surrounding realism in feminist drama, see Schroeder 1999.

4 Bryan's comments refer to the story "A Jury of Her Peers," but they are equally valid for the play *Trifles*.

5   *Trifles* was included in Judith Barlow's *Plays by American Women, 1900–1930* (1981), Sandra Gilbert and Susan Gubar's *Norton Anthology of Literature by Women* (1985), and C. W. E. Bigsby's *Plays by Susan Glaspell* (1987).

6   In her later *The Outside* (1917) and the novel *Fugitive's Return* (1929) Glaspell's women protagonists also choose silence as a form of rebellion against patriarchal society's banishment of women to invisibility.

5 Key plays II: *The Verge*

1   Wycherly had been brought in to professionalize the haphazard directing of the Players' productions at the same time as Nina Moise; she directed Pendleton King's *Cocaine* in 1917 (on the same bill as Glaspell's *The People*) but had never acted for the Provincetown Players. She was the first professional actor to participate in a Provincetown Players production.

2   Henry O'Neill moved on to Hollywood, where he played in more than 150 movies, including *Tortilla Flat* and *The Wings of the Eagles*.

3   See Sarlós 1982: 204–06 for a detailed description of the dome.

4   The *hanamichi* or "flower paths" run through the audience and provide means of access to the main stage for the actors.

6 Life and ideas

1   In his study *The Theater of Trauma*, Michael Cotsell examines many of Treadwell's plays as expressions of her traumatic childhood (Cotsell 2005: 275–85).

2   In her largely autobiographical novel *Hope for a Harvest*, Treadwell writes of her younger self as escaping tensions with her mother by similarly sleeping outdoors on the ground under a locust tree (Dickey and López-Rodríguez 2006: 246–47). The novel contains repeated passages reflecting her family's prejudices toward her ethnicity.

3   The League had been formed in 1920 by Ruth Hale and Jane Grant. Members of its executive committee formed at the first meeting included a number of prominent theater figures, including Zona Gale, Susan Glaspell, Ida Rauh, Mary Shaw and Michael Strange (née Blanche Oelrichs), the latter the current wife of John Barrymore (Stannard 1977: 191–92). Other prominent members of the committee included Charlotte Perkins Gilman, Anita Loos and Heywood Broun (Anon. 1921).

4   Merrill Schleier states that about this time Treadwell also had an affair with Arthur Cravan, a Dadaist author, well-known ex-boxer and husband of Mina Loy (Schleier 2005: 253n).

5 Roché was an art collector, diplomat, and representative of the French High Commission. Wood, a noted painter, actress, lover of Roché and Duchamp, acted in one of Treadwell's early plays, *Claws*, in 1918. Parker, a lifelong friend of Treadwell, served as associate editor of *Current Opinion* and wrote for and edited several art magazines. Other regular guests at the Arensbergs' but with less lasting ties to Treadwell included Francis Picabia, Albert Gleizes, William Carlos Williams, Djuna Barnes, Alfred Kreymborg, Mina Loy and Man Ray, among many others (Crunden 1993: 409–43). The Arensberg's salon would typically convene after dinner and the theater, lasting until the early morning hours (Naumann 1980: 18).

6 See Naumann 1999 for a photo of Arensberg's assisted *With Hidden Noise*, now housed, like much of the Arensbergs' modern art collection, at the Philadelphia Museum of Art. The location of Treadwell's version is not known. Naumann also believes Treadwell assisted Duchamp in an English–French cryptogram accompanying the piece (*ibid.*: 66–67).

7 Of course, O'Neill's Broadway plays often built up a critical reputation first through their productions by the Provincetown Players, an avenue that may have similarly aided Treadwell, had she chosen to work within the little theater movement.

7 Early plays

1 The play was originally composed under the title "Mrs. Wayne." Thematically, this title reflects the woman's complete lack of identity except as that in the socially defined role of wife.

2 For further discussions of Treadwell's use of expressionist techniques, see Dickey 1999, Walker 2005, and López-Rodríguez 2006.

3 Treadwell's husband, however, was no fan of psychoanalysis, dismissing it as "foolishness" (McGeehan 1931: 231).

4 This individuation process includes a transcendental phase in which one develops the capacity to unify opposite tendencies of one's personality. With this in mind, *To Him Who Waits* could be seen as an attempt by Treadwell consciously to recognize disparate aspects of her personality. For a discussion of Treadwell's attraction to Jung and rejection of Freudian psychoanalysis as practiced in the United States, see López-Rodríguez 2006: 129–35.

5 Toni (Antonia) Wolff was a patient and longtime lover and collaborator of Carl Jung, their relationship beginning in 1914. Wolff's "Few Thoughts," written in 1934, was published in *Spring* (1941), 81–103 and elaborated upon in her 1956 book *Structural Forms of the Feminine Psyche* (Zurich: Spring Publications). For a discussion of Wolff's theories, see Douglas (1990): 203–07.

6   *The Eye of the Beholder* was produced on a bill titled "Drama under the Influence" from 23 February–24 March at the Gunston Theatre II in Arlington. In addition to *Trifles*, other plays on the bill included works by Dorothy Parker, Eulalie Spence, Rita Wellman, Gertrude Stein, and Susan Glaspell and George Cram Cook. For a description of the performance, see Dickey 2007.

7   See Ross 1936: 65 for the origin of this term.

8   Broadway and later plays

1   Treadwell's work in Hollywood was particularly handicapped by the fact that the director and star, not the writer, dominated the film industry. As in her writings for the commercial theater, she resisted advice for revision. As the architect Clarence S. Stein wrote in 1938 to his wife, Aline MacMahon, a former Broadway actress who by the late 1930s had two dozen films to her credit: "The whole problem is Sophie Treadwell. If she doesn't want your criticism, talk to her about the weather" (Stein 1998: 382).

2   The serial was prompted by recent passage of the Red Light Abatement Act by the state of California that threatened closure of property used for prostitution, in effect creating large populations of homeless prostitutes, especially in Treadwell's San Francisco (see Dickey and López-Rodríguez 2006: 23–24).

3   As noted in Chapter 6, Treadwell and Strange were both members of the Lucy Stone League around the time of this lawsuit.

4   See Dickey 1995 for a detailed account of the events surrounding this lawsuit.

5   Treadwell was also an active member of the contract committee of the Dramatists Guild (Anon. 1935). Her most notable triumph in advocacy for dramatists' rights was her ability in 1933 to become the first Western playwright to secure production royalty payments from the Soviet Union (Anon. 1933b). See Chapter 9 for details on her trip to the USSR.

6   Hopkins also produced and directed the premiere of *Machinal* on Broadway (see Chapter 9).

7   The novel *Hope for a Harvest* remains unpublished, although its first chapter appears in Dickey and López-Rodríguez 2006).

9   Key plays I: *Machinal*

1   For more descriptions and photos of the Broadway production, see Parent 1982.

2   The 1931 London production of *Machinal*, retitled *The Life Machine*, met with censorship from the Lord Chamberlain, leading to an initial private production at the Arts Theatre Club before

transferring to the Garrick Theatre in London's West End. British critics nearly unanimously disliked the sordidness of the play's subject, often singling out the sympathetic depiction of the Young Woman's extramarital affair as morally indecent.

3   For a detailed discussion of this production's background and staging, see Dickey 1997b. While Tairov's production was in performance, a second production of the play went into rehearsal in Russia. Reuben Simonov staged the play at the Vakhtangov Theatre in the fall of 1933, changing the title to *Ellen Jones* (Leyda 1934).

4   The set featured a reduced-scale house raised on stilts. As the action progresses, the house first cracks open to reveal a family and later explodes, forcing the characters onto the open stage.

5   This paper, delivered at a 2005 conference, has just been published under the same title in *South Atlantic Review* 71.3 (Summer 2006): 4–14.

10   Key plays II: *Intimations for Saxophone*

1   The stage premiere was preceded, however, by two broadcasts on BBC Radio 3 on 1 December 1996 and in September of the following year. The broadcast featured Fiona Shaw and was most likely an outgrowth of her work with Stephen Daldry on *Machinal* for the National Theatre (BBC 2005). The producer of the radio broadcast was Kate Rowland, who had previously directed *Machinal*, and shared her notes and research with Daldry prior to his production (Lesser 1997: 228–29).

2   The University of Arizona manuscript used for quotations in this summary is paginated according to act–page and act–scene–page.

3   *Enduring Passion* was a work by Marie C. Stopes that was published first in London in 1928 and then in New York in 1931. Stopes was a pioneer in the birth-control movement in Great Britain and published a number of taboo-breaking books and controversial plays on marriage, sexual practices and contraception.

4   This manuscript variant may be found at the University of Arizona Library Special Collections, ms. 124, box 13. Other manuscripts housed under this call number replace Kartner with a violinist named Hyer and move the action from Vienna to Rio de Janeiro.

5   That trilogy, titled in English translation *The Maurizius Case* (1929), *Etzel Andergast* (or *Doctor Kerkhoven* in the American edition) (1932) and *Joseph Kerkhoven's Third Existence* (1934), presents Kerkhoven as a former provincial general practitioner whose insight into human behavior and holistic treatment methods contributes to his rise as a noted specialist in psychology and neurology. I am indebted to Michael Kinghorn for pointing out the connection between Wassermann and Kartner.

Bibliography

Introduction

Archer, W. (1921) "Great contributions of 'little theatres' to our drama's future," *New York Post*, 24 February.

Aston, E. (1995) *An Introduction to Feminism and Theatre*, London: Routledge.

Austin, G. (1990) *Feminist Theories for Dramatic Criticism*, Ann Arbor: University of Michigan Press.

Barlow, J. E. (1995) "Susan's sisters: the 'other' women writers of the Provincetown Players,' in L. Ben-Zvi (ed.) *Susan Glaspell: essays on her theater and fiction*, Ann Arbor: University of Michigan Press, 259–300.

Black, C. (2002) *The Women of Provincetown, 1915–1922*, Tuscaloosa and London: University of Alabama Press.

Chansky, D. (2004) *Composing Ourselves: the little theatre movement and the American audience*, Carbondale: Southern Illinois University Press.

Chicago, J. (1975) "Womanhouse – performances," in R. Drain (ed.) *Twentieth Century Theatre: a sourcebook*, London: Routledge, 128–32.

Cixous, H. (1977) "Aller à la mer," in R. Drain (ed.) *Twentieth Century Theatre: a sourcebook*, London: Routledge, 133–35.

Craig, E. G. [1905] "The art of the theatre: the first dialogue," in J. M. Walton (ed.) (1983) *Craig on the Theatre*, London: Methuen, 52–71.

Drain, R. (ed.) (1995) *Twentieth Century Theatre: a sourcebook*, London: Routledge.

Friedman, S. (1984) "Feminism as theme in twentieth-century American women's drama," *American Studies* 25.1: 68–89.

Gainor, J. E. (2001) *Susan Glaspell in Context: American theater, culture, and politics 1915–1948*, Ann Arbor: University of Michigan Press.

Glaspell, S. (1927) *The Road to the Temple*, New York: Frederick A. Stokes.

Kenton, E. (1997) "The Provincetown Players and the Playwrights' Theatre, 1915–1922," *The Eugene O'Neill Review* 21.1 and 2: 16–160.

Keyssar, H. (1996) "Drama and the dialogic imagination: *The Heidi Chronicles* and *Fefu and Her Friends*," in H. Keyssar (ed.) *Feminist Theatre and Theory*, London: Macmillan, 109–36.

Kiper, F. (1914) "Some American plays from the feminist viewpoint," *Forum* 51 (June): 921–31.

Murphy, B. (1987) *American Realism and American Drama, 1880–1940*, Cambridge: Cambridge University Press.

Ozieblo, B. (2000) *Susan Glaspell: a critical biography*, Chapel Hill: University of North Carolina Press.

Reinelt, J. (1996) "Beyond Brecht: Britain's new feminist drama," in H. Keyssar (ed.) *Feminist Theatre and Theory*, London: Macmillan, 35–48.

Schroeder, P. (1996) *The Feminist Possibilities of Dramatic Realism*, London: Associated University Presses.

Susan Glaspell

For a complete bibliography of works by Susan Glaspell, including non-print sources and archival resources, see the bibliography on the Susan Glaspell Society website: <www.susanglaspell.org>.

For an annotated bibliography of reviews of Glaspell's plays from 1916 to 1992 and for citations prior to 1975, see Mary E. Papke (1993), *Susan Glaspell: a research and production sourcebook*, Westport, Conn.: Greenwood Press.

For a constantly updated bibliography of secondary critical sources from 1975 to the present, see the bibliography on the Susan Glaspell Society website: <www.susanglaspell.org>.

Agate, J. (1926) *The Contemporary Theatre*, London: Chapman and Hall.

Alkalay-Gut, K. (1984) "Jury of her peers: the importance of trifles," *Studies in Short Fiction* 21.1: 1–9.

—— (1995) "Murder and marriage: another look at *Trifles*," in

L. Ben-Zvi (ed.) *Susan Glaspell: essays on her theater and fiction*, Ann Arbor: University of Michigan Press, 71–84.

Anon. (1918a) "'Pokey' is a joy at the Comedy," *New York Times*, 24 January.

—— (1918b) "'Woman's Honor' acted," *New York Times*, 21 May.

—— (1919) "Funereal drama and childish skit in the Village," *New York Herald*, 24 March.

—— (1920a) "Review of *Plays* by Susan Glaspell," *Independent*, 11 December.

—— (1920b) *The Freeman*, 11 August, unidentified clipping in the Susan Glaspell Papers in the Henry and Albert Berg Collection, New York Public Library.

—— (1921a) "Behind the scenes," *New York Evening Telegram*, 31 October.

—— (1921b) "Claire – superwoman or plain egomaniac? A no-verdict disputation," *Greenwich Villager*, 30 November.

—— (1921c) "Philosophers wrestle with 'The Verge' while bread burns," *Greenwich Villager*, 23 November.

—— (1922) "Susan Glaspell's 'Chains of Dew' is sharp satire," *New York Herald*, 28 April.

—— (1925a) "A London letter: the situation unchanged," *Yorkshire Post*, 3 April.

—— (1925b) "Personalities and powers: Susan Glaspell," *Time and Tide*, 27 March, 294–95.

—— (1925c) "Pioneer Players: last subscription performance," *Morning Post*, 30 March.

—— (1925d) "The drama of Susan Glaspell," *Illustrated London News*, 11 April.

—— (1925e) "The Pioneer Players: *The Verge* by Susan Glaspell," *Daily Telegraph*, 30 March.

—— (no date) "The Verge," undated, unsigned clipping in the Susan Glaspell Papers in the Henry and Albert Berg Collection, New York Public Library.

Aston, E. (1997) "Performance review: *The Verge*," *Theatre Journal*, 49.2: 229–31.

Atkinson, J. B. (1927) "Pioneer traditions," *New York Times*, 20 March.

Bach, G. and Harris, C. (1992) "Susan Glaspell – rediscovering an American playwright," *Theatre Journal*, 44.1: 94–96.

Barlow, J. E. (ed.) (1981; rev. edn 1985) *Plays by American Women: 1900–1930* [originally titled *Plays by American Women: the early years*], New York: Applause Theatre Book Publishers.

Ben-Zvi, L. (1995) "'Murder She Wrote': the genesis of Susan Glaspell's *Trifles*," in L. Ben-Zvi (ed.), *Susan Glaspell: essays on her theater and fiction*, Ann Arbor: University of Michigan Press, 19–48.

—— (2005) *Susan Glaspell: her life and times*, New York: Oxford University Press.

Ben-Zvi, L. and Gainor, J.E. (Forthcoming) *The Complete Plays by Susan Glaspell*, Jefferson, NC: McFarland.

Bigsby, C. W. E. (1982) *A Critical Introduction to Twentieth-Century American Drama*, Cambridge: Cambridge University Press.

—— (1987) Introduction in C. W. E. Bigsby (ed.) *Plays by Susan Glaspell*, Cambridge: Cambridge University Press, 1–31.

Billington, M. (1996) "*The Verge*," *Guardian*, 11 April.

Black, C. (2002) *The Women of Provincetown, 1915–1922*, Tuscaloosa and London: University of Alabama Press.

—— (2005) "'Making queer new things' queer identities in the life and dramaturgy of Susan Glaspell," *Journal of Dramatic Theory and Criticism*, 20.1: 49–64.

Blon, K. T. von. (1933) "*Alison's House* presented," *Los Angeles Times*, 22 February.

Bottoms, S. J. (1998) "Building on the abyss: Susan Glaspell's *The Verge* in production," *Theatre Topics*, 8.2: 127–45.

Boyce, N. (1994) "Constancy," in B. Ozieblo (ed.) *The Provincetown Players: a choice of the shorter works*, Sheffield: Sheffield Academic Press, 52–63.

Broun, H. (1916) "Best bill seen at the Comedy," *New York Tribune*, 14 November.

—— (1917) "In wigs and wings: looking up, down and around with the Provincetown Players: Susan Glaspell and *The People*," *New York Tribune*, 18 March.

—— (1919) "Realism has special thrills of its own," *New York Tribune*, 30 March.

Bryan, P. (1997) "Stories in fiction and in fact: Susan Glaspell's 'A Jury of Her Peers' and the 1901 murder trial of Margaret Hossack," *Stanford Law Review*. 49: 1293–363.

Bryan, P. and Wolfe, T. (2005) *Midnight Assassin: a murder in America's heartland*, Chapel Hill, NC: Algonquin Books.

Carpentier, M. C. (2001) *The Major Novels of Susan Glaspell*, Tallahassee: University Press of Florida.

—— (ed.) (2006) *Susan Glaspell, New Directions in Critical Inquiry*, Newcastle: Cambridge Scholars Press.

Carpentier, M. C. and Ozieblo, B. (eds.) (2006) *Disclosing*

Intertextualities: the stories, plays, and novels of Susan Glaspell, Amsterdam: Rodopi.

Castellun, M. (1921) "*The Verge*, daring venture in drama by Susan Glaspell," *New York Call*, 16 November.

Corbin, J. (1917) "Little theatre plays," *New York Times*, 11 November.

—— (1918) "The one-act play," *New York Times*, 19 May.

—— (1919) "Seraphim and cats," *New York Times*, 30 March.

Cummins, G. D. (1925) "*The Verge*: Miss Thorndike's views on her new play," *Yorkshire Post*, 13 February.

Denton, M. (2005) Review of *Inheritors* at www.nytheatre.com, 19 November 2005. Available at <http://www.metropolitanplayhouse. org/InheritorsReview.htm> (accessed 2 December 2006).

Deutsch, H. and Hanau, S. (1931; rpt. 1972) *The Provincetown: a story of the theatre*, New York: Russell & Russell.

Dickinson, W. (1921) "*The Verge* – bad insanity clinic," *New York Evening Telegraph*, 15 November.

Drucker, R. (1919) "Provincetown Players show their best," *New York Times*, 20 April.

Fetterley, J. (1982) "Reading about reading: 'A Jury of Her Peers,' 'The Murders in the Rue Morge,' and 'The Yellow Wallpaper,'" in E. A. Flynn and P. Schweickart (eds.) *Gender and Reading: essays on readers, texts, and contexts*, Baltimore: Johns Hopkins University Press, 47–64.

Fishbein, L. (1982) *Rebels in Bohemia: the radicals of* The Masses, *1911–1917*, Chapel Hill: University of North Carolina Press.

Flanagan, H. (1940; rpt. 1985) *Arena: the story of the Federal Theatre*, New York: Limelight Editions.

Fletcher, C. V. (2006) "'The rules of the institution': Susan Glaspell and sisterhood," in M. C. Carpentier and B. Ozieblo (eds.) *Disclosing Intertextualities: the stories, plays, and novels of Susan Glaspell*, Amsterdam: Rodopi, 239–56.

Frank, S. (2003) "On 'The Verge' of a new form: *The Cabinet of Dr. Caligari* and Susan Glaspell's experiments in *The Verge*," in A. Gewirtz and J. J. Kolb (eds.) *Experimenters, Rebels, and Disparate Voices: the theatre of the 1920s celebrates American diversity*, Westport, Conn.: Praeger, 119–29.

Friedman, S. (1995) "Bernice's strange deceit: the avenging angel in the house," in L. Ben-Zvi (ed.) *Susan Glaspell: essays on her theater and fiction*, Ann Arbor: University of Michigan Press, 155–63.

Gainor, J. E. (2001) *Susan Glaspell in Context: American theater, culture, and politics 1915–1948*, Ann Arbor: University of Michigan Press.

—— (2006) "*Woman's Honor* and the critique of slander per se," in M. C. Carpentier (ed.) *Susan Glaspell, New Directions in Critical Inquiry*, Newcastle: Cambridge Scholars Press, 66–79.

Gilbert, S. M. (1986) "What do feminists want? A postcard from the volcano," in E. Showalter (ed.) *The New Feminist Criticism: essays on women, literature, and theory*, London: Virago, 29–45.

Gilbert, S. M. and Gubar, S. (eds.) (1985) *The Norton Anthology of Literature by Women*, New York: Norton.

Glaspell, S. (1909) *The Glory of the Conquered*, New York: Frederick A. Stokes.

—— (1911) *The Visioning*, New York: Frederick A. Stokes.

—— (1914) "The rules of the institution," *Harper's Monthly Magazine*, January, 198–208.

—— (1915) *Fidelity*, Boston: Small, Maynard.

—— (1916; rpt. 1994) *Suppressed Desires*, in B. Ozieblo (ed.) *The Provincetown Players: a choice of the shorter works*, Sheffield: Sheffield Academic Press, 34–51.

—— (1917) "A Jury of Her Peers," *Everyweek*, March.

—— (1919; rpt. 1924) *Bernice: a play in three acts*, London: Ernest Benn.

—— (1920a) *Chains of Dew*, unpublished typescript, copies deposited in Library of Congress, Washington, DC.

—— (1920b; rpt. 1987) *The Outside*, in C. W. E. Bigsby (ed.) *Plays by Susan Glaspell*, Cambridge: Cambridge University Press, 47–55.

—— (1920c; rpt. 1987) *Trifles*, in C. W. E. Bigsby (ed.) *Plays by Susan Glaspell*, Cambridge: Cambridge University Press, 36–45.

—— (1920d; rpt. 1929) *Woman's Honor*, in S. Glaspell, *Trifles and Six Other Short Plays*, London: Ernest Benn, 83–102.

—— (1921; rpt. 1987) *Inheritors*, in C. W. E. Bigsby (ed.) *Plays by Susan Glaspell*, Cambridge: Cambridge University Press, 103–57.

—— (1922; rpt. 1987) *The Verge*, in C. W. E. Bigsby (ed.) *Plays by Susan Glaspell*, Cambridge: Cambridge University Press, 57–102.

—— (1926a; rpt. 1929) *Close the Book*, in S. Glaspell, *Trifles and Six Other Short Plays*, London: Ernest Benn, 47–65.

—— (1926b; rpt. 1929) *The People*, in S. Glaspell, *Trifles and Six Other Short Plays*, London: Ernest Benn, 29–43.

—— (1927) *The Road to the Temple*, New York: Frederick A. Stokes.

—— (1928a) *Brook Evans*, New York: Frederick A. Stokes.

—— (1928b; rpt. 1931) *Tickless Time*, in J. Hampden (ed.) *Ten Modern Plays*, London: Thomas Nelson & Sons, 121–44.

—— (1929) *Fugitive's Return*, New York: Frederick A. Stokes.

—— (1930) *Alison's House*, New York: Samuel French.

—— (1931) *Ambrose Holt and Family*, New York: Frederick A. Stokes.

—— (1939) *The Morning Is Near Us*, New York: Frederick Stokes.

—— (1942a) *Norma Ashe*, Philadelphia: Lippincott.

—— (1942b) Typescript of autobiographical notes in the Sheaffer–O'Neill Collection, Charles E. Shain Library, Connecticut College.

—— (1945) *Judd Rankin's Daughter*, Philadelphia: Lippincott.

—— (no date) *Springs Eternal*, unpublished, undated typescript, copy deposited in the Susan Glaspell Papers, Henry and Albert Berg Collection, New York Public Library.

Glaspell, S. and Matson, N. (1927) *The Comic Artist: a play in three acts*, New York: Frederick A. Stokes.

Gluck, V. (2005) "Reviews: Inheritors," Backstage.com, 22 November. Available at: <www.metropolitanplayhouse.org/InheritorsReview. htm> (accessed 2 February 2006).

Griffith, H. (1925) "The week's theatres: 'The Verge,'" *Observer*, 5 April.

Hampden, J. (1928; rpt. 1931) "Acting notes," in J. Hampden (ed.) *Ten Modern Plays*, London: Thomas Nelson & Sons, 225–50.

Hapgood, H. (1939; rpt. 1972) *A Victorian in the Modern World*, Seattle: University of Washington Press.

Hewison, R. (1997) "*Inheritors*," *Sunday Times*, 2 March.

Hinz-Bode, K. (2006a) *Susan Glaspell and the Anxiety of Expression: language and location in the plays*, Jefferson, NC: McFarland & Co.

—— (2006b) "Susan Glaspell and the epistemological crisis of modernity: truth, knowledge, and art in selected novels," in M. C. Carpentier (ed.) *Susan Glaspell, New Directions in Critical Inquiry*, Newcastle: Cambridge Scholars Press, 89–108.

Hornblow, A. (1917) "Mr. Hornblow goes to the play," *Theatre*, January.

Ibsen, H. (1892; rpt. 1987) *The Master Builder*, in *Four Major Plays*, trans. James McFarlane, Oxford: Oxford University Press, 265–355.

Irwin, I. H. (1922) "Ines Haynes Irwin turns light on Susan Glaspell," *Public Ledger*, 13 May.

Kenton, E. (1997) "The Provincetown Players and the Playwrights'

Theatre, 1915–1922," *The Eugene O'Neill Review*, 21.1 and 2: 16–160.

Kingston, J. (1996) "Growing pains: *The Verge*," *The Times*, 3 April.

Kolodny, A. (1986) "A map for rereading: gender and the interpretation of literary text," in E. Showalter (ed.) *The New Feminist Criticism: essays on women, literature, and theory*, London: Virago, 46–62.

Langner, L. (1952) *The Magic Curtain*, London: Harrap.

Lauter, P. (1983) "Race and gender in the shaping of the American literary canon," *Feminist Studies*, 9: 435–63.

Le Gallienne, E. (1934) *At Thirty-Three: autobiography*, London: John Lane, Bodley.

Lewisohn, L. (1921) "Drama – *The Verge*," *Nation*, 14 December .

—— (1922) *The Drama and the Stage*, New York: Harcourt, Brace & Co.

—— (1931) *Expression in America*, London: Thornton Butterworth.

Macgowan, K. (1921) "The new play," *New York Evening Globe*, 15 November.

Macgowan, K. and Jones, R. E. (1923) *Continental Stagecraft*, London: Benn Brothers.

Makowsky, V. (1993) *Susan Glaspell's Century of American Women: a critical interpretation of her work*, New York: Oxford University Press.

—— (1999) "Susan Glaspell and modernism," in B. Murphy (ed.) *The Cambridge Companion to American Women Playwrights*, Cambridge: Cambridge University Press, 49–65.

Malone, A. E. (1924) "Susan Glaspell," *Dublin*, September.

Malpede, K. (1995) "Reflections on *The Verge*," in L. Ben-Zvi (ed.) *Susan Glaspell: essays on her theater and fiction*, Ann Arbor: University of Michigan Press, 123–27.

Molnar, M. (2006) "Antigone redux: female voice and the state in Susan Glaspell's *Inheritors*," in M. C. Carpentier (ed.) *Susan Glaspell: New Directions in Critical Inquiry*, Newcastle: Cambridge Scholars Press, 37–44.

Murphy, B. (2005) *The Provincetown Players and the Culture of Modernity*, Cambridge: Cambridge University Press.

Nietzsche F. (1883; rpt. 1987) *Thus Spoke Zarathustra*, Harmondsworth: Penguin.

Noe, M. (1981) "Region as metaphor in the plays of Susan Glaspell," *Western Illinois Regional Studies*, 4.1: 77–85.

—— (1983) *Susan Glaspell: voice from the heartland*, Macomb: Western Illinois University Press.

—— (1995) "*The Verge*: *l'écriture féminine* at the Provincetown," in

L. Ben-Zvi (ed.) *Susan Glaspell: essays on her theater and fiction*, Ann Arbor: University of Michigan Press, 129–44.

Noe, M. and Marlowe, R. (2006) "*Suppressed Desires* and *Tickless Time*: an intertextual critique of modernity," in M. C. Carpentier and B. Ozieblo (eds.) *Disclosing Intertextualities: the stories, plays, and novels of Susan Glaspell*, Amsterdam: Rodopi, 51–62.

O'Neill, E. (1921) "Damn the optimists!," *New York Tribune*, 13 February.

Ozieblo, B. (2000) *Susan Glaspell: a critical biography*, Chapel Hill: University of North Carolina Press.

—— (2006a) "Silenced mothers and questing daughters," in M. C. Carpentier and B. Ozieblo (eds.) *Disclosing Intertextualities: the stories, plays, and novels of Susan Glaspell*, Amsterdam: Rodopi, 137–57.

—— (2006b) "Susan Glaspell and the modernist experiment of *Chains of Dew*," in M. C. Carpentier (ed.) *Susan Glaspell, New Directions in Critical Inquiry*, Newcastle: Cambridge Scholars Press, 7–24.

Papke, M. E. (1993) *Susan Glaspell: a research and production sourcebook*, Westport, Conn.: Greenwood Press.

—— (2006) "Susan Glaspell's last word on democracy and war," in M. C. Carpentier (ed.) *Susan Glaspell, New Directions in Critical Inquiry*, Newcastle: Cambridge Scholars Press, 80–88.

Parker, R. A. (1921) "Drama – plays domestic and imported," *Independent*, 17 December.

Peters, A. D. (1924) "Susan Glaspell: new American dramatist," *Daily Telegraph*, 19 June 1924.

Rathbun. S. (1921) "Spanish operetta, musical comedy and two dramas arrive Thanksgiving week," *Sun*, 19 November.

Roberts, R. E. (1925) "A great playwright," *Guardian*, 17 July.

Robertson, J. F. (1925) "The drama of Susan Glaspell: the memoirs of Sir J. Forbes Robertson," *Illustrated London News*, 11 April.

Rodier, K. (1995) "Glaspell and Dickinson: surveying the premises of *Alison's House*," in L. Ben-Zvi (ed.) *Susan Glaspell: essays on her theater and fiction*, Ann Arbor: University of Michigan Press, 195–218.

Rohe, A. (1921) "The story of Susan Glaspell," *Morning Telegraph*, 18 December.

Royde-Smith, N. G. (1926) "The drama: the American play," *Outlook*, 9 January.

Sarlós, R. K. (1982) *Jig Cook and the Provincetown Players: theatre in ferment*, Amherst: University of Massachusetts Press.

Schroeder, P. (1996) *The Feminist Possibilities of Dramatic Realism*, London: Associated University Presses.

Schroeder, P. R. (1999) "Realism and feminism in the Progressive Era," in B. Murphy (ed.) *The Cambridge Companion to American Women Playwrights*, Cambridge: Cambridge University Press, 31–46.

Schwarz, J. (1986) *Radical Feminists of the Heterodoxy: Greenwich Village 1912–1940*, Norwich, Vt.: New Victoria Publishers.

Shafer, Y. (1995) *American Women Playwrights 1900–1950*, New York: Peter Lang.

Shaughnessy, N. (2004) "The disappearing subject in Susan Glaspell's auto/biographical theatre," in M. B. Gale and V. Gardner (eds.) *Auto/Biography and Identity: women, theatre and performance*, Manchester: Manchester University Press, 39–57.

Shay, F. (1921) "Drama," *Greenwich Villager*, 23 November.

Sievers, W. D. (1955) *Freud on Broadway: a history of American psychoanalysis and the American drama*, New York: Hermitage House.

Smith, A. (1922) "The new play," *New York Evening Globe*, 28 April.

Stein, K. F. (1987) "The women's world of Glaspell's *Trifles*," in H. K. Chinoy and L.W. Jenkins (eds.) *Women in American Theatre*, New York: Theatre Communications Group, 253–56.

Valgemae, M. (1972) *Accelerated Grimace: expressionism in the American drama of the 1920s*, Carbondale: Southern Illinois University Press.

Waterman, A. (1966) *Susan Glaspell*, New York: Twayne.

—— (1979) "Susan Glaspell's *The Verge*: an experiment in feminism," *Great Lakes Review*, 6.1: 17–23.

Woollcott, A. (1921) "The play – Provincetown psychiatry," *New York Times*, 15 November.

—— (1922) "The play," *New York Times*, 28 April.

Young, S. (1921) "Susan Glaspell's *The Verge*," *New Republic*, 7 December.

Zatkin, N. (1927) "Glaspell play at 14th Street," *New York Daily Telegraph*, 9 March.

Sophie Treadwell

For an annotated bibliography of all of Treadwell's writings and reviews of her plays, see Jerry Dickey (1997) *Sophie Treadwell: a research and production sourcebook*, Westport, Conn.: Greenwood Press.

Addams, J. (1913) *A New Conscience and an Ancient Evil*, New York: Macmillan.

Anon. (1921) "Wives debate right to maiden names," *New York Times*, 18 May.

—— (1925) "*O Nightingale*," *Picture Play*, July, clipping, Sophie Treadwell Papers, University of Arizona Library Special Collections (UALSC from hereon), ms. 318, box 12.

—— (1928) "The New York stage: expressionism," *Guardian*, 19 December.

—— (1929) "*Ladies Leave*, at the Hopkins, is modern problem comedy," *New York American*, 3 October.

—— (1933a) "*Lone Valley* on a morning after," unsourced clipping, 14 March, Billy Rose Theatre Collection at the New York Library for the Performing Arts, Lincoln Center.

—— (1933b) "Soviet royalty on play won by US dramatist," *New York Herald Tribune*, 28 August.

—— (1935) "News of the stage," *New York Times*, 28 December.

—— (2005) "Arena Stage: *Intimations for Saxophone*," *Potomac Stages*. Available at: <www.potomacstages.com/Arena.htm> (accessed 31 January 2005).

Anderson, M. C. (2000) *Pancho Villa's Revolution by Headlines*, Norman: University of Oklahoma Press.

Atkinson, B. (1933) "The play: desire in *Lone Valley*," *New York Times*, 11 March.

Barlow, J. E. (1981) *Plays by American Women: the early years*, New York: Avon Books.

Barnes, C. (1990) "Perfect period piece," *New York Post*, 16 October.

Beaufort, J. (1990) "Atmospheric revival of murder drama captures '20s mood," *Christian Science Monitor*, 31 October.

Benchley, R. (1925) "Drama: coasting," *Life*, 7 May: 22.

Billington, M. (1993) "Theatre," *Country Life*, 28 October, clipping, Royal National Theatre, London.

Black, C. (2002) *The Women of Provincetown, 1915–1922*, Tuscaloosa and London: University of Alabama Press.

Blanchard, J. (2005a) "Modern themes permeate lost Treadwell work," *Washington Times*, 28 January. Available at: <www.washington times.com/functions/print.php?StoryID=200501...> (accessed 3 February 2005).

—— (2005b) "Soul of *Saxophone* rings flat amid sleek and stylized staging," *Washington Times*, 29 January.

Blankenagel, J. (1946) "Jakob Wassermann's conception and treatment of character," *Modern Language Quarterly*, 7: 3–20.

British Broadcasting Corporation (BBC) (2005) *Intimations for Saxophone*, programme catalogue. Available at: <catalogue. bbc.co.uk/catalogue/infax/programme/DA+95695_6> (accessed 2 November 2007).

Broun, H. (1922) "The new play," *New York World*, 15 December.

Calta, L. (1960) "*Machinal* opens at Gate March 9," *New York Times*, 10 February.

Chaney, J. (2005) "The battle of the saxes," *Washington Post*, 18 February. Available at: <www.washingtonpost.com/wp-dyn/articles/A32476-2005Feb17.html> (accessed 21 May 2006).

Chansky, D. (2005) "Sax and the city," *New York Theatre Wire*. Available at: <www.nytheatre-wire.com/dc05023t.htm> (accessed 3 May 2006).

Cohn, R. (1993) "At *Machinal*," *Plays International*, December: 17.

Coleman, R. (1936) "*Plumes in the Dust* a pageant of Edgar Allan Poe," *New York Daily Mirror*, 7 November.

Corbin, J. (1922a) "Americans in Mexico," *New York Times*, 15 December.

—— (1922b) "The critic and his orient," *New York Times*, 24 December.

Cotsell, M. (2005) *The Theater of Trauma: American modernist drama and the psychological struggle for the American mind, 1900–1930*, New York: Peter Lang.

Craig, J. (1922) "*Gringo*: new Sophie Treadwell play a story of banditry and tangled affections in Mexico," *New York Mail*, 15 December.

Cros, Caroline (2006) *Marcel Duchamp*, London: Reaktion Books.

Crunden, R. M. (1993) *American Salons: encounters with European modernism, 1885–1917*, New York: Oxford University Press.

Cummings, S. T. (2006) *Remaking American Theater: Charles Mee, Anne Bogart and the SITI Company*, Cambridge: Cambridge University Press.

Cushman, H. (1929) untitled, unsourced clipping, 3 October, Billy Rose Theatre Collection at the New York Public Library for the Performing Arts, Lincoln Center.

de Rohan, P. (1928) "*Machinal* ugly but great play," *New York American*, 8 September.

Dickey, J. (1995) "Sophie Treadwell vs. John Barrymore: playwrights, plagiarism, and power in the Broadway theatre of the 1920s," *Theatre History Studies*, 15: 67–86.

—— (1997a) *Sophie Treadwell: a research and production sourcebook*, Westport, Conn.: Greenwood Press.

—— (1997b) "Sophie visits Russia: Tairov's production of *Machinal* and Treadwell's awakenings in *The Promised Land*," *Women and Theatre: Occasional Papers*, 4: 1–17.

—— (1997c) "The 'real lives' of Sophie Treadwell: expressionism and the feminist aesthetic," in J. C. Reesman (ed.) *Speaking the Other Self: American women writers*, Athens: University of Georgia Press, 176–84.

—— (1999) "The expressionist moment: Sophie Treadwell," in B. Murphy (ed.) *The Cambridge Companion to American Women Playwrights*, Cambridge: Cambridge University Press, 66–81.

—— (2003) "Sophie Treadwell's summer with Boleslavsky and lectures for the American Laboratory Theatre," in A. Gewirtz and J. J. Kolb (eds.) *Experimenters, Rebels, and Disparate Voices: the theatre of the 1920s celebrates American diversity*, Westport, Conn.: Greenwood Press, 111–18.

—— (2005) Interview with Michael Kinghorn, Washington, DC, 27 January.

—— (2007) "The American Century Theater production of *Trifles* and *Suppressed Desires*," Susan Glaspell Society. Available at: <www.academic.shu.edu/glaspell/performances.html> (accessed 30 April 2007).

Dickey, J. and López-Rodríguez, M. (eds.) (2006) *Broadway's Bravest Woman: selected writings of Sophie Treadwell*, Carbondale: Southern Illinois University Press.

Dickey, J. *et al.* (2001) "The Sophie Treadwell Collection," University of Arizona Library Web Exhibit, Arizona Board of Regents. Available at: <www.library.arizona.edu/branches/spc/treadwell> (accessed 12 May 2007).

Doughty, L. (1993) "Pillage idiot," *Mail on Sunday*, 23 October.

Douglas, C. (1990) *The Woman in the Mirror: analytical psychology and the feminine*, Boston: Sigo Press.

Duchamp, M. (1989) *The Writings of Marcel Duchamp*, eds M. Sanouillet and E. Peterson, New York: Da Capo Press.

Dudley, B. (1929) "*Ladies Leave*," *New York Evening World*, 2 October.

Eye of the Beholder, The (2007), director Steven Scott Mazzola, The American Century Theater, Arlington, Va., 17 March.

Fadiman, W. J. (1935) Letter to Arthur Hopkins, 12 December, UALSC, ms. 124, box 9, folder 6.

Fox, A. M. (1993) "Variations on a theme: *For Saxophone* by Sophie Treadwell," *Text and Presentation: The Journal of the Comparative Drama Conference*, 14: 41–45.

Gabriel, G. (1936) "Poets in plays: from Poe to Byron," *New York American*, 15 November.

Gainor, J. E. and Dickey, J. (2005) "Susan Glaspell and Sophie Treadwell: staging feminism and modernism, 1915–1941," in D. Krasner (ed.) *A Companion to Twentieth-Century American Drama*, Oxford: Blackwell, 34–52.

Gassner, J. (1949) *Twenty-five Best Plays of the Modern American Theatre, Early Series*, New York: Crown.

Gibbs, W. (1941) "Ants and grasshoppers," *New Yorker*, 6 December: 46.

Glaspell, S. (1928) *Brook Evans*, New York: Frederick A. Stokes.

Gleeson, E. T. (1915) "Actress and author share big triumph," *San Francisco Bulletin*, c. 1–2 February, clipping, UALSC, ms. 318, box 9.

Goldman, E. (1916, 2nd edn; first pub. 1911) *Marriage and Love*, New York: Mother Earth Publishing.

Gore-Langton, R. (1993) "The enigma behind the Broadway hit," *Daily Telegraph*, 15 October.

Graham, T. (2007) "Drama under the influence," *Washington City Paper*. Available at: <www.washingtoncitypaper.com/display.php?id=898> (accessed 10 April 2007).

Hagerty, B. (1993) "*Machinal* the marvellous," *Today*, 18 October.

Hammond, P. (1925) "Do you use your husband's name?," *Liberty Magazine*, 17 January, 1.37: 45.

—— (1926) "Oddments and remainders," *New York Tribune*, 31 January.

—— (1933) "The theaters," *New York Herald Tribune*, 11 March.

Harris, P. (2005) "*Intimations for Saxophone*," *Variety.com*, 14 February. Available at: <www.variety.com/review/VE111792 6187?categoryid=33&cs=1&query=intimations+for+saxophone &display=intimations+for+saxophone> (accessed 3 May 2006).

Hassell, G. (1993) Review of *Machinal*, *What's On*, 27 October, reprinted in *Theatre Record* (1993), 8–21 October, 13: 1186.

Heck-Rabi, L. (1976) "Sophie Treadwell: subjects and structures in 20th century American drama," Dissertation, Wayne State University.

Hepple, P. (1993) "Ghosts in the *Machinal*," *The Stage and Television Today*, 28 October.

Hopkins, A. (1918; rpt. 1931) *How's Your Second Act?: notes on the art of production*, New York: Samuel French.

Intimations for Saxophone (2005), director Anne Bogart, Arena Stage in association with SITI Company, Fichandler Theatre, Washington, DC, 26 January.

Jackson, D. M. (2007) "Drama under the influence," *DC Theatre Scene*. Available at: <www.dctheatrereviews.com/2007/02/27/drama-under-the-influence/> (accessed 2 November 2007).

Jones, A. (1980; rpt. 1996) *Women Who Kill*, Boston: Beacon Press.

Jones, J. (1994) "In defense of the woman: Sophie Treadwell's *Machinal*," *Modern Drama*, 37: 485–96.

Jones, R. E. (1928) "The artist's approach to the theatre," *Theatre Arts Monthly*, 12: 629–34.

—— (1937) Letter to Sophie Treadwell, 24 October, UALSC, ms. 318, box 5, folder 13.

—— (1940) Letter to Sophie Treadwell, 26 April, UALSC, ms. 124, box 1, folder 11.

—— (1941) *The Dramatic Imagination*, New York: Theatre Arts Books.

—— (n.d.) Letter to Sophie Treadwell, undated, UALSC, ms. 318, box 5, folder 13.

Keating, M. (1967) "*He Doesn't Want to Play* ought not to," *Tucson Daily Citizen*, 26 July.

Kinghorn, M. (2005) "Return from obscurity: Treadwell's *Saxophone*," *Arena Stage: Intimations for Saxophone*, program book, Washington, DC: 12–13.

Kirkpatrick, M. (1990) "Domestic tragedy," *Wall Street Journal*, 26 October.

Kissel, H. (1990) "She's a victim, so's audience," *New York Daily News*, 16 October.

Koiransky, A. (1935) Letter to Sophie Treadwell, 17 July, UALSC, ms. 124, box 1, folder 12.

—— (1944) Letter to Sophie Treadwell, 7 January, UALSC, ms. 124, box 1, folder 12.

Kramer, Dale (1949) *Heywood Broun: a biographical portrait*, New York: Current Books.

Krentzlin, D. (2007) "'DUI': punch-drunk love," *Examiner.com*. Available at: <www.examiner.com/a-604160~_DUI__Punch_drunk_love.html> (accessed 30 March 2007).

Kwolek-Folland, A. (1994) *Engendering Business: men and women in the corporate office, 1870–1930*, Baltimore, Md.: Johns Hopkins University Press.

L., M. (1925) "*The Sapphire Ring* good drama; *O Nightingale* is sprightly," *New York Daily News*, 16 April.

Langner, L. (1951) *The Magic Curtain*, New York: E. P. Dutton & Company.

Lesser, W. (1997) *A Director Calls*, Berkeley: University of California Press.

Levy, J. (2005) "*Saxophone* a medley of tastes," *Daily Colonial*, 31 January. Available at: <www.dailycolonial.com/go.dc?p=3&s=418> (accessed 2 August 2005).

Leyda, J. (1934) "News from Moscow," *Theatre Arts Monthly*, 18: 282.

Littell, R. (1928a) "Chiefly about *Machinal*," *Theatre Arts*, 12: 774–80.

—— (1928b) "The play: *Machinal*," *New York Evening Post*, 8 September.

Lockridge, R. (1928) "*Machinal*, murder and motives," *New York Sun*, 1 October.

Longacre, B. (1929) "*Ladies Leave*," *New York Standard Union*, 2 October.

López-Rodríguez, M. (2006) "Sophie Treadwell, Jung, and the mandala: acting a gendered identity," in B. Ozieblo and M. D. Narbona-Carrión (eds.) *Codifying the National Self: spectators, actors and the American dramatic text*, Brussels: P.I.E.–Peter Lang, 123–36.

Lutes, J. M. (2006) *Front Page Girls: women journalists in American culture and fiction, 1880–1930*, Ithaca, NY: Cornell University Press.

McDermott, D. S. (1984) "Creativity in the theatre: Robert Edmond Jones and C. G. Jung," *Theatre Journal*, 36.2: 212–30.

Machinal (1990), director M. Greif, New York Shakespeare Festival, video recording, Theatre on Film and Tape Archive, New York Public Library for the Performing Arts, Lincoln Center.

McGeehan, W. O. (1910) Letter to Sophie Treadwell, 4 July, UALSC, ms. 318, box 5, folder 19.

—— (1931) *Trouble in the Balkans*, New York: Dial Press.

Macleod, G. (1999) "The visual arts," in M. Levenson (ed.) *The Cambridge Companion to Modernism*, Cambridge: Cambridge University Press, 194–216.

Madden, R. (1937) Letter to Sophie Treadwell, 2 April, UALSC, ms. 124, box 13, folder 9.

Mantle, B. (1928) "*Machinal* – the perfect exhibit," *New York Daily News*, 8 September.

—— (1933) "*Lone Valley* an author's orphan," *New York Daily News*, 11 March.

——— (1936) "Plumes in the theatre: the biography of Edgar Allan Poe," *New York Sunday News*, 15 November.

Markey, M. (1928) "Panorama of plays and players," *New York's Illustrated News Weekly*, 1 October, clipping, UALSC, ms. 318, box 13.

Markov, P. A. (1935) *The Soviet Theatre*, New York: G. P. Putnam's Sons.

Marks, P. (2005) "Arena's *Saxophone*: a very slender reed," *Washington Post*, 31 January. Available at: <www.washingtonpost.com/wp-dyn/articles/A50184-2005Jan.30.html> (accessed 21 May 2006).

Mazer, C. M. (1998) "The *Machinal* Machine." Available at: <www.english.upenn.edu/~cmazer/machina2.html> (accessed 9 June 2007).

Minwalla, F. (2005) "Playing a 'lost' saxophone," *American Theatre*, 22: 9.

Modjeska, H. (1908) Letter to Sophie Treadwell, 23 July, UALSC, ms. 318, box 5, folder 23.

Munch, J. (2005) "Stage haze," *MetroWeekly*, 3 February. Available at: <www.metroweekly.com/arts_entertainment/stage.php?ak=1433> (accessed 3 May 2006).

Naumann, F. (1980) "Walter Conrad Arensberg: poet, patron, and participant in the New York avant-garde, 1915–20," *Philadelphia Museum of Art Bulletin*, 76: 1–32.

——— (1994) *New York Dada, 1915–23*, New York: Harry N. Abrams.

——— (1999) *Marcel Duchamp: l'art à l'ère de la reproduction mécanisée*, Paris: Éditions Hazan.

Nightingale, B. (1993) Review of *Machinal*, *The Times*, 19 October, reprinted in *Theatre Record* (1993), 8–21 October, 13: 1184.

Noe, M. (1995) "*The Verge*: *l'écriture féminine* at the Provincetown," in L. Ben-Zvi (ed.) *Susan Glaspell: essays on her theater and fiction*, Ann Arbor: University of Michigan Press, 129–42.

Nordern, B. (1993) "Death in metroland," *Times Literary Supplement*, 22 October.

Norton, E. (1941) "Stirring play at Colonial," *Boston Globe*, 1 April.

O'Mahoney, J. (1993) "Til death do they partake in," *Irish Post*, 6 November.

Parent, J. (1982) "Arthur Hopkins' production of Sophie Treadwell's *Machinal*," *Drama Review*, 26: 87–100.

Pelizzon, V. P. and West, N. M. (2005) "Multiple indemnity: film noir, James M. Cain, and adaptations of a tabloid case, the disappearing of the death chamber," *Narrative*, 13.3: 211–37.

Pettitt, G. A. (1973) *Berkeley: the town and gown of it*, Berkeley: Howell-North Books.

Pollack, A. (1928) "The theaters," *Brooklyn Eagle*, 8 September.

Rich, F. (1990) "A nightmarish vision of urban America as assembly line," *New York Times*, 16 October.

Riley, W. J. (1929) "*Ladies Leave*," *Billboard*, 12 October.

Ross, I. (1936) *Ladies of the Press: the story of women in journalism by an insider*, New York: Harper & Brothers.

Rousuck, J. W. (2005) "Noteworthy *Saxophone* is a tale of self-discovery," *Baltimore Sun*, 29 January. Available at: <www.baltimoresun.com/features/bal-to.saxophone29jan29,1,197...> (accessed 3 February 2005).

Rubinstein, R. (1933) "A word from the Soviet theater on its production of *Machinal*," *New York Herald Tribune*, 28 May.

S., A. (1925) "At the 49th Street Theatre: *O Nightingale*," *New York World*, 16 April.

Schleier, M. (2005) "The skyscraper, gender, and mental life: Sophie Treadwell's play *Machinal* of 1928," in R. Moudry (ed.) *The American Skyscraper: cultural histories*, Cambridge: Cambridge University Press, 234–54.

Scott, D. A. (1991) "Undiscovered treasure: an actor's search brings *Machinal* to life," *American Theatre*, January, 7: 36–37.

Shafer, Y. (1995) *American Women Playwrights, 1900–1950*, New York: Peter Lang.

Shaw, R. (1993) "Theatre," *Tablet*, 20 November, clipping, Royal National Theatre, London.

Sobel, B. (1933) "*Lone Valley* is presented at Plymouth," unsourced, undated clipping, UALSC, ms. 318, box 12.

Stannard, U. (1977) *Mrs. Man*, San Francisco: GermainBooks.

Steed, T. (1995) "Sophie Treadwell," in W. W. Demastes (ed.) *American Playwrights, 1880–1945: a research and production sourcebook*, Westport, Conn.: Greenwood, 427–36.

Stein, C. S. (1998) *The Writings of Clarence S. Stein: architect of the planned community*, ed. K. C. Parsons, Baltimore, Md.: Johns Hopkins University Press.

Stickland, L. (1994) "*Machinal*'s National exposé," *Live!*, January: 42–43.

Stone, P. N. (1925) "Many-sided Sophie Treadwell places playwright side first," *New York Herald Tribune*, 26 April.

Stopes, M. C. (1931) *Enduring Passion*, New York: G. P. Putnam's Sons.

Strand, G. (1992) "Treadwell's neologism: *Machinal*," *Theatre Journal*, 44.2: 163–75.

Tancheva, K. (2003) "Sophie Treadwell's play *Machinal*: strategies of reception and interpretation," in A. Gewirtz and J. J. Kolb (eds.) *Experimenters, Rebels, and Disparate Voices: the theatre of the 1920s celebrates American diversity*, Westport, Conn.: Praeger, 101–10.

Thielman, S. (2005) "*Intimations for Saxophone*," *CurtainUp.com*. Available at: <www.curtainup.com/saxophone.html> (accessed 21 May 2006).

Tilles, D. (1993) "TyroTalents: David Gallo," *Theatre Crafts International*, 27: 20.

Torda, T. J. (1977) "Alexander Tairov and the scenic artists of the Moscow Kamerny Theater 1914–1935," Dissertation, University of Denver.

Treadwell, S. (*c*. 1905) *A Man's Own*, unpublished typescript, UALSC, ms. 124, box 5, folder 9.

—— (1908) "The Story of Muh Life by One Who Has None," unpublished typescript, UALSC, ms. 318, box 20, folder 7.

—— (*c*. 1909) "She heard the call of the blood of her fathers," unsourced clipping, UALSC, ms. 318, box 7, folder 2.

—— (1915a) "How I got my husband and how I lost him" (Chapter 54), *San Francisco Bulletin*, undated clipping, UALSC, ms. 318, box 9.

—— (1915b) *Sympathy*, unpublished typescript, UALSC, ms. 124, box 5, folder 9.

—— (1915c) "Women in black," *Harper's Weekly*, 31 July: 111–12.

—— (*c*. 1915–18) *To Him Who Waits*, unpublished typescript, UALSC, ms. 124, box 5, folder 9.

—— (1918) *Madame Bluff*, unpublished typescript, UALSC, ms. 124, box 5, folder 6.

—— (1921a; rpt. 2006) "A visit with Villa: a 'bad man' not so bad," *New York Tribune*, 28 August; reprinted in J. Dickey and M. López-Rodríguez (eds.) *Broadway's Bravest Woman: selected writings of Sophie Treadwell*, Carbondale: Southern Illinois University Press, 44–67.

—— (1921b) "Mexico's dislike for us is long standing: a source of aggravation is our discourtesy," *New York Tribune*, 2 January.

—— (1921c) *Rights*, unpublished typescript, UALSC, ms. 124, box 7, folder 2.

—— (1922) *Gringo*, unpublished typescript, UALSC, ms. 318, box 17, folder 1.

—— (1923) "Villa's voice, the voice of Mexico, rings from the lips of José Ruben," unsourced clipping, UALSC, ms. 318, box 12.

—— (1924a) Letter to Walter Hampden, 25 November, UALSC, ms. 124, box 6, folder 8.

—— (1924b) "Mexico, international puzzle, land of doubt and imitation, begins new era under Calles," *New York Herald Tribune*, 16 November.

—— (1924c) "The mirage of Mexico," typed notes, UALSC, ms. 124, box 2, folder 2.

—— (1925) *O Nightingale*, unpublished typescript, UALSC, ms. 124, box 8, folder 3.

—— (*c.* 1928) *Machinal*, unpublished typescript, UALSC, ms. 124, box 11, folder 1.

—— (*c.* 1928–29) *Machinal*, unpublished typescript, UALSC, ms. 124, box 11, folder 2.

—— (1934) *For Saxophone*, unpublished typescript, Manuscript Division, Library of Congress.

—— (1936) *Plumes in the Dust*, unpublished typescript, UALSC, ms. 124, box 6, folder 7.

—— (*c.* 1936a) *For Saxophone*, unpublished typescript, UALSC, ms. 124, box 13, folder 6.

—— (*c.* 1936b) *Intimations for Saxophone*, unpublished typescript, Billy Rose Theatre Collection at the New York Public Library for the Performing Arts, Lincoln Center.

—— (1941) "I remembered a big white house," *New York Herald Tribune*, 14 December.

—— (1942a) *Hope for a Harvest*, New York: Samuel French.

—— (1942b) Letter to Pat [Duggan?], July, UALSC, ms. 124, box 13, folder 9.

—— (1943) Letter to Alexander Koiransky, 19 November, UALSC, ms. 124, box 1, folder 12.

—— (1947) Letter to Marie Darrach, 5 October, UALSC, ms. 124, box 10, folder 1.

—— (1949a) "A tourist among the ruins," *New York Herald Tribune*, 11 June.

—— (1949b; rpt. 1993) *Machinal*, in J. Gassner (ed.) *Twenty-five Best Plays of the Modern American Theatre*, *Early Series*, New York: Crown, 495–529; reprinted in S. Treadwell (1993) *Machinal*, London: Nick Hern Books.

—— (1958) Personal diary, 1 January, UALSC, ms. 318, box 3, folder 1.

—— (1969) Letter to Gerald Brenan, 16 August, UALSC, ms. 318, box 4, folder 11.

—— (2006a) *Ladies Leave*, in J. Dickey and M. López-Rodríguez (eds.) *Broadway's Bravest Woman: selected writings of Sophie Treadwell*, Carbondale: Southern Illinois University Press, 140–97.

—— (2006b) *The Eye of the Beholder*, in J. Dickey and M. López-Rodríguez (eds.) *Broadway's Bravest Woman: selected writings of Sophie Treadwell*, Carbondale: Southern Illinois University Press, 133–39.

—— (n.d.a) Scrapbook 1, UALSC, ms. 318, box 7, folder 1.

—— (n.d.b) "Toni Wolff: a few thoughts on the process of individuation in women," unpublished typescript, UALSC, ms. 124, box 2, folder 1.

—— (n.d.c) untitled typescript, UALSC, ms. 124, box 2, folder 1.

Waldorf, W. (1929) "*Ladies Leave*," unsourced clipping, 2 October, UALSC, ms. 318, box 12.

Walker, J. A. (2005) *Expressionism and Modernism in the American Theatre: bodies, voices, words*, Cambridge: Cambridge University Press.

Wassermann, J. (1932) *Doctor Kerkhoven*, trans. C. Brooks, New York: Horace Liveright.

Wattenberg, R. (1995) "Sophie Treadwell and frontier myth: western motifs in *Machinal* and *Hope for a Harvest*," in M. Maufort (ed.) *Staging Difference: Cultural Pluralism in American Theatre and Drama*, New York: Peter Lang, 339–50.

Watts, Jr., R. (1933) "Moscow sees *Machinal* and approves of it," *New York Herald Tribune*, 18 June.

—— (1936) "The theaters," *New York Herald Tribune*, 7 November.

Weiss, K. (2005) "Sophie Treadwell's *Machinal*: electrifying the female body," paper presented at the Technology, Media and Culture in the Space Between, 1914–1945 Conference, Montreal, 27–29 May.

Willeford, G. P. (n.d.) "The life of General Francisco Villa at ex-hacienda la Purísima Concepción de el Canutillo." Available at: <www.ojinaga.com/canutillo/> (accessed 30 May 2002).

Winer, L. (1990) "Sophie Treadwell's everywoman revival," *New York Newsday*, 16 October.

Woollcott, A. (1922) "The incautious Miss Treadwell," *New York Herald*, 24 December.

Worrall, N. (1989) *Modernism to Realism on the Soviet Stage: Tairov – Vakhtangov – Okhlopkov*, Cambridge: Cambridge University Press.

Writers' Program, California (1941) *Berkeley: the first seventy-five years*, Berkeley: Gillick Press.

Wynn, N. (1982) "Sophie Treadwell: the career of a twentieth-century American feminist playwright," Dissertation, City University of New York.

—— (1991) "Sophie Treadwell: author of *Machinal*," *Journal of American Drama and Theatre*, 3.1: 29–47.

Young, S. (1928) "Joy on the mountains," *New Republic*, 31 October: 299.

Index